Public Intellectuals,
Radical Democracy
and Social Movements

Studies in the Postmodern Theory of Education

Joe L. Kincheloe and Shirley R. Steinberg
General Editors

Vol. 276

PETER LANG
New York • Washington, D.C./Baltimore • Bern
Frankfurt am Main • Berlin • Brussels • Vienna • Oxford

Carmel Borg and Peter Mayo

Public Intellectuals, Radical Democracy and Social Movements

A BOOK OF INTERVIEWS

PETER LANG
New York • Washington, D.C./Baltimore • Bern
Frankfurt am Main • Berlin • Brussels • Vienna • Oxford

Library of Congress Cataloging-in-Publication Data
Borg, Carmel.
Public intellectuals, radical democracy and social movements: a book of interviews /
Carmel Borg, Peter Mayo.
p. cm. — (Counterpoints: studies in the postmodern theory of education; v. 276)
Includes bibliographical references.
1. Democracy. 2. Radicalism. 3. Social movements. 4. Intellectuals—Interviews.
I. Mayo, Peter. II. Title.
JC423.P8838 321.8—dc22 2007024887
ISBN 978-0-8204-7076-4
ISSN 1058-1634

Bibliographic information published by **Die Deutsche Bibliothek**.
Die Deutsche Bibliothek lists this publication in the "Deutsche
Nationalbibliografie"; detailed bibliographic data is available
on the Internet at http://dnb.ddb.de/.

Cover design by Joni Holst

© 2007 Peter Lang Publishing, Inc., New York
29 Broadway, 18th floor, New York, NY 10006
www.peterlang.com

All rights reserved.
Reprint or reproduction, even partially, in all forms such as microfilm,
xerography, microfiche, microcard, and offset strictly prohibited.

Table of Contents

Preface — vii

Introduction — ix

Reflections from a Third Age Marriage: A Pedagogy of Reason, Hope and Passion
Interview with Nita Freire — 1

Nicaragua: Past and Present
Interview with Maria Hamlyn Zuniga — 15

Women, Peace and Middle East Politics
Interview with Nahla Abdo — 23

Lula, Freire, Liberation Theology
Interview with Frei Betto — 33

Popular Education, Social Movements and Story Telling
Interview with Chris Cavanagh — 41

Human Rights, Social Justice and Civil Society
Interview with Magda Adly — 49

Popular Education and Social Change
Interview with Jane Thompson — 61

Curriculum as a Political Text
Interview with William Pinar — 77

School Exclusion, Educational Engagement and Social Equity
Interview with Paul Cooper   87

Theatre of the Oppressed: Italian Initiatives
Interview with Roberto Mazzini   99

Lorenzo Milani and the Barbiana Legacy
Interview with Edoardo Martinelli   107

Literacy, Micro-States and Postcolonialism
Interview with Didacus Jules   125

A World That Can Be—Democracy, Education and Participatory Budgets
Interview with Sergio Baierle   141

Critical Environmental Education 'Justice in Trade' and the No-Global Movement
Interview with Vincent Caruana   153

Trade Union Education in an Age of Globalization
Interview with John Fisher   167

From Madness to Consciousness: Redemption through Politics, Art and Love
Interview with Antonia Darder   181

Fascism, Colonialism and the Promise of Critical Education
Interview with Luiza Cortesão   207

Preface

Radical Insurrection and Dialogue

Insurrection is a word that has invaded the discourse of the twenty-first century. It has been negatively attached to civil unrest and directed in large part to the Middle East. In this short preface, I am proposing that critical teachers retrieve the word from the forces of the neo-liberal guardians of the status quo and re-create it within our own pedagogy. We are in need of an insurrection that proclaims to educators and scholars that we are willing to rise from our grassroots to retrieve intellectualism, critical discourse, and social justice from the dusty treatises of writers and activists past and present who have been buried under the political machines of apathy, right-wing agendas, and hegemonic administration.

As those who participate in insurrection, we claw our way through the volumes of governmentally mandated ways to construct educational institutions. As twenty-first century insurrectionists we critically read the world, in the process demanding that those who engage in the act of pedagogy recognize that we have the right and responsibility to promote rigor, depth, and disobedience in our teaching and in the lives of our students.

An essential earmark of any insurrection involves *naming* that which is hegemonic, inappropriate, dominant-ideologically inscribed, and covertly motivated by the logic of capital. For many decades, educators and scholars have been gagged by the chloroformed rags of positivism that are shoved down our throats by those that know less than nothing about education. As those who claim to be engaged in the critical pedagogy of children, youth, and adults, we are honor-bound to name forces of power that attempt to strangle socially just educational praxis. Additionally, we are integrity-bound to respect the differences between ourselves, to engage in dialogue in order to clarify alternative views, and to not devour our own.

A practice of the WASPish dominant cultures of Western Europe and North America has been to *not* name oppression, to *be polite,* and to suck *it* up. Informed by non-Western ways of seeing the world, critical academics and teachers refuse to not *name* that which is oppressive, unjust, inhumane, and scientistic. The interviews in this volume shout out insurrection by naming those responsible for the less than mediocre education that today's global children are receiving. The interviewees beg us to recognize the forces that continue to pervert just efforts to make education equitable and fair. This book is a valiant triumph over the silencing of difference and dissent. It exemplifies more than a decade's worth of thought, and reminds us of the notion of intellectual revolution, the reinvention of praxis. Many of us mourn the loss of a critical intelligentsia, especially in North America. This book reminds us that we still have those who are willing to speak out, to teach, and to reveal the dirty secrets of the status quo. Do not take this book lightly, for it contains the voices of those who lay the foundation of our critical pedagogical insurrection.

Shirley R. Steinberg
Director, The Paulo and Nita Freire International
Project for Critical Pedagogy

Introduction

Against the backdrop of a hegemonic, global economic arrangement that has spawned astounding disparities in wealth, this book foregrounds seventeen intellectuals who are engaged in resisting corporate values and in promoting social justice and human dignity. Ranging from socially engaged professors with a track record in grassroots involvement to popular educators, the interviewees challenge the manufactured consent, produced by armies of intellectuals organic to dominant ideologies, reminding us that strategic silence and/or indifference reproduce/s a common-sense arrangement where critical "reading of the word and the world" (Freire, 1987) is relegated to the periphery.

In the process of creating new agendas for critical discussion, the interviewees draw our attention to the fact that hegemony is never complete; it "is never done" (Miliband, 1982). In their engagement with counter-hegemonic world-views, they advocate the need for a more thorough understanding of the origins and mechanisms of false consciousness that capitalism and its technologies of oppression can generate. Ideology, considered by social agents organic to dominant structures and discourses as dead and buried, is considered by a number of interviewees as fundamental to the process of transformation.

This book is about critique and possibility. It is an attempt to help readers understand that oppression cannot be reduced to a simplistic formula of cause and effect. Oppression, as developed in this book, is multifaceted, multi-levelled, constantly shifting and is deeply rooted in social relations. For those who are searching for "lessons for better democracy" (Gret and Sintomer, 2005), this book provides ample leads into the process of challenging and dismantling oppression, both locally and globally. What might come across as a disjointed collection of interviews is, in fact, a coherent attempt to understand how different social actors, playing in different social theatres, at a specific historical moment, understand, cope with and address asymmetrical relationships of power. Their interviews represent specific ways of knowing the world and acting against the grain of cynicism, paralysis and social indifference.

For those who are searching for a viable vision other than that driven by consumption, this book provides them with ample opportunities for constructing utopias of possibility inspired by a tradition of social activism, critical theory and pedagogy. The deliberate choice of interviewees, most of them known for their dual commitment to transformative reflection and action, should convince sceptics that another type of world is possible; a world where theory and practice combine to produce a type of citizenship that sits uncomfortably with the current status quo; a citizenship which longs and works for self—as well as collective—transformation.

This work foregrounds the centrality of committed intellectuals to the process of moulding an alternative view of citizenship. Such intellectuals consider the challenges generated by their operational spaces as opportunities for democratic engagement and actual transformation. Their struggle is to reclaim authentic democracy within their public sphere. The fact that the interviewees hail from different geographical locations points at the potential for genuine democracy as an international, social movement; a world-wide counter-hegemonic movement that truly endangers the taken-for-grantedness of neo-liberalism.

The importance of excavating "subjugated knowledges" is emphasised by many of the interviewees. Authentic democracies must come to terms with the collective memories, sufferings, "common-sense" knowledge, voices and experiences, cultural relations and interests of subordinated individuals and groups. As indicated in various parts of the book, failing to surface and affirm, albeit critically, the authentic narratives and subjectivities of those who have been buried under the weight of consensual, read hegemonic, knowledges and experiences, is tantamount to personal and collective colonization.

The pedagogy of this book—chapters based on interviews—reaffirms our commitment towards forms of authorship that call attention to the importance of dialogue as an emancipatory tool. It is through multi-levelled, dialogical encounters, firmly rooted in the day-to-day struggles, and communicated in accessible languages, that oppressions can be named, shamed and, eventually, tackled. Such a pedagogical paradigm is impregnated with critical reflection and with informed decoding of what is fabricated as given, static and inevitable.

Authentic dialogue, as most interviewees affirm, implies horizontality, solidarity and an understanding of knowledge as public. With the institutions of civil society currently soaking in highly individualistic and competitive waters, dialogue as the pedagogy of life and as a powerful counterpoint to social relations generated by neo-liberalism, is both desirable and urgent.

The public intellectuals interviewed are various and are situated in different parts of the world including Brazil, Canada, England, Italy, Malta, Portugal,

St. Lucia and the rest of the Caribbean, and the United States. The issues include the 'participatory budget' in Porto Alegre, trade union education, fascism and colonialism, popular education, social movements, women's issues, the emancipatory power of story-telling, revolutionary settings, curriculum development, 'justice in trade', ecological issues and so forth.

These issues attest to the range of struggles taking place in various parts of the world which involve forms of community activism and educational projects that serve as an antidote to the current Neo-liberal scenario.

Some of the interviewees are well known. Others are less known particularly outside the contexts in which they operate. Whether the interviewee was well known or not was of no particular concern to us since our intention in this work is to foreground the struggles in which they are involved. Many of the public intellectuals involved belong to a social movement and it is this sense of movement that they embody. We do recognise, however, that we are dealing with 'persons in process', and for this reason we sought as much as possible to insert questions that will provide the reader with a sense of their biographical trajectories, indicating the sources of influences in their lives, the tough choices made and the strength of their commitment.

We also sought to revisit contexts that, not so long ago, had captured the imagination of activists, internationalists and educators in different parts of the world. It is for this reason that we inserted an interview, carried out electronically in 2005, with a popular health educator who had worked in Nicaragua. Furthermore, we revisited an interview with Frei Betto we originally carried out in Brazil in 1998 to update it in light of such occurrences as a change in the papacy and the conclusion of Lula's first term of presidency in Brazil. These two and the interview with Sergio Baierle concerning the participatory budget in Porto Alegre and other issues under Lula's presidency serve as a 'reality check' to help us avoid romanticising situations that capture our imagination and offer much hope.

In addition we also pay tribute to two key educators and thinkers who have been inspiring a number of social activists in various parts of the world. These are Lorenzo Milani, who founded the School of Barbiana in Tuscany, Italy, and the Brazilian educator, Paulo Freire. We interviewed two persons who have lived close to them namely Edoardo Martinelli, one of Don Milani's pupils at the School of Barbiana, and Paulo Freire's widow, Nita Freire.

We have sought to provide a mixture of discussions centring around issues related to the so-called 'old' and 'new' social movements although this is a dichotomy that does not go down well with us.

There is a mixture of face to face interviews carried out in countries such as Italy and Brazil and interviews carried out through electronic networking. We sought to cover as large a range of issues as is possible in a book such as this, although we do not claim to be exhaustive in that geographical distance and inability to secure the right contacts prevented us from interviewing people engaged in struggles in sub-Saharan Africa and in Chiapas, to name but two areas. We are confident, however, that other books in the same format and dealing with similar issues will follow and continue to bring other struggles to the fore, besides taking these debates further.

References

Gret, M. and Sintomer Y. (2005). *The Porto Alegre Experiment; Learning Lessons for Better Democracy*, London; Zed Books.

Miliband, R. (1982). *Capitalised Democracy in Britain*, Oxford University Press.

Reflections from a Third Age Marriage; A Pedagogy of Reason, Hope and Passion

Interview with Nita Freire

It had been almost a year since Paulo Freire (1921-1997) suddenly passed away and several activities, marking this first anniversary, were being organised in Brazil. We were in São Paulo to join an international gathering of educators, community activists and scholars participating at the 1st International Paulo Freire Forum organised by the Instituto Paulo Freire. Meanwhile, in Freire's native Nord-este, particularly in the city of Recife, the city for which Paulo always had a special passion, the Movimento dos Sem Terra (the Movement of Landless Peasants—MST), was organising another commemorative event in honour of a person they regard as an important source of inspiration. We had been barely a day in the Brazilian megalopolis when we caught up with Paulo Freire's widow, Professor Ana Maria Araújo Freire (Nita Freire), at her residence, not far from the Pontifical Catholic University (PUC) where Paulo Freire taught.

The interview, kindly organised on our behalf by the Maltese Dominican priest, Frei Joao Xerri, took place a couple of hours before Nita Freire was to catch the plane for Recife in order to be present at the MST commemorative event. Its availability in English is the result of a truly collaborative Maltese-Brazilian effort which involved Frei Joao as interlocutor throughout the interview (he had been working in Brazil since 1974), Frei Sergio Abreu as transcriber of the text and Lilia Azevedo as translator.

We are convinced that your husband, Paulo Freire, was immersed in a number of political and pedagogical projects at the time of his passing away. Can you tell us something about his concerns at the time and the projects he had in mind?

Paulo had many dreams and projects, for his life, for his work and which concerned the world in general. He wanted very much to live and because of this we thought that these dreams and projects might give him many years of life—more than is normally possible. Unfortunately, there was no exception in his case.

There is one thing, perhaps only one, that provides me with some consolation following his death, a consolation for these unfulfilled dreams and the sadness of not having him near me: the fact that he died in full activity, at the height of his wisdom and of his ethical, political and pedagogic thought. It wouldn't be fair if Paulo had died when he wasn't any more the extraordinary thinker and achiever that he was. This is, I repeat, the basis for my acceptance of this terrible thing: the death of a beloved one, such as Paulo was for me.

Some of these projects involved writing books and articles; giving courses and seminars; doing interviews; visiting dear friends and places again; listening to good music, eating dishes he liked, drinking good wine. In a word, to "live love," "fulfill my political tasks," "to know and to feel that I am here in this world, so difficult but at the same time so delightful"!

In April last year we had gone to the USA, at the invitation of Harvard University, for Paulo to give classes in the first semester (September 97 to January 98). He organized the bureaucratic matters and the last details of the programme for the course he was to co-teach with Donaldo Macedo. The course was to be about the knowledge necessary for a progressive teaching practice, basically the reading of "Pedagogia da Autonomia": *Pedagogy of Autonomy*.[1] The project was for an eminently critical course and there were already a great number of students interested in this less alienated way of "reading" the world. Paulo and Donaldo were very happy with the enthusiasm shown in anticipation of the course.

Paulo had begun to talk with the professors of the University where he had been teaching since 1980—the Catholic University—PUC—of São Paulo—about his project of writing a book about an educational curriculum, in its most ample and critical form. He spoke about carrying out the project even before his trip to the USA. The book would be about the act of teaching-learning, the seriousness of studying, evaluation, etc.

He was obstinate about writing about neo-liberalism with another member of the PT (*Partido dos Trabalhadores*—Workers' Party), from the State of Minas Gerais. He never tired of condemning the proclaimed **fatalism,** with which the neo-liberals justify the historical route they themselves have traced to attain their objectives, as an inexorable force against which there is nothing to be done. They say that this is the natural course of human socio-economic and political evolution and there is no way and even no reason for changing it. He said: "Fatalism is only understood by power and by the dominant classes when it interests them. If there is hunger, unemployment, lack of housing, health and schools, they proclaim that this is a universal trend and so be it! But when the stock market falls in a country far away and we have to tighten up our belts, or if a private national bank has internal problems due to the inability of its directors or owners, the State immediately intervenes to "save them." In this case, the "'natural,' 'inexorable,' is simply put aside." He wanted to clarify and denounce this more complete and perverse form of capitalism, because he felt it was his duty as an educator.

During his last years, Paulo always denounced, in his speeches, the horror of neo-liberalism that denies history, ideology, the existence of social classes, the better to invade, oppress and exploit those who have less, either persons or countries, for the purpose of **announcing** better times for all. He was concerned with the number of persons who let themselves be deceived by neo-liberal slogans and so become submissive and apathetic when confronted with their former dreams. Paulo used a metaphor for this situation: "They have gone to the other side of the river!"

He used to say, like Ionesco's character at the end of the play "Rhinoceros": "I am a man, I refuse to be a rhinoceros." When Paulo said this, he meant that he would never be converted to this distorted way of being in the world. "I will stay alone in this world, Nita, but I will never ally myself to the neo-liberal principles." I am sure—we are all sure—that Paulo would never go to the other side of the river!

Travelling all over this immense Brazil we saw and cooperated with a very large number of social movements of different sizes and natures, but who had (and continue to have) a point in common: the hope in their people's power of transformation. They are teachers—many of them are "lay": embroiderers, sisters, workers, fishermen, peasants, etc., etc., scattered all over the country, in favelas, camps or houses, men and women with an incredible leadership strength, bound together in small and local organizations, but with such a latent potential that it filled us, Paulo and me, with hope for better days for our people. Many others participated in a more organized way in the MST (Movimento dos Sem Terra: *Movement of Landless Peasants*), the trade unions, CUT (Central Única dos Trabalhadores), and CEBs: *Christian Base Communities*. As the man of hope he always was, Paulo knew he would not remain alone. Millions of persons, excluded from the system, are struggling in this country, as they free themselves from oppression, to liberate also their oppressors.

Paulo died a few days after the arrival of the MST March in Brasília. On that April day, standing in our living-room, seeing on the TV the crowds of men, women and children entering the capital in such an orderly and dignified way, full of emotion, he cried out: "That's it, Brazilian people, the country belongs to all of us! Let us build together a democratic country, just and happy!"

Such was Paulo during the last days of his life—the same as when he was a boy in Jaboatão, going hungry. Then he thought of struggling against injustice. He spent his life showing how, through education, one can eliminate injustice and build a really democratic society.

Since we do not know Portuguese and so can only have access to Paulo Freire's thought through translations, we ask: what are we losing, as a result?

Ah! I think you lose a lot, not because of the translators, who are usually very good, but because Paulo's language was so rich. Since he mastered the Portuguese language with such precision and beauty, he had the ability to recreate words, give them new meanings and even create new words. Paulo's language is so rich, strong and radical that it becomes impossible to provide an absolutely faithful translation. By the way, this is the difficulty translators have with any writer. With Paulo it becomes a challenge that goes beyond a translator's capability. Paulo says a lot through his language, which is completely his own and is, at the same time, poetical and precise. His ideas are universal because they refer to and deal with the problems of men and women, but the language he used is deeply Brazilian. Perhaps this is why he said: "I write in Brazilian and not in Portuguese!" You see, he certainly said this because of the radical way in which he said and wrote what he thought.

Conscientização (to make someone aware of his own reality); **quefazer** (What-to-do); **oprimido** (someone who is oppressed); **denúncia-anúncio** (denunciation-annunciation); **pronunciar o mundo** (to proclaim the world); **leitura do mundo** (to read the world); **boniteza** (prettiness); **paciência impaciente** (impatient patience) and hundreds of other words he used were recreated by him and so carry the political specificity of his language. He used words of such beauty and plasticity, organized in phrases and these in turn in the context of the totality of the text, with such aesthetic and political force that, I repeat, they cannot be transposed so easily into other languages because a language cannot be translated literally. And it is important to emphasize that his language is extraordinarily beautiful, rich and full of his particular way of being.

Paulo was not using the word **conscientização** any more (conscientização did not exist as a Portuguese word. D. Helder Câmara used it, but it was Paulo who filled it with such meaning). This was because of the criticism he had received from those who understood it to be an idealistic concept. However, lately, he used to tell me he was going to use it again, because he found it to be very rich: it indicates movement, the beginning of an action, preparation of the action that must follow. In no way did it indicate a sense of "spontaneity" or "voluntarism." Neither did it imply that unchecked action or idealism was among its ingredients. In short, he did not intend it to convey a sense lacking in or separated from true political praxis, the praxis that reaches for theory, and goes back to it, illuminating it.

Denounciation was a worn-out word, with an aggressive and ugly connotation, that of a persecution of someone or something, of a condemnation or reproof of an unjust or unscrupulous act made by the other person. Paulo rescued this word, giving it the meaning of the moment in which a person becomes aware of a certain problem and, with this awareness, there already appears, dialectically, the possibility of change, of revelation (un-veiling), of hope (if men and women want it and are able to do it, rendering it concrete in a "viable original," which is also a very rich category created by Paulo), through the dialectical pair to which he gave the name of **announciation.**

I chose these words, from among others I could cite, to show how Paulo "loaded" his phrases with a beautiful and difficult subtlety.

Another problem for translators who did not know Paulo well is the fact that his language is loaded with his feelings, since he never provided a dichotomy between reason and emotion. Paulo was a radically coherent man: what he said contained what he felt and thought and this is not always easy to translate. There are emotions whose meaning can only be well perceived, understood and felt inside a certain culture. And we Brazilians are unique in this way. I think this is so, isn't it?

Without any prejudice, I think it is difficult for translators who have only studied the Portuguese language, albeit accurately, to express Paulo in all his aesthetic and even cultural-ideological richness. I say so because the academicism of many persons from the so-called rigorous cultures who study him leads translators from these languages to be very concerned with the fidelity of the form, the word they use, leaving aside other words that could seem to be too full of feelings and so should be avoided, because after all "Paulo was a philosopher of education and not a novelist." And so unwittingly the "careful" translator can*not* do exactly what Paulo did: choose words recreated by an imagination in love with the knowledge and the beings of the world, which represents one of his humanist marks on the world.

I can provide an example here. First World intellectuals said to me: "Don't cry, don't become emotional! You are giving a scientific speech, an academic work in surroundings where there is no place for emotions!" Can you imagine? I was in Hamburg, at a Congress for Adult Education where everything, or almost everything, turned around Paulo. The conference paid great homage to him. His ideas and his name filled the atmosphere of the meeting. And I had lost Paulo less than three months before! The terrible sense of loss was strongly reflected in the form of working I had learnt exactly from him: to say what one felt when thinking. Why would it be wrong to think, crying? Can it be true that when we cry we lose our reason? I felt and could not even control myself to stop crying, but I knew I was thinking. And so, why control myself? That is the question!

Paulo was a man who was never ashamed to say that everything he knew came from his curiosity, awakened by his feelings, by what his skin said, his intuition aroused, his emotion dictated.

From there he went on to deep and reflective thought, to that which had been aroused in him from different sources. Intuition, as a principle, derived from his sensibility to see what was in the world, which obviously required the use of reason and the exacting steps of science to constitute as historical scientific truth. One can here speak of *an intuition rigorously systematized*. After all, intuition or emotion, without the necessary discernment that comes from a serious and deep questioning, from an exacting reflection, leads to distortions and misunderstandings.

For Paulo, intuition or emotion, or both, provided the beginning of knowledge. They provided the beginning of the curiosity that slowly becomes an *epistemological curiosity*.

Paulo always criticized the use of an absolutely emotional speech. Here are a few examples: the explosive words with which, during the fifties and beginning of the sixties, the Brazilian left manifested the need for changes in our society: "Let us kill the bourgeoisie, take over their factories and expose their heads on the street posts." He never tired of saying that these highly aggressive speeches were terribly imprudent and could not lead the revolution to its goal. And this could not happen also because it could well be that the proclaimers themselves did not really want to do what they proclaimed. And, even if a few really wanted it to occur, feeling this desire, it was impossible, in the Brazilian context, to be applied to the bourgeoisie as a whole.

There are limits even to the expression of our emotions, most of all when it is a matter that requires scientific accuracy: I wish to make this very clear. Paulo never maintained that emotion should subjugate reason. But he also vehemently rejected the opposite 'academicist' view.

Finally, for Paulo, **starting** from emotions necessarily implied that they be controlled, filtered and elaborated to become the starting point for the construction of lucid ideas and humanizing actions. And this should never entail the generation of emotions that distort the sense of BECOMING, which is the true ontological destiny of men and women. Let emotion be the "starting motor" of systematized knowledge.

I met Paulo when I was almost four years old (he was 17, a late follower of the 2nd grade in my father's high-school) and so I was able to perceive all through his life that he allied his immense intelligence and his charismatic character to the will to educate his own abilities and virtues. These virtues include coherence, tolerance and respect, which are embedded in his words, in his political-ideological humanistic discourse, and which his translators must learn. And they must be learnt in all their magnitude and with all their ethical weight! And this is not easy.

Even though this is not entirely pertinent to your specific question, I would like to emphasize these qualities of Paulo in his everyday actions. When he asked me to write the Notes in his books, *Pedagogia da Esperança* (*Pedagogy of Hope*), *Cartas a Cristina* (*Letters to Cristina*) and *À sombra desta mangueira* (*Under the shadow of this mango-tree*), he totally respected my condition as writer and researcher. I read the text and wrote the Notes according to criteria chosen by myself. Only one of them was written at his request, "A turma do lenço" (*The handkerchief band*) because his father had taken part in this movement and he knew almost nothing about this subject. This research gave me a lot of trouble but I managed to do it.

I can provide another example of the respect Paulo had for persons and cultures. In Europe, we observed professors who presented their "Freirean way" of teaching adults to read and write. Surprised by what I saw and heard, I said: "Paulo, this is a far cry from what you have been proposing!!!" He answered: "Nita, you are not making allowances for the differences in culture, for what conditions them."

I don't know if it is clear why I have talked about so many things. I want to say that to respect another person and other cultures requires many other qualities and not just knowing the author's language. Here's another example: "What is to be done"? Paulo would say: **"what-to-do"**! How interesting, isn't it? It is a rich, deep political category that indicates action with commitment. Now, how can a translator, who knows the language but not Paulo's tongue— i.e., his way of speaking, understand this subtlety of expression?

Paulo's texts are so "wet"—this is another of Paulo's fantastic expressions— that I am afraid his metaphors will not be well understood. Neither would be his way of "reading the words," which also carry a certain typically Brazilian sensuality that he enjoyed so much. I repeat: language is culture.

The translators who were able to translate him faced a very difficult task and should rejoice, because the pleasure of reading a text from Paulo in Portuguese, or better still, in Brazilian, is unique. Let's hope they were able to overcome all these barriers in their translations!

At a 1977 conference on Adult Education, held in England, one of us heard a professor say that Paulo once told him that he was not happy with the English translation of *Pedagogy of the Oppressed*. We find this hard to believe. What is your reaction?

Paulo wrote "Pedagogia do oprimido" while living in Chile. "He wrote it in his head." By this I mean that Paulo's thought, based upon his practice, his theoretical knowledge and his sensibility, created his ideas without his ever putting them down on paper. The moment he felt he had finished what he wanted to say about a particular subject, he sat down and wrote his ideas.

He inaugurated this way of writing, from which he seldom deviated, with the "Pedagogia do oprimido". And so, in one particular year, 1967, he mentally elaborated his book. He wrote it down on paper in a single effort during his 15-day holiday, because he already had it in his head.

He gave the originals to his great and dear friend, Ernani Maria Fiori, to write the preface. Fiori was a great philosopher. A few days later, with an extraordinary essay in his hands—"Aprenda a dizer suas palavras": *Learn to pronounce your words*—that presents Paulo's book, Fiori said: "Paulo, this is a fantastic thing! But I believe you should round off the work with a political analysis of what you said in these three chapters."

Paulo spent a few months reading and studying all he could muster about political science, and, at the same time, writing the fourth chapter. This took months and the few hours he had left each day, after working for so many hours. He told me he wrote while travelling by car in the then dusty roads of the Chilean hinterland, or even in the simple hotels that did not always have adequate lighting.

This was how he finished his "Pedagogia do oprimido" in 1968. He and Elza, his first wife, said to each other: " If we manage to have a Chilean edition of 3,000 copies, it will be splendid." For political reasons, this edition was not produced.

A friend then took the originals to a great American theologian, Richard Shaull, who read them and said to Paulo something like this: "This book will cause a revolution in the world. It came at a good moment to support political practices in many areas, including Liberation Theology!" He wrote the preface for the American edition and indicated a young countrywoman of his who, having lived and worked in Rio for many years, having even married a Brazilian, had systematically studied the Portuguese language. This woman is Myra Ramos. Paulo told me that, with a unique dedication, she translated the originals, consulting him every time she had a doubt: "Is this good or not? Is this really what you are saying?"[2]

It is true that many persons criticize the translation she made, saying that many things could be improved, but Paulo never accepted this criticism. He always answered that Myra had done it carefully and with his approval. During the last years many persons had asked Paulo to have a new translation made, saying that after 20 years it could be "updated." But Paulo always rejected this argument, remaining faithful to the translation and the translator. He did agree in part saying: "There are possibly things to be improved, in my text also, but both will remain as they are. I must only correct some distortions I made, due to the "machista" vision I had then, insisting that when I said MAN, I was also including WOMEN in this category. I have already authorized all the editors to change this, but nothing else shall be changed, and I include Myra's translation in this or 'nothing'." That's the truth. That was how Paulo understood what had been accurately and seriously done at a certain moment in a person's intellectual journey, even though he respected those that differed from him and chose other forms of treating their texts.

He said: "If I want to say something better, I write another text saying it more carefully, in a more proper and profound manner, saying what I had not said before, because I now know more about it. I re-elaborate what I already said in other texts. I don't like to go around changing what I wrote, according to the historical developments or because my awareness of the themes I treated is clearer and more lucid."

I ought to point out that Paulo's work began with a small report—some 5 or 6 pages—he wrote for the Second National Congress of Adult and Adolescent Education. And practically everything is already there in these writings of 1958. He went on growing intellectually and politically and his initial ideas continued to be, in a sense, re-elaborated, because he made his first writings become more profound, more complex, more radical.

Anyhow, this was how Paulo saw the act of writing and of translating: as a fact, historically dated.

One of the challenges for us as critical educators is to move outside the academy and make our mark in the 'public sphere.' Carmel was very much involved in the drafting of the preliminary document for a new national curriculum which is intended to render the Maltese educational system more democratic, guided by the principles of equity, inclusion and entitlement. We are also both involved in a parental empowerment and education project in a working class area of Malta. We are therefore very interested to learn, during our stay here in São Paulo, about Freire's work as Education Secretary in the Erundina Municipal Government. What, in your view, were Paulo's major achievements as Education Secretary?

About your question on Paulo's work in the Municipal Bureau of Education in São Paulo, I would say briefly—although it requires a long answer—that he worked very much and seriously to 'Change the face of the school.' This means: to make it really popular because it would be happy, pretty, efficient, agreeable. To this end, he would be counting upon the participation of the educational agents (teachers, students, directors, supervisors, people in charge of pedagogic orientation, guards, people in charge of the meals, cleaners, janitors, mothers and fathers of the students, etc.).

For this purpose, Paulo delegated initiatives to his advisors and the leaders of the Núcleos de Ação Educativa: *Educational Action Centers* (the former Delegacias de Ensino: *Teaching Precincts*); he signed cooperation agreements with the PUC-SP (*Catholic University of São Paulo*), with the USP (*São Paulo State University*) and with the UNICAMP (*University of Campinas*) to improve educational practice. And so the curriculum for the schools underwent a revolutionary change. It was put at the service of the popular classes because it was born out of the needs and desires of the communities who frequented the schools, enriched by the systematic knowledge which had been elaborated.

Paulo created a really loving dialogue in this small world that he directed from January 1989 to May 1991, because all of those who took part in it, directly or indirectly, could discuss, demand, improve themselves, suggest and create new things and, for the most part, decide.

The formation of all the educational agents, in particular that of the teachers, was of great concern. Other concerns were: the contents of the curricula, de-compartmentalisation of knowledge ; the act of teaching-learning, seen as an indivisible act (this means that when professors are teaching they are also learning with their students and , while they are learning, they are teaching the professor); the valorization of the **menino popular**: *child of the people* as a person with her or his own knowledge. This concept even triggered off academic discussions. In response to someone who pointed out this fact, Paulo argued: "It is possible that sociology does not have this category, but the fact that the **menino popular** (*child of the people*) exists is indisputable! These children are in the streets, in the favelas, among the underemployed and exploited... and, most of all, out of school". I cannot fail to mention also the School Councils among other collegiate bodies established during Paulo's administration.

Paulo created MOVA—Movimento de Alfabetização de Adultos e Jovens (*Adult and adolescent literacy movement*), which is today the model for POPULAR EDUCATION in many municipalities and progressive governments in the country. This movement led to the organization of the First Adult Literacy Students Congress. This is, to date, the only congress of its kind in the world. It was held on the 16 December 1990, and 3,000 students participated.

Once the PT was no longer in government in the city of São Paulo (the original interview was held in April 1998), what was left, in the immediate aftermath of the PT's municipal electoral defeat, of the reforms which Paulo and his team had introduced?

Little is left, and yet contradictorily there is much left to be said. When Paulo left the Bureau in order to go back to writing, his work, based on the idea of a committed education, primarily concerned with the popular masses, who attend public schooling in Brazil, was taken up by Mario Sergio Cortella in Mayor Luiza Erundina's Democratic Government of São Paulo. When this extraordinary mayor's term of office ended, a man from the extreme right took over the government of São Paulo and immediately began to enjoy the benefits of the former administration. Authoritarian acts reappeared, especially in the educational area. The voices of the illiterate, directors, teachers, students and parents were silenced. Punishments came back and also threats and persecutions; in a word, he changed the educational practice into something consistent with his own political practice—the consistency **of** and **for** the absurd, but consistent, nevertheless!

However, the fruits of the real democratic school remained; even though they have been denied since January 1993, they are still there, because they came with enough strength to stay. And they will reappear at the first sign of a progressive government, that is, one which is in favour of and not against the popular classes. The testimony of a great many teachers from the municipal schools in São Paulo made this clear to Paulo.

Teachers are "stubborn" people who do not lose hope! Patiently impatient, they wait as Paulo waited for the right time to reinvent, once again, the education for citizenship they had learnt to make available for their pupils, mainly through Paulo's practice as secretary. He left more than a seed. He left a tree with fruits and flowers, which, though submerged for the time being, will opportunely emerge with the same force of the dream with which it was planted by Paulo. I am sure of this!

It would have been most unfair, in an interview such as this, to focus exclusively on Paulo and not on your own work also. You are an established academic and activist in your own right. Can you tell us something about your own work?

I had been giving classes in different universities in São Paulo (Moema Faculty, which was later closed, Catholic University of São Paulo, São Marcos University) and in some teacher formation courses, when I married Paulo. It was a "third age" marriage, and we didn't want to be far from each other. We wanted to be always close to each other, touching, caressing each other, talking about everyday matters or about educational problems and the world. Paulo used to say: "We have no time to lose!" A touch of Brazilian culture, not so common nowadays but still very strong in Paulo, made him say: "Look here,

Nita, I can't see why you are always away from home! We got married in order to be always together, didn't we? Whom will I talk to during my moments of reflection if you are always busy preparing and giving classes?"

This is why he asked me to stay with him, to study and work with him. It was really unthinkable, or too difficult, for him to remain a long time alone while I was running from one university to the other, either during the day or, most of all, in the evenings (São Paulo is a dangerous city, there is a real problem of personal security).

And so, I gave up the work that was linked to my formal jobs. I understood it was a legitimate desire of his and that it would be important also for me to enjoy, as much as I could, his tender, intelligent, loving presence.

I presented my Master's thesis, a work he had supervised, even though, because of our marriage, he was not a member of the examining board and neither, to my great frustration, did he appear officially as Supervisor. I acquired other credits and received my doctorate in 1994. As I have already said, I wrote the notes that explain the context which Paulo addressed in three of his books: *Pedagogia da esperança*, *Cartas a Cristina* and *À sombra desta mangueira*. I published three books of my own: *Analfabetismo no Brasil*—Illiteracy in Brazil (Cortez Editors), *Centenário de nascimento de Aluizio Pessoa de Araújo*—The Hundredth anniversary of the birth of Aluizio Pessoa de Araújo (Editora do Autor: Author's Publishing House) and *Nita e Paulo: Crônicas de amor*—Nita and Paulo: love chronicles (Editora Olho d'Água: Olho d'Água Publishers). I have had many articles published in magazines in Brazil and abroad, particularly after Paulo's death.

My work in the field of the history of education, during these 10 years of daily living and sharing with Paulo, enabled me to delve deeply into Paulo's thoughts and so I became able to understand, with greater clarity and propriety, the revolutionary power of his understanding of education. I learned every day, listening to him or discussing his writings with him.

All of a sudden, when he was full of engagements, projects and life, there came the heart attack that took him away. He smoked many cigarettes a day. His organism was compromised, undermined by nicotine. One of the kidneys was not functioning any more; he had a brain ischemia and his blood pressure was controlled by drugs. Unfortunately his whole circulatory system was weakened, but we never thought he could die so soon.

As you can see, the immense pain of losing days so intensely lived, which Paulo's death stole from me, did not paralyse me. Rather, I wished him to continue in me in several ways, including my writing about both of us and about what he thought as an educator. And I wished this, not only because of what the first hours of the 2nd May 1997 represent in my life—a terrible moment of loss, amazement and pain, that does not even allow us the capacity to truly realize what is happening; the sensation is that our own life is ending. When I was able to think, I decided that I should continue to think what Paulo thought. Reliving what we had lived. "Thinking him" my way, with my own resources. This means that I continue to work so that Paulo's real legacy, his authentic liberating thought,[3] is not erased or distorted.

This year, a group of friends, the majority of whom I got to know through Paulo, because they were old friends of his or had worked with him, approached me so that we can create together the Movimento Paulo Freire Vivo: *Paulo Freire Alive Movement.*

The main purpose is to divulge as much as possible Paulo's ideas, either by assisting popular communities to recreate him faithfully and adequately,[4] or by encouraging the setting up of documentation and theoretical study centers by admirers of Paulo and his work, because this is a huge task which therefore requires—it is important to emphasize—a collective and committed effort.

Notes

1. The book has been published in the U.S. as *Pedagogy of Freedom: Ethics, Democracy and Civic Courage*, Lanham, Maryland: Rowman & Littlefield, 1998.
2. Nita: The work related to the translation of *Pedagogia do oprimido* coincided with the period during which Paulo lived in Cambridge, USA, when he taught at Harvard university, between April 1969 and February 1970. Myra lived in a city nearby and she never hesitated to phone him to ask for help whenever difficulties arose with the translation. So the first edition of this book by Paulo came out in 1970 and in English. Only in 1975 was it possible to find a way of getting around the Brazilian censorship and to publish it in Brazil.
3. Nita: On July 1st of this year, as I was revising this interview for publication, I had the pleasure of hearing from Dra. Isabel Capeletti, the Coordinator of the Programa de Pós-Graduação em Educação—Currículo (Post-Graduate Programme on Education—Curriculum), the news of the creation, at the Catholic University of São Paulo / PUC, of the "Cátedra Paulo Freire" (Paulo Freire Chair). This will offer students, following a Master's or doctoral degree programme at PUC or other univerisities in Brazil, courses about the work and thoughts of Paulo Freire. I had the honour of being invited to give the inaugural course, between August and December 1998.
4. Nita: The "Escola de Samba Leandro de Itaquera": Leandro de Itaquera Samba School, in São Paulo, chose 'the life and work of Paulo Freire' as their theme for the February 1999 Carnival. As his widow, an expert on the subject and a member of the *Movimento Paulo Freire Vivo*, I helped them in an advisory capacity.

Translated by Lília Azevedo, August 1998

Nicaragua: Past and Present

Interview with Maria Hamlyn Zuniga

The Nicaraguan revolution captured the imagination of several persons all over the world in the 80s because of the great promise it held out for building a socially just society. A truly international movement emerged in support of the Nicaraguan revolution comprising groups from various parts of the world. Attempts were, however, made to destabilize the revolutionary government through an internal civil war known as the Contra War. In the meantime great initiatives were introduced in the areas of education, including popular education, and health. This early period in the revolution will always be remembered for the Mass Literacy Crusade that took place. However things changed drastically since then as Maria Hamlyn Zuniga, a popular educator who worked in the field of popular health education in Nicaragua, explains in the following interview which is an extension of another interview one of us carried out with her in Toronto in 1991. The updated interview was carried out in February 2005.

In your view to what extent did popular education help change social relations in Nicaragua soon after the 1979 revolution?

Popular education was fundamental to the transformation from a dictatorship to a new society based on equality and justice for all.

At one point over one third of the Nicaraguan population, over one million people, were involved in some form of education. The formal education from pre–school to adult education was free and universal. There were over 45,000 popular educators involved in carrying out programmes in the communities around the country continuing the efforts of the literacy crusade in spite of the counter revolutionary war.

Informal education was to be found in every sector with thousands of people taking part in workshops and education for living in the transition from the dictatorship to a more just and equal society.

In health over 100,000 persons, especially women and youths, were involved in the popular health brigades working on health promotion and prevention in all the municipalities, towns and rural areas of the country.

These popular education programmes depended, to a large degree, on the generosity and support provided as a result of international solidarity.

Soon after the Sandinista defeat during the 1990 elections, the former Nicaraguan literacy crusade coordinator and Minister of Education, Fernando Cardenal, is on record as having said that it was only then that Nicaragua was beginning to move away from 'banking education'. What does this mean to you?

Actually, that quote could not have been after 1990. In 1984 P. Fernando Cardenal was named Minister of Education after having successfully led the Literacy campaign in the first years of the Revolution. He stated, at that time, that there needed to be a revolution in education, and that all education had to be based on the principles of popular education that is 1. Based on the reality of each situation, fully aware of the economy of survival and the terrible situation of poverty and lack of sufficient resources available to the country; and, 2. All teachers would have to make use of their creativity to carry out the popular education principles in their schools and communities.

Education for liberation and transformation means leaving behind the concept of banking education through which one receives information, memorizes it, feeds it back at an examination, and promptly forgets it. Banking education in Nicaragua was common, even for those who had the privilege of an education. It took a great deal of effort to change the patterns and practices of teachers and other educators during the revolution, thus the comment by P. Cardenal when he took on the responsibility of the Ministry of Education.

Liberating education, based on the Paulo Freire Model, was the basis for the popular education in Nicaragua in all sectors. It was the basis for our work in popular health education and led to the active role of community members in changing their lives and their conditions during the RPS. However, there was always the tendency towards expecting the orientations for the educational programmes to come from the Ministry of Health rather than being developed at the local level as a response to the particular situation.

Has anything been salvaged from the Sandinista projects in education and health?

There is what some people call "social capital" that was salvaged, at least for a number of years. Those who were popular educators, health brigadistas, and others, maintained for years, even after the defeat of the Sandinistas, their commitment to the programmes of literacy training or being involved in the health campaigns for vaccination programmes, for control of vectors that cause diseases such as dengue and malaria. Because of the passage of years, many of those persons are now older and not as active. But the essence of the education reform is still alive, even if it is dispersed.

The popular education model and the "social capital" model have not been destroyed by the present neoliberal model. It is not capable of destroying the organizational capacity of the people that was a constant during the RPS when youths and adults became aware of their capabilities and the need to make a change. This is a social, political and educational awareness that still lives on, especially in the processes of decentralization and the turning over of power and programmes to the municipal governments. People continue to give their time generously to training programmes, workshops, educational programmes of different types, still making use of popular education principles. However these programmes are dispersed in the territories. In terms of the official programmes and priorities of the Ministries of Health and Education at the national level, little remains of these nationwide programmes.

To what extent have the Nicaraguan health and education systems suffered through structural adjustment programmes (SAPs)?

Absolutely. From 1990 on the excessive requirements of the Breton Woods institutions we have witnessed the total dismantling of the programmes of the RPS, including restructuring and privatization under the guise of "modernization" of the health and education sectors.

Nicaragua is among the most highly indebted nations in the world. It has the most severe poverty in Latin America after the regrettable state of Haiti. This year, 2005, Nicaragua will have an external debt of $4,185 million which is equivalent to 90% of the GNP expected for the year. It has a comparable internal debt because of government decisions which have favoured the banking sector over all other sectors, and in particular the social sector which is in a disastrous situation—$3,370 million equivalent to 80% of the GNP. Even with programmes for reducing or alleviating the external debt, the major part of the funds that are generated are used for maintaining the strength of the international reserves in the Central Bank.

Approximately 49% of the population are considered unemployed or under employed and over 16% of the population that could be considered economically active are not expected to generate income this year, 2005.

An analysis of the expenditures in health in Nicaragua demonstrates that the family is spending more than the government on health services. Have a look at these figures:

	2000	2001	2002
Expenditures MINSA/ GNP	2.4%	2,3%	2.6%
Expenditure Households/GNP	3.6%	3.6%	9.9%

Source: Office of National accounts in Health, Ministry of Health, Nicaragua.

Further examples of this are seen in the following data related to the basic salary of teachers in Central America where the salary of the teachers covers only about 75% of the basic requirements for a family of four:

Basic salary of a teacher in Central America in 2004

                            Primary   /   Secondary

Guatemala   US$ 462.30 / US$ 486.73

El Salvador   US$ 564.00 / US$ 621.00

Honduras   US$ 275.00 / US$ 325.00

Nicaragua   **US$ 085.00 / US$ 097.00**

Costa Rica   US$ 407.95 / US$ 423.40

Panamá   US$ 515.00 / US$ 630.00

What are the challenges facing health workers like you in the current neo-liberal scenario?

- Constant attacks against NGOs since 1996 during the Aleman presidency when severe measures were taken against individuals and organizations.
- Lack of public funds for the Ministry of Health programmes because of the severe reductions in social programmes and budgets due to SAPs and the so called "Poverty Reduction Strategies." The budget approved by the National Assembly is totally inadequate.
- Poorly paid health workers and ancillary personnel in the government sector.
- Marked reduction in overseas development aid to NGOs. Health is not considered a priority for bilateral donors nor for the international NGOs that were active in Nicaragua in the past. Multilateral donors, WB/IMF, implement programmes that intensify the structural adjustments and vertical programmes that do not provide support for health systems, per se.
- Burnout.

What important shifts have occurred within the Sandinista movement in view of the new political local, regional and global scenario in which they find themselves, a scenario which is markedly different from the one they faced in 1979?

The major shift is in the ethics and morals of the leadership of the Sandinista Party, the "cupola." There is an increasingly severe and dangerous polarization between persons and groups who maintain the ideals of General ACS and those who support Daniel Ortega. The latter and the group that is closest to him have become part of the new entrepreneurial class, the new oligarchy in Nicaragua, which maintains power and privilege without regard for the poverty and the misery in which the vast majority of the population are living. In part, this is the result of the fact that nobody was prepared for the defeat, the changes, and the abuses that followed the fall of the Sandinistas from power in 1990.

During the last five years, the corruption of both of the "caudillos," Daniel Ortega and former President Arnoldo Aleman, has resulted in mutual protection between the two leaders. There is no debate of ideas or preparation of party platforms based on reality. The official Sandinista party structure has made a political pact with the Liberal party. This pact affects all aspects of political life and all the powers of the state. It makes it impossible for any alternative political parties to reorganize and become an alternative for those who are not satisfied with the present political parties and want to bring about change.

Who provides a counter-hegemonic voice in Nicaragua?

The official Sandinista Party cannot be considered a counter-hegemonic voice at present. It is considered by many to have abandoned the real struggle for justice in Nicaragua and to be a traitor to the workers, peasants and the poor.

Different forces of civil society now exercise that role. NGOs, the community based organizations and the social movements are the counter-hegemonic forces today. This includes environmental organizations and groups, citizens' groups struggling against the privatization of water, electricity and social security, human rights organizations, religious organizations, local and regional networks, as well as groups and persons who have been active in the World Social Forum. All of these individuals and groups believe that another world is possible and are working to bring about justice and peace in Nicaragua.

However, NGOs still exercise too much 'protagonismo' in the civil society sphere. They need to be willing to support and develop the community organizations and the social movements so that the latter are better able to act on their own behalf.

Much of the literature concerning the Sandinista years in government attaches importance to the emergence of mass organisations such as the health workers union, agricultural workers, teachers' union, etc. How strong has the social movement sector been since then, and what role, if any, is it playing in contemporary Nicaraguan politics?

Those "official" mass organizations have been totally taken over by the official party and obey the dictates of Daniel Ortega. Several leaders are now members of the national party directorate and are members of the national Assembly. They play an active role in national politics, but are not representative of the masses in any sense of the word.

The presence of priests in the old Sandinista leadership sheds light on the role of the Church in Nicaraguan society. What role is the Church, or its different factions, playing today?

We witness the role of the hierarchy of the Catholic Church in giving support to the pact between the two major parties and in particular, giving unconditional support to the two caudillos.

There is still an active group of liberation theologians and many persons who are part of basic Christian communities, that are not accepted by the hierarchy, but who continue to denounce injustices and to be prophetic voices in the situation of misery that characterizes Nicaragua today.

From where would a person committed to change in Nicaragua derive his/her resources of hope?

- The humility and hard work of the majority of the people, especially the women, who struggle to overcome poverty, violence, repression and depression through their work and an everlasting sense of humour of the Nicaraguan people give one hope.
- There is a constant struggle not to go backward, not to fall into depression and disillusionment, but to struggle to keep working towards a better life and better conditions.
- The expressions of commitment to change that are coming about because of the processes of decentralization, of the development of the municipalities and the diverse and dispersed local expressions of power and political action have resulted in a renewal of spirit at this level, which is very different from what is occurring at the national level.

Women, Peace and Middle East Politics

Interview with Nahla Abdo

*N*ahla Abdo is a prominent Palestinian peace activist currently residing in Canada but who has been carrying out consultancy work in Palestine with the Palestinian Ministry of Women Affairs. In this interview she discusses a whole range of issues with regard to Middle East politics, the women's movement in the Arab world, Islamophobia, Islam, peace prospects in Palestine, the post-9/11 situation, multiculturalism, curriculum development in Palestine, religious tolerance and a variety of other issues. She is a Professor of Sociology at Carleton University, Ottawa, Canada.

In one of his conversations with David Barsmian, Edward Said speaks of a growing women's movement" in the Arab world. How would you assess this comment?

Throughout the Arab world and for several decades now, individual and small groups of women have been very active in demanding their social, legal and political rights. Changes in local and global politics, including the stifling regimes throughout the Arab world, the first Gulf War, the American colonial invasion of Iraq, Israeli continued settler colonial occupation of Palestine, and the overall Western (mainly American) demonization and attacks against Islam and Muslims, have undoubtedly contributed to a greater sense and need by Arab civil society institutions to take their issues in their hands. In various Gulf countries, women began to demand a presence and representation in decision-making processes, participation in electoral processes and they began to present serious challenges to existing Shari'a based legal systems in the Arab world.

In addition to various local campaigns and women's NGOs established to fight against violence against women, we have witnessed different attempts being made to establish regional (especially Middle Eastern and North African) institutes to raise consciousness against violence against women, such as the Arab Women's Court established in Rabat Morocco in 1996 as a symbolic body to voice public concerns over the issue, and the Arab institute, Aisha, which is a network for Arab women activists in gender issues.

It goes without saying that due to the historical, political and quite specific circumstances of the Palestinians, the Palestinian women's movement stood up as a particularly strong movement, leading in some areas. This is partly demonstrated by the establishment of the first ever Ministry of Women's Affairs in the Middle East. It is worth noting here that the so-called only democracy in the Middle East (Israel) lags very much behind on gender issues. Israel does not have a Ministry of Women's Affairs (MoWA), nor even a solid civil society gender institute, independent of the racist policies of the state. It is in this sense that one can say that the Arab world has been witnessing a bourgeoning women's movement.

You have been involved in consultancy work in Palestine with the Ministry for Women's Affairs. Can you tell us something about this work?

My experience as a consultant to the Palestinian Ministry of Women's Affairs has proven to be a most fulfilling one. I joined MoWA during the early stages of its establishment, working for the first month or so without an office, a computer or even staff as the building of the infrastructure of MoWA was underway. I participated in the process of interviewing and appointing staff, which proved to be extremely professional, based on the principles of transparency, accountability and professionalism. I contributed to the capacity building of the Ministry, through intensive workshops on gender research and gender consciousness. Such workshops were attended by almost all staff at the Ministry (women and men). Enthusiasm by all participants for learning and advancing their knowledge was demonstrated through the diligent homework participants did during these workshops. The troubles and extreme difficulties placed by Israeli occupation, roadblocks, military checkpoints and recently the Apartheid Wall, could not stand in the face of the Ministry staff who came from various parts of the West Bank. Some of the staff who travel for several hours (e.g., from Hebron, Nablus) would begin their morning at 5 a.m. and would go through multiple military check-points. If not successful, they would take the side roads, climbing hills, going through muddy and rocky streets to make it to work.

With this high level of determination on the part of the Ministry staff, I was convinced that MoWA deserves my utmost contribution and commitment. My major contribution to the Palestinian Ministry of Women's Affairs was in drafting the strategy of the Ministry. Considering the principles on which the Ministry was established, it became clear that the Ministry is not to function as an arm of the Palestinian National Authority removed from the concerns of women and the poor. Quite to the contrary, at the outset, the strategy of MoWA was clearly based on two fundamental principles: working closely with Palestinian civil society institutions and most importantly the different women's organizations; and lobbying other governmental and official bodies for changing policies, practices and perceptions of Palestinian women. A full dialogical, transparent and democratic process was established to discuss the Ministry's strategies, share it with women's institutions and organizations. Multiple drafts of the Ministry's strategy, the short term and the long term, were presented at national conferences with the presence of representations from almost all women's groups (including official and NGOs). Feedback was re-incorporated and a more advanced version of the strategy would be developed and shared again. The commitment of Ms. Zahira Kamal, the Minister, her other consultants and the Ministry at large, to turning MoWA into a model institution, provided a great incentive for all.

The choice of MoWA to focus on advancing women's rights to participate in the economic, political, and social life and its commitment to change oppressive laws against women was appreciated by the office of the Prime Minister, leading to the full adoption of its strategy. It is interesting to note that the Minister is not a member of the ruling Fateh party, which, despite some allegations about electoral irregularities, has won the Presidency after the death of Arafat. Not being a Fateh member has recently raised some concerns as to whether the Minister herself would survive the new elections. But the serious work, commitment and historical activist record of the Minister proved her deservedness of the post. Yet, the concern or rather fear comes from Israeli settler colonial presence in the occupied territories and the tremendous obstacles it places on Palestinians in general and its assault on civil and official institutions more specifically. One only needs to remember how Israel destroyed Palestinian infrastructure, invaded and destroyed the Ministry of Education, with Israeli soldiers urinating in the Ministry's offices, ruining and stealing educational programs and projects.

Provided the foundational principles, on which the Palestinian Ministry of Women's Affairs was established, are adhered to, I am confident that this Ministry could function as a major asset for improving Palestinian women's conditions with the potential of becoming an Arab/Middle Eastern model institute to follow.

A particular form of racism—Islamophobia—has been present, in several parts of the world, for a number of years. This situation has been exacerbated by the events in the US of September 11, 2001 and in Madrid on March 11, 2004. In your view, how can educators and cultural workers help combat Islamophobia?

Islamophobia has been around for several decades now, but the events of 9/11, followed by the American invasion of Afghanistan, the military destruction and colonialism in Iraq, Israeli continued racist destruction of Palestinian society and current threats on Iran and Syria, have unleashed a more intensified attack and organized campaigns against Islam and Muslims. The intensity of such campaigns largely led by American neo-conservatives, Christian evangelists and Zionists is unprecedented. The power (economic and military) placed in the hands of such groups has reached almost every aspect of Arab and Muslim societies; from sheer military force used in invading and destroying countries and civilizations; to massacres under the pretext of fighting Islamic fanatics, Jenin/Palestine, Fallojah/Iraq, to mention just a few; to increased curtailing of democratic rights and civil liberties and a particular attack on education institutions.

It is possible to argue that a full scale campaign intended to curtail and diminish freedoms of speech and expression in both media and academia has gripped the Western world and especially North America. Direct attacks on anti-racist activist faculty members and students, is witnessed in many universities and higher educational institutions throughout North America. Intensive campaigns to monitor faculty members engaged in critique of racists, US and anti-Israeli oppressive policies and practices, for the purpose of punishing those faculty members and students, for example, the infamous Daniel Pipe campaign, and similar Israeli-based campaigns have gained solid support, status, and funding from the US and Israeli governments.

Although such campaigns have caused a lot of trouble and inconveniences for various faculty members, not to mention life-threats, and various forms of attacks made on members of faculty in various North American universities including attacks on me, such campaigns have not necessarily detracted from the resolve and commitment of critical, anti-racist faculty members and students, to continue their fight towards a just life free of many forms of oppression.

Educators in both the West and the East have and continue to play an important role in raising new generations conscious of the need to live in a true—and not American or Israeli type of—democracy, in a world that adheres to and respects international laws and rules; a world where international bodies like the UN and the International Criminal Court can be respected and not highjacked by Zionist and U.S. interests. Educators can play a major role in advancing people's right to live in a fair and dignified world, in promoting gender equality and fighting discrimination based on class, ethnic and religious differences.

Unfortunately, globalization has brought some benefits to certain members of various societies, including state and government academics. Here I find Gramsci's perception of the intellectual as having a crucial role in the context of creating a counter hegemonic rule, to be paramount. This notion, re-enforced by Edward Said's concept of the "exilic intellectual" should serve as an eye-opener to all academics and educators concerned with bringing reason, rationality, sanity and justice to a so-called global system that appears to have lost all perspective. The "exilic intellectual", whether in or outside of academia is the one who uses her/his critical and analytical faculties and commitment to combine academia with activism in order to change the world and bring true justice, equality and sensibility to our world.

How do you conceive of Islam?

As a Palestinian born and raised in Nazareth, I grew up with the understanding that Islam and Muslims, like Christianity and Christians, represent a faith which expresses the private relationship between the individual and their God. Muslims and Christians practise different yet similar rituals, including fasting, praying. They both celebrate their Holy days separately and together. In Nazareth, which until recently was made up of almost equal number of Muslims and Christians, the same names to the two major Holy days are used: Eid el-Kabir (the big Eid) for Muslims, known as Al-Adha, and Eid el-Kabir, also known as Easter among Christians, and Eid el-Saghir (the small Eid), also known as Ramadan for Muslims and Eid el-Saghir, also known as Christmas for Christians. Muslims and Christians lived (and continue to live) in the same neighbourhoods, and in many aspects they participate in both religious festivities. I started this with my personal experience to suggest that at the community, popular level Islam is void of political interest.

Instead, it is the state, the polity, rather than the religion itself, which has turned Islam into a political statement and political movement. Both Arab and Muslim states along with the imperialist interests of the US and the colonial settler ambitions of the Israeli state and the world Zionist movement, I believe, have been behind the rise of Islamicism or political Islam as we witness it today. It is these political interventions and the limited class and imperialist self-interests, used to justify vicious attacks against Muslims, which have also led to the emergence of fanatic Islamicists.

I find it particularly disheartening that racist, imperialist powers have succeeded in turning world attention to Islam as the villain, while the danger of the Christian, Jewish, and Hindu racist and fundamentalist character and practice goes unrecognized and underplayed. If anything, this means that the cycle of violence, racism and discrimination would only grow: imperialist powers pressure Arab and Muslim states; the latter, instead of democratically dealing with their societies' conflicts and factionalism, intensify such conflicts and place more pressure on Islamic groups; more Islamic organizations and groups grow within Arab and Muslim societies fighting back the regime. In the process of all of this Arab and Muslim women turn out to be the primary victims of this cycle of violence. The economic dependence of various Muslim and Arab countries on the West (particularly the US), along with the World Bank and IMF programmes of structural adjustment have led to increased economic troubles, political, social and even cultural dependence of various states on imperial powers. In an attempt to carry out such policies many states found themselves in need of re-enforcing emergency rules, inherited from British colonial times, as means to control the public and any attempt at political activism challenging such policies.

Lack of democracy, dictatorial rule, high unemployment rates and worsening living conditions make fertile grounds for the emergence of conservative social forces such as the various Islamic and Islamicist organizations which have mushroomed in the recent years throughout the Arab and Muslim countries.

The above analysis suggests that there is not one homogenous notion of Islam, but a multiplicity of Islams, depending on the meaning and context of such notions. Unfortunately, however, US and Israeli imperialist powers, for geo-political and ideological reasons, insist on advancing a totalitarian homogenous and a-historical notion of Islam to brand all Arab and Muslim countries and civil societies with terrorism and fanaticism.

When defending the rights of Arabs and Muslims in multicultural societies, we are often confronted by such arguments as 1) the tolerance shown by western societies towards Muslims is not reciprocated by similar tolerance in predominantly Muslim countries towards people professing a different religion or life style 2) women are oppressed within the Muslim culture, being denied basic human rights. How would you respond to this in the context of promoting a society characterized by interethnic solidarity and conviviality?

There is a partial truth in your statement that Western multicultural societies demonstrate more tolerance towards the rights of Arabs and Muslims. First, I would like to say that the concept of multiculturalism must be problematized and not be taken at face value. After all, most Western 'multicultural' states are settler colonial states (e.g., the US, Canada, Australia, Israel, etc.). While claiming multiculturalism as a form of liberal democratic means of dealing with their diverse ethnic, national and religious groups these states have all been established on the ruins of the respective countries' indigenous inhabitants, the natives.

In fact, as a Palestinian living half of my life in Israel, I was often hounded with such statements: "You should be proud of living in a democratic country"; "If you were in an Arab country you would be in jail for criticizing the state or for your feminist activism"; "Aren't you proud of being Israeli"? and so on. I always resented such a simplistic understanding of liberal democracy and multiculturalism. I always wondered how could anyone make such a statement when the whole system/rule/state being defended has been essentially based on the extermination, destruction and ruin of the indigenous Palestinians.

Still, I did and continue to recognize that the very liberal democratic forms of governing adopted by such countries undoubtedly encourage and promote a certain level of freedom which spins off and spills out, mostly unintentionally and un-planned, to all citizenship. I realize that such limited, yet found, liberties and freedoms are absent in many—if not most—Arab and Muslim countries where democracy is absent and the concept and practice of citizenship is not developed. I realize that the collusion between political Islam and the state throughout the Middle East has placed tremendous pressures on women, depriving them of their basic human and democratic rights in the legal, economic, political, social and cultural spheres.

The answer to above forms of discrimination and lack of tolerance could be achieved through the development of a true democratic system based on respect of international laws, UN conventions and genuine democracy.

Are liberal and Islamic opposed and mutually exclusive terms?

Not necessarily. If and when Islam is conceived of as a religion, I see no reason why one cannot speak of liberal Muslims, the same way they would speak of liberal Christians or liberal Jews. Muslim liberal discourses have firmly been entrenched in the legal system of some Arab/Muslim countries like Tunisia for example. Moreover, Sheikh al-Qaradawi, often featured on al-Jazira and the well-known Sheikh Al-Azhar from Egypt are well known for their liberal interpretations of social and gender phenomena in the Arab/Muslim societies.

A term like Islamicist, which refers to a political Islamist movement with a conservative social agenda, on the other hand, could be seen as in opposition to liberal ideology. Here the terms liberal and Islamic can be mutually exclusive. In other words, the determining factor in assigning a particular identity and character to a movement or a social thought would be the power-base and power relations which dictate the dynamics of each phenomenon or set of ideas.

How do you read the Palestinian question? How is the Palestinian Uprising affecting the plight of Palestinian women?

This question is somewhat problematic. The plight of Palestinian women is not a consequence of the Palestinian national resistance expressed in the first (1987-92) and second (2000-) Intifada (uprising). If anything both Intifadas are themselves a reaction to the Israeli military occupation, the Israeli settler colonial policies, its land grab, Apartheid Wall, military checkpoints, roadblocks, economic devastation and political oppression. Palestinian women's full participation and active involvement, particularly in the first Palestinian Intifada, has been fully documented. In fact, this involvement proved a catalyst for raising women's social and political consciousness and for opening their eyes to their domestic/gender plight. This was true until the rise of Hamas in the last 2-3 years of the first Intifada. The political vacuum and economic devastation under which Palestinians have been living have undoubtedly led to the emergence of Hamas (much stronger in the Gaza Strip than in the West Bank). The chaos and political vacuum, especially in Gaza have largely contributed to the growth of a socially conservative, politically strong movement. Women's suffering, especially in Gaza, is partly due to the reign of Hamas. It is quite interesting today—after the new local and presidential elections—to see how social-gender relations and women's position would change, especially with the successful election of about 20 (almost 17% of the total number of elected members) women as members of the local councils. Incidentally, the local elections in the West Bank have also produced very encouraging results, as over 60 members of the total elected representatives were females.

Having said that, one cannot deny the need for fundamental changes in the socio-economic, political and cultural structure of the Palestinian society in order for women to enjoy their rights and live in a law-abiding society. As long as Palestine is under occupation and cannot enjoy a sovereign, independent status, I think Palestinian human rights in general and women's rights in particular will always be jeopardized.

How is the Palestinian curriculum dealing with the current political reality? Are women visible in Palestinian syllabi and textbooks?

Earlier in the interview I referred to the Israeli destruction of the Palestinian infrastructure and the particular assault on the Ministry of Education. The late Professor Ibrahim abu-Lughod spent years on developing the Palestinian new curriculum and textbooks, one that is more Palestinian, instead of the earlier Egyptian—for Gaza—and Jordanian—for the West Bank—to be adopted by the Palestinians in the occupied territories. This curriculum which is in place in Palestinian schools, has a highly improved pedagogical system and materials, which takes up issues of gender, class, ethnicity and history in a progressive and positive manner. While I am sure there is a lot more to be done around the Palestinian curricula in terms of gender issues—not unlike other curricula, including in liberal democracies such as the US—the visibility of productive women, professional, political women and women in leadership positions are more pronounced in the Palestinian curricula than before.

I am cognizant of the Israeli and US media frenzy which for several years has tried to disseminate fabrications and lies about Palestinian education and denounce it as hate literature. In fact, since then a number of studies have concluded that the hate campaign was more political and ideological in nature than expressing real curricular issues. In fact, studies about the Israeli curriculum in schools have largely concluded its racialized, racist and exclusionary character, particularly in terms of its evasion of the presence and history of the Palestinians even when such curricula are used in schools which Palestinian citizens attend.

As critical thinkers we all know the meaning of "Blaming the Victim". The onus is almost always placed on the victim to prove his/her innocence, while the victimizer often gets away with murder. A more suitable question in this regard would be to ask about Palestinian textbooks and curriculum in comparison with that developed by the occupiers and which has been practised for the last 5 decades or so!

Is education an effective antidote to militarism?

Education, in principle, is an effective antidote not only to militarism but also to most social and political ills. Yet, here again the question is who is the target? Who are our subjects? The society, which is militarized to the teeth, is not the Palestinian but the Israeli society. This is where every young (over 18) girl and boy are conscripted and taught to use weapons to kill. Palestinian society is largely demilitarized. Unlike the Israelis, Palestinian citizens in Israel and Palestinians in the occupied territories, unlike the Israeli (Jewish) society, are not part of a militarized culture. We need anti-racist, anti-militarized forms of education to replace the entrenched culture of militarism. This should be integrated into the curricula and textbooks of Israeli school children. This is one effective way to dissuade Israeli youth from getting inside the cycle of violence and demonizing the other, a demonisation they inculcate as part of their cultural upbringing.

You are well known for your peace activism in your adopted country Canada and elsewhere. What educational measures have been effective in Canada to provide a counter-discourse to the dominant one concerning the war in Iraq?

Since the racist American invasion and destruction of Iraq, the civilization, the country and the people, many educators and students have organized various talks, conferences and workshops to unlearn the U.S hate campaign against Iraq and counter it with the actual imperialist interests in the area. Other workshops have focused on the hypocritical position of the U.S as it is trying to push "democracy" through the gun.

Despite the extreme difficulties under which progressive and critical academics are operating these days with the constant threat on freedom of expression, the voice of many educators for peace, justice and respect of international laws remains high. The problematic here is that which could have been assumed earlier, i.e., liberal democratic freedom of expression. As a given, it is not a given any more. In fact, recent changes in the Canadian position on international issues have negative effects on extending the voice of reason. Canada is developing somewhat draconian policies aimed at restricting critical expression and especially in so far as the US and Israel are concerned. The assault on civil rights and domestic liberties is having its toll on several educators, including some in ivy-league universities in the US, such as Columbia. Without going into any details here suffice it to mention that educators do not and cannot work in a vacuum. They need the right political environment to effect true societal changes. In the absence of such healthy conditions, such as we are currently experiencing, I find the role of intellectual and educator to be somewhat difficult. This does not mean that the voice of reason, humanism and justice is totally silent, it just means that more energy and sacrifices are required on the part of the intellectual and educator to make their voices heard.

Lula, Freire, Liberation Theology

Interview with Frei Betto

*C*arlos *Alberto Libanio Christo, popularly known as Frei Betto, is a leading left wing Brazilian activist and thinker. Originally from Belo Horizonte (he now resides in São Paulo), Frei Betto is a lay dominican friar who has made a name for himself as a journalist and popular educator. He has for years been involved in popular education in the Christian Base Communities (Comunidade de Base) especially among metallurgical workers in São Bernardo do Campo. He is also closely connected to one of the two most vibrant movements in Latin America, the Movimento dos Sem Terra (Movement of Landless Peasants). His books in Portuguese, Spanish and Italian cover a wide range of subjects, including a volume (translated into Italian) consisting of a series of interviews on the topic of 'Christianity and Revolution' with Fidel Castro. A former key figure in the Brazilian student movement, he was arrested, following the 1964 military coup in Brazil, for activities deemed "subversive." These and other experiences, including popular education experiences, are captured in a book with Paulo Freire and Ricardo Kotscho which is available in Portuguese and Italian, the title in Portuguese being* Essa Escola Chamada Vida *(Attica, 1984).*

Frei Betto shared some of his views, concerning the church, Paulo Freire, postmodernism and Neo-liberalism, in an interview with us carried out in a São Paulo restaurant in the very early hours of Tuesday, April 28, 1998 after we had accompanied him to a long talk he gave to a group of industrialists in the Brazilian megalopolis. We were in São Paulo to attend the first International Paulo Freire Forum organized by the Paulo Freire Institute on the first anniversary of the Brazilian educator's death. The interview was made possible through the help of Frei João Xerri, OP, known in Brazil as Frei João, who acted as interlocutor throughout the interview. Most of Frei Betto's responses were translated from Portuguese to English by Lilia Azevedo. We updated the interview in 2004 by adding three new questions, the ones concerning Frei Betto's work in popular education in São Bernardo do Campo and elsewhere, Lula's presidency and the pontificate of Pope John Paul II. These were translated by Helen Hughes. We thank Frei João Xerri for making this update possible.

What memories do you have of Paulo Freire as a person, thinker, activist and Christian?

During many periods of our lives I was on intimate terms with Paulo Freire and I consider myself his disciple. For more than 20 years I worked in popular education based upon his method and we wrote a book together, with the participation of journalist Ricardo Kotscho. The first thing that impressed me about Paulo Freire was that, ever since his experience with workers in the State of Pernambuco, he allowed himself to be educated by the workers, before presuming to be their educator. Based upon his experience of faith as a Christian, he had an attitude of listening and even of compassion, which intellectuals who do not have a Christian sensibility usually do not have towards simple and poor people. This allowed Paulo to develop his method of a pedagogy for oppressed people. He was a simple person, an unpretentious intellectual, who never wished to show off his erudition, who did not favour one person over another in any relationship. I remember him telling me how he had entered a store that sold neckties in Switzerland and could not get anyone to help him. After some time he complained and the employee said that nobody paid attention to him because he would not have enough money to buy any of those ties. He related this anecdote as a joke, laughing, to show the prejudices that exist in Europe regarding Latin Americans. He was a very consistent person. A few months before his death, I had lunch at his home. Talking about people who change their convictions, their political parties, he banged on the table and said: "Betto, I have made up my mind to die a Christian and a member of the PT (Workers' Party)." He was someone who loved to pray. I met Paulo through his first wife, Elza; I was there when she died and I preached at her funeral mass. What impresses me most about Paulo is the fact that all his life was dedicated to making the 'little ones,' the oppressed people, the subjects of history. I feel that he died happy because he was able to watch the start of this in the Brazilian process and also in South Africa and Nicaragua, where the popular forces, in some way, managed to have a great influence on the situation (conjuntura).

What effect did Paulo Freire have on the Left in Latin America?

If the CIA questioned me—by inflicting torture—to say who was responsible for all the popular struggles in Latin America during the last 40 years, I would point out Paulo Freire as the one person responsible. By this I mean that, thanks to him, the "left" in Latin America not only changed from an elitist, pseudo-intellectual left, who imported models from Spanish anarchism or Soviet communism, to a popular left, that reconciles revolutionary posture and Christian faith, also reconciling Christian faith and Marxist analysis, but also developed into one which generates a mystique that includes all popular culture, songs, religiosity, feasts, food and the dream of a new society. I ask myself if this would have been possible without Paulo Freire. He was the one who greatly launched this process. He was the one who furnished us with the "road map." The people built the road, but the person who gave us the map of how the 'little ones' can become the subjects of history, how a simple peasant, a simple worker can become a great political leader, was Paulo Freire.

Your book with Paulo Freire and Ricardo Kotscho, *Essa Escola Chamada Vida*, has not, as yet, been translated into English. Can you convey to readers like ourselves, who do not understand Portuguese, your feelings concerning this book project?

I like it very much and consider it an important book. I have a great regard for this book which was written in 1985. It was an evaluation of many years of work in popular education. It was suggested by journalist Ricardo Kotscho and we decided to have a talk to evaluate our work in popular education. It is a book in which, by talking and telling stories, we convey to the reader the nature of our work with the popular classes, the social movements, the trade unions, the Christian Base Communities, the Church pastorals for the popular classes. It is a huge success in Brazil. It is still being sold and greatly helps people understand the practice of popular education. It is not a theoretical book; it addresses the way popular education is lived, is experienced.

Can you tell us something about your work as a popular educator in São Bernardo do Campo and elsewhere?

I worked in São Bernardo do Campo from 1979 to 2002. I worked as advisor to the Workers' Pastoral and the Metal Workers' Trade Union in the area known as ABC (*Santo André, São Bernardo, São Caetano, three cities in the metropolitan area of São Paulo*—translator's note).

I developed an intense activity of popular education according to Paulo Freire's method: in the Pastoral field, by linking faith and politics, spirituality and social activity, struggle for justice and a life of prayer; in the trade union, by helping the leaders to develop a critical analysis of reality, to define tactics and strategies for the struggle, to internalise ethical values and to speak in public.

How would you assess Lula's presidency thus far?

It is necessary to understand that Lula did not bring about a revolution; he won an election within rules defined by the Brazilian oligarchy. Lula did not attain, take over, power; he gained the government, and has to govern in permanent tension with the Congress, where he has only 30% of support and with the judiciary that in Brazil is very conservative. And so the Lula government is marked by paradox: on the one hand, progressive social policies, such as "Zero Hunger"; a daring foreign policy, such as the rejection of the Free Trade—AFTA—proposal by USA, and on the other, a neoliberal macroeconomic policy, submitted to the dictates of the International Monetary Fund, which drains the wealth of the country. In spite of difficulties, Brazil is better off with Lula than without him.

How strong is Liberation Theology at the moment?

On the one hand, Liberation Theology is weak at the moment. After the fall of the Berlin Wall and the pressures from the Vatican, there have been no great advances and in some measure it "dis-articulated" itself because of a lack of support. On the other hand, themes that belonged exclusively to Liberation Theology are today addressed even in documents by the Pope. Suddenly, the Vatican publishes a document about Land Reform which could be signed by any Liberation theologian. We now say that Liberation Theology is no longer a ghetto in the Church, but a leaven that has been "irradiated" so that one can no longer perceive the leaven because it has irradiated itself. Anyone who can cook can distinguish the leaven from the dough at the moment of mixing, but afterwards this is no longer possible.

In a way, Liberation Theology is present as a method, as a sensibility towards social questions and the poor in the general Church theology, because the Vatican's disappointment with neo-liberalism, with the situation of the countries of the late Soviet Bloc, induces it to favour this concern about destitution and poverty.

I would say that Liberation Theologians were marginalized, but Liberation Theology ended up by being incorporated into the official theology of the

Church with all the contradictions that this official theology has, because it still carries great conservative weight.

Whenever we refer to the concept of the 'Prophetic church' in our country, we are told that this concept is important for Latin America but not for the kind of society we live in or for Europe in general. What would be your reaction to this?

First of all, I find this kind of argument rather funny. In fact, I find it ridiculous. The feeling I get in certain European countries—though not in Malta—is that today there are more tourists than believers in the churches. It seems to be a sort of museum-church, a nostalgic church; the people go to the celebrations because they want to listen to the Gregorian music and not because they want to pray and be committed to the Gospel. I am afraid that the European Church will be too late in discovering the importance of a popular pastoral, of Liberation Theology. It is a Church that is much closer to a monarchic model than to the evangelical inspiration. This can be seen in the statements of European cardinals and bishops, who talk much more about the Pope than about Jesus. These are small linguistic symptoms that clearly reveal the state of affairs.

Now that Pope John Paul II has just passed away and has been replaced by Pope Benedict, how would you assess the former Pontiff and latter's papacy to date?

I would say that John Paul II's pontificate was, *overall*, positive.

He was a pope whose head was turned to the right and whose heart was turned to the left. He was an orthodox in matters of doctrine and progressive in social or political matters. The proof is that he never severed the relations between the Holy See and Gaddafi's Libya, Saddam Hussein's Iraq and Fidel Castro's Cuba. In the last years, John Paul II advanced even more, condemning the USA's war on Iraq, criticizing the present model of globalization, defending the pardoning of the external debts of the poorer countries.

As for Benedict XVI it is still too early to evaluate him.

How would you describe Pope John Paul II's visit to Cuba in 1998?

A courageous visit, because he received a lot of pressure not to go to Cuba. The fact that he went was a recognition of the Cuban Revolution. He was Cuba's strongest supporter, at the time, against the American blockade; he declared himself emphatically against the blockade and, for the first time, and in Cuba, he criticized neo-liberal capitalism. He gave Cuba an international visibility that the country only had achieved in 1962, during the missile crisis. His visit was considered by the Cuban people and the government as most positive for the country. The Pope did not go there to canonize the revolution. He went to strengthen the Catholic Church, to undermine Cuban socialism. However, he did act with such diplomacy, in a certain sense, that this did not affect the character of the visit. It was only affected by a Cuban bishop who made a very strong statement against the Revolution. But since the Pope did not endorse this statement, the visit proved to be very positive for Cuba and its relations with the Vatican, though not so much for the relations between the Cuban government and the Catholic Church in Cuba.

The revolutionary movements in Central America entered a stage of 'compromise' or 'concertación'. All the parties sit around a table to engage in dialogue. What is your view of the situation?

This happened basically because of two factors. First, the failure of the Sandinista Revolution and second the fall of the Berlin wall. These two great references were lost, and today to start an armed struggle in Latin America is really suicide because before being a military war, an armed struggle is an ideological war and we have lost our ideological references. Even though the motive for our struggle—which is the existence of stark poverty—has increased, our cultural, utopian and idealistic references have disappeared and it will take some time to recuperate them. And it is not stark poverty that causes a revolution, because if it were, Haiti would already be in post-socialism. What causes the revolution is a culture of ethic values and this culture was lost with the fall of the Berlin wall and the failure of the Sandinista Revolution.

Which are the most expressive popular movements in Brazil today, and what sort of links have been developed between these movements and the Catholic Church?

The most expressive movement today is the *Movimento dos Sem Terra* (MST)—the Movement of Landless Peasants. One should also not disregard the PT—the Workers' Party—which had many mayors, besides congressmen and congresswomen, senators and some governors. One should neither disregard the importance of CUT—Central Única dos Trabalhadores (Unique Trade Unions Central Organization) and the "Central de Movimentos Populares"

(Popular Movements Central Organization). But MST is the most representative because it addresses a very urgent and important question: land reform. Now, to ask what is the relation between the Church and these movements, is the same as asking where does the water end and the grape juice begin in the wine. Everything is so mixed in Brazilian history: I myself helped to prepare many of these leaders by means of the Church. It is difficult to find a popular leader today in Brazil who did not enter into his militancy through the door of a popular pastoral. The Church is the great seed-bed for popular leaders in Brazil. It is difficult for people locked in European Cartesianism to understand this.

Some postmodern thinkers, exhibiting a nihilistic and paralyzing streak, have announced the 'end of history,' positing what Freire calls the 'ideology of ideological death.' What is your reaction to this?

This is a typical description of neo-liberal ideology, which is modern and preaches post-modernism, is well consolidated from a strategic point of view and preaches fragmentation. This ideology has great strategy for the future and preaches immersion in the present and disregard for the future. This is exactly it: it is an ideology that preaches the death of ideology. I think this is all nonsense, because human beings need dreams, need utopia and there is no ideology, no system that can stop this force. Dostoyevsky was right when he said: 'The most powerful weapon of a human being is his conscience' and this nobody can destroy.

I think it ridiculous when they preach that there is no ideology any more, in order to be able to state that the only ideology is the neo-liberal one. I think that it is a matter of time before we witness the eruption of a world movement to rescue utopias.

We have just accompanied you to a talk you delivered to industrialists in São Paulo. Many people from industry whom we know tend to subscribe to a neo-liberal point of view. They have a mindset which is at odds with the kind of utopian vision developed by people like Paulo Freire and yourself. How do you engage in dialogue in such a context?

One of my principles is that if the persons are open to dialogue I do not refuse to talk to them; I will go anywhere and present my positions, whether the people like it or not. In the specific case of this evening, they were entrepreneurs whose thinking is already close to that of the PT, and so of an alternative project for Brazil, not linked to neo-liberalism, which makes it much easier to dialogue. However, a short time ago I had a three-hour conversation with very high level entrepreneurs. It was a difficult, hard talk but the result was also very good because with these people I never discuss specific questions related to their pragmatism, but I always try to discuss fundamental questions, of which many times they are not even aware. And so, the fact that I do have this awareness and can help them to perceive this key to the understanding of reality is always productive in the end.

How does one develop a pedagogy of hope in this day and age?

It is not easy. I would say that today there are two ways for us to maintain hope: from a subjective, personal point of view, through the mystic experience of a very strong interiorization, which then allows us to have a critical view of our own awareness of the system and then of the system itself. The second way is to participate in collective movements which are alternative and potentially revolutionary. Because if I keep myself locked up inside my house, if even though I have an awareness I do not participate, and am not an "accomplice" to expectations or hopes for change, I will not have hope. But the fact that I am linked to the MST or to political projects that still dream of something different gives me strength to struggle. Now, after a certain period, that has nothing to do with age but depends upon an experience, we interiorize in such a way that my personal identity can only be consolidated in the frame of this social project. When one makes this "marriage" it is very difficult to turn back, because it would really mean that one is committing suicide; it is what I call vital suicide. This is what keeps us alive, standing up and always ready to die for the ideals that nurture our hope.

You said, in today's talk with industrialists, that we should salvage some aspects of Cartesian thought while seeking to overcome some of its limitations. Can you elaborate?

I think it would be very difficult to overcome, but the contradictions are so great that the fact that we assume new perspectives and new paradigms helps to enhance these contradictions and so to attenuate the strength of the Cartesian thought. Here I speak for instance of Liberation Theology, which today is working in an ecological and holistic dimension, surpassing Cartesianism. We are not going to overcome it or reject it, but to surpass it. And this is very positive.

Popular Education, Social Movements and Story Telling

Interview with Chris Cavanagh

Chris Cavanagh is a committed popular educator from Canada. He has for years been involved in a variety of popular education projects including the 'Naming the Moment' project in Toronto. Inspired by Latin American experiences and writings, among others, he has been quite active in the North American popular education scene. In this interview, he speaks about the major sources of influence on his popular education work, the kind of work he has carried out over the years, the role of popular education as an antidote to neo-liberal policies in education, the richness of story-telling as a popular education tool, the role of social movements and prospects for popular education in North American society.

Can you tell us something about those writers, educators and movements that have influenced and continue to influence you in your work as a popular educator?

Writers, educators and movements, eh? That's quite a spread. I am such a voracious reader that listing those writers and educators who are major influences on me would fill a substantial bibliography. So I'll just note the first few that come to mind. One writer who was an early influence on me and who continues to inspire me is Eduardo Galeano. You could say that his *Open Veins of Latin America* is one of the founding documents of my political consciousness. And Galeano's trilogy *Memories of Fire* stretched my heart and soul into new shapes. Not surprisingly, I was heavily influenced by liberation struggles in Latin America and the Caribbean. The music of Victor Jara and the

Nuevo Cancion movement was part of my teen years which were overshadowed by the US-backed coup against the Chilean Allende government. Che, Castro, Costa Gavras' film 'State of Siege' about the Tupamaro guerrillas in Uruguay—these were the things that formed the landscape of my teenage imagination. Add to that the anti-nuclear movement and the feminist movement and you have most of the midwives of my adult consciousness. In my twenties I became an anti-apartheid activist and Nicaraguan solidarity activist as well as doing social justice and anti-poverty work in Montreal. It was also in the early 80s that I came across the work of Paulo Freire and began to discover the world of popular education. As a social movement, popular education is a tricky thing. It's more like a thread within many social movements, each of which includes both very authoritarian and emancipatory means of learning, leadership and participation. I have always resisted authoritarian relationships and approaches to learning, having had my fill of these in primary and secondary school. I witnessed first-hand the dehumanising effects of this approach to education—institutions that were filled with equally miserable students and teachers. In high school I actually had a number of teachers who were obvious alcoholics. But mostly I remember the daily indignities of a mass education that was more about obedience and conformity than learning. As I think of it now I realize that schooling, for me, was, unfortunately, a war on my imagination. And I fought back by reading fiction—mostly science fiction and fantasy but also Dickens and Austen. I also had early encounters with Sartre and Camus who, to a sad 17-year-old, offered powerful and sustaining explanations of the world. My influences continue to be various. I've come to see that when I look at those social movements, writers and educators that have influenced me they can mostly be grouped together under the rubric anti-colonial. So let me add some more writers and educators: women of colour, poets and theorists have been a huge influence on me including Audre Lorde, Gloria Anzaldua, Maria Lugones and the prolific bell hooks; the poets Pablo Neruda, Federico Garcia Lorca, Denise Levertov and Grace Paley are constant companions; educators who I continue to learn from include dian marino, Myles Horton, and the many scholars in the Freirean tradition.

What are the major issues confronting popular educators in Canada and the US today?

First, popular education is confronted by the same issues confronting any movement for social change. But two issues concern me particularly: authoritarian culture and resources. By authoritarian culture I refer to that of both Left political movements and education in general. Popular education is fundamentally anti-authoritarian and challenges dominant power relations. It's not as simple as being anti-hierarchical nor is it proposing laissez-faire alternatives. The processes of popular education are extremely effective for increasing people's capacities to function democratically and with critical mindedness. And as these capacities increase and are more widely shared by groups of people, the weaknesses of traditional authoritarian practices of leadership and learning begin to be exposed. And, not surprisingly, there is resistance from those sectors and individuals most wedded to authoritarian practices. This is most pernicious when it comes to Left culture, which fancies itself committed to liberation and resistance to oppression. And yet Left culture too often includes oppressive behaviours, suppressing dissent and being anti-democratic in the belief that it must take on the forces of the Right (especially neoliberalism, nowadays) on its own terms. Popular education is mutually exclusive of authoritarian education and seeks new relations of power and knowledge that are authoritative and humble.

As for resources, popular education is at a critical conjuncture in that it is becoming increasingly wellknown as a better means of learning, leadership and movement building. And, therefore, many individuals and various social movement sectors turn to popular education for the creative solutions they feel can be found there. However, popular education, like most social movements, suffers from a scarcity of resources. This scarcity is no accident however and has a long history worth examining closely. The danger confronting popular education in the coming years is that of expectation out of step with the willingness to commit adequate resources. Especially since choosing to do things differently from the norm, which popular education is most definitely doing, requires more resources, more time, more commitment than traditional means. It is characteristic of hegemony to sabotage effective means of social change by placing unrealistic expectations upon it. The failure to meet those expectations is then cleverly used to claim that that particular approach to social change is a dead end and can, in future, be ignored. Popular educators cannot afford to be naïve about these hegemonic tactics and must meet these challenges head on.

What in your opinion should be some of the key attributes of a popular educator?

From my earliest reading of Paulo Freire I learned of faith, hope, humility, love and critical mindedness. A quarter century on and I still find this quintet of attributes/values a powerful set to reflect on and learn. I could write an essay on each of these and certainly see them with much more complexity than I did 25 years ago. And, perhaps similar to Freire, I feel that love is one of the most important qualities of the educator committed to emancipation. Love is an essential component of compassion and solidarity. It is that which imagines a better world in which all can live to realize the full potential of their lives. The popular educator has a special obligation to love, both the people with whom they work as well as to love the potential of those people. When all around is bleak and hard and the struggle for a better world seems to lead on endlessly towards a horizon we never seem to reach, it is love that can sustain us. Which means that the popular educators must also love themselves. Otherwise, it is not solidarity with the oppressed that we practice but altruism. I have also learned to add to the critical mindedness that Freire writes about, the Buddhist notion of mindfulness—the awareness of one's thoughts and actions in the here and now—being present to oneself. I think the educator who can practise both critical mindedness and mindfulness is one who can mobilize a wonderful capacity to teach and learn with others. And, of course, there's curiosity. I had a friend who was a great teacher and I remember being surprised once about her harsh opinion of a mutual friend who had been studying with her and was now elsewhere. My friend said she was glad this mutual friend had moved on because she had no curiosity. And I had to admit that she was correct in this judgement. Curiosity is the imagination in action. And an attribute that all popular educators must cultivate.

You have been engaged in 'Naming the Moment' projects in Canada. Can you tell us what form this project takes?

Naming the Moment was a ten-year project of the Jesuit Centre for Social Faith and Justice and was an extremely successful popular education community organizing tool. From year to year, the project would identify a critical theme that related to life in Toronto and then organize a series of workshops from September through the Spring of the following year. Dozens of community activists, educators and workers would attend to participate in democratic, systematic and participatory exploration of the theme. These themes included aboriginal sovereignty, anti-racism, homelessness and poverty and more. Naming the Moment has, at its core, a process of democratic conjunctural analysis, identifying and examining the movement of key forces (economic, political, cultural and so on) and their impact on various structures of society. The democratic nature of the process allowed participants to advocate for various actions according to the needs of the moment and to also recruit allies. As a popular education process 'Naming the Moment' drew on a wide range of means of dialogue from common small-group discussions to the use of popular theatre, visual art and song. And, as with popular education,

Interview with Chris Cavanagh

it took more time and resources than more conventional processes of community organizing. The project ended in 1996 and has since been practised intermittently by the Catalyst Centre, which has continued to develop it as a community organizing tool.

You also carried out work around the area of story telling. In what way can story telling constitute a transformative force?

Now this is something very close to my heart. Storytelling is a tremendously powerful medium, pedagogy and much more. It is something so pervasive in human culture that we often fail to notice its presence and power. Look at all the world's major religions—each has at its heart a story. One that, sadly, people are willing to fight, kill and die for. Stories define societies, cultures, communities. They act as social-cultural glue. Our histories are all, of course, stories and there has been much scholarship in the last twenty years that looks critically and sceptically at who wrote the various canonical histories and for whom and in what interests they were written. Post-modernism (in its progressive aspects) and post-structuralism have injected a healthy scepticism about the grand narratives to which we grant normative power. Popular education is a practice that structures and applies this post-structural scepticism in a democratic and rigorous fashion to enable people to tell new and better stories—recovering personal and community histories that have disappeared or were subjugated and subordinated to the dominant (or hegemonic) narratives. It also develops our collective capacities to imagine different stories about where we might be going in the decades we might yet have to live—assuming we survive the imminent crises of peak oil, global warming, extreme neo-liberalism and the ever-present militarisation of our beleaguered world—let's not forget that most of the nuclear weapons of the 20th century still exist.

How are ecological issues becoming an integral feature of popular education in this day and age?

Now this is an interesting question. I'm not sure that "ecological issues" are an integral feature of popular education. And I'm uncertain if this is even an emerging trend. This is perhaps ironic of me to say since I am teaching a popular education class at the Faculty of Environmental Studies at York University. And, of course, I do believe that so-called "ecological issues" should be an integral part of popular education. However, popular education has emerged out of the struggles defined largely by class and thus aimed at supporting peoples' efforts to self-organize in the face of economic and political oppression. Environmental and ecological issues have, of course, always been part of this. But do they constitute a focus of popular education efforts such that we can talk about them as "integral"? I am unsure. What I see of the environmental movement in Canada is that it is still largely a middle class and white movement. It is not one that has a strong class analysis nor does it come even close to being anti-capitalist. In fact some sectors of the environmental movement seek to accommodate to capitalist production, arguing for how economically beneficial ecological issues can be if packaged properly. Even if this isn't that large a part of the environmental movement, I would say that the greater part of the environmental movement lacks any critical take on capitalist production. Not that I'm letting the socialist economies of the former Soviet bloc off the hook (some of the worst environmental exploiters and polluters of the planet)—but their day is past and we now have an almost uniform neoliberal world to contend with. I would say that there are numerous experiments integrating popular education with ecological issues—not always using the term "popular education"—such as the much-lauded Chipko movement, the global justice activism of Starhawk, the resistance to the Narmada Dam in India, food activism in Canada to name a few. But we have a long way to go.

What viable response can popular education offer to counter the all-pervasive influence of neoliberal politics in mainstream education?

Popular education must unrelentingly look at power and resistance to unjust uses of power. It must do this in both content and practice. It must walk the talk and model the very ethics and values that it analyses and teaches. Popular education must also beware of the almost inevitable moment of co-optation—one which I am, ironically, contributing to by teaching a popular education course in a major university. The day will come when you will be able to get first, a certificate and eventually, bachelor's and master's degrees in "popular education." And once it has become a certified field of practice it will then be subject to political and state regulation. On that day, it will cease to be a force for social change. This is not something that we should be afraid of. For the mainstreaming of popular education could also be part of creating a more just society. But we cannot be naïve about this. We must be vigilant to ensure that the ethics of justice and compassion and love remain vital within popular education. Neoliberalism needs a fragmented world to prosper fully—it requires liberal individualism. This is anathema to popular education which recognizes the complex relationship between power and subjectivity that

Foucault has done so well to elaborate. Popular education promotes collective learning and action—it resists the fracturing of society into nothing more than a linear equation of one person plus one person plus one person ad infinitum. Popular education must name the world more truthfully, honestly and compassionately than does neo-liberalism. Perhaps that's the most succinct, if coded, thing to say of it.

Which progressive social movements seem to be capturing the imagination in Canada today?

The most active and visible over the last couple of years has been the movement to legalize same sex marriage. And, despite conservative opposition, it looks like this movement has won. But more than that, it's hard to say that there is any one social movement capturing the "imagination in Canada". There are, of course, numerous active social movements. But it doesn't feel like any one of them, save for the same sex marriage fight, deserves the qualifier "capturing." The feminist, environmental, anti-poverty, aboriginal sovereignty and anti-globalization movements are all active. But none is grabbing headlines at the moment.

To what extent is popular education a feature of the work carried out by these movements?

Within any social movement including the organized labour sector you will find some individuals and a few non-profits familiar with and favourable towards popular education. But I wouldn't say that popular education is thriving. It has cautious respect. Too many people interpret it as gentler, kinder facilitation or better democratic process. On the one hand, there isn't a strong consciousness of how profoundly challenging of dominant power relations popular education is. On the other hand, I do think that there is an awareness, albeit somewhat subconscious, when it comes to those who fund social movement work. It is very difficult, if not in, many cases, impossible, to secure funding for popular education work. The dominant (or hegemonic) norm remains one that insists on concrete, measurable outcomes and thus favours funding issues and not processes. Popular education necessarily resists predicting concrete outcomes since the emphasis is on facilitating a democratic, creative and dialectical process of naming the world in order to change it. To presume what that naming will be and include, and what action the participants might then choose would deny freedom. So popular education continues to be seen as a nice process. You might say that popular education suffers by being "damned with faint praise," an effective means of controlling, if not regulating, its revolutionary potential. I do think its influence will continue to grow slowly. But unless it gets a break, it will be a long slow process.

Earlier on, you mentioned the Catalyst Centre. Can you tell us something about this centre with which you have been involved for a number of years?

The Catalyst Centre is a deliberate and conscious effort both to institutionalise and to democratise popular education—to give it the concrete resource of an address that can be found by interested individuals and institutions. There are such popular education institutions in Quebec and elsewhere in the world. But, despite many practitioners in English Canada there are few institutions that identify as popular education groups. Catalyst started in the late 90s after a number of other popular education groups had gone the way of the history books—these included the Doris Marshall Institute for Education and Action (DMI) and the Naming the Moment Project. Catalyst is connected with these organically, housing some of the archives of both DMI and the Moment Project. At Catalyst we aim to walk the talk, democratically practising within an anti-oppression framework. Our desire is to contribute to strengthening the capacity of social movements to practise freedom. We are less interested in ameliorating any particular oppression than in sharing the means by which people in communities can name and resist oppressions for themselves. Practically speaking we get asked to do a great deal of facilitation and curriculum development for many non-profits and trade unions. It's a tough walk.

Human Rights, Social Justice and Civil Society

Interview with Magda Adly

Magda Adly is a leading social activist in Egypt. A medical doctor by profession, she has suffered imprisonment for her political activities and continues to work for an NGO deeply involved in the struggle for rehabilitation of victims of violence. In this interview, she dwells at length on her political struggles over the years, her experience of incarceration, prospects for the democratization of Egyptian society and the emergence of civil society.

Can you provide readers with an account of your engagement in the struggle for social justice in Egypt over the years?

This really provides me with a good chance to revive very old memories and try to understand what was happening and what factors conditioned our choices. I was born in 1953, that is nine months into the Egyptian revolution against the British colonist. It was a golden period in our modern history and it appeared thus to those born at that time. President Nasser's speech about freedom, independence, equality, and social justice captured this generation's imagination and influenced our attitude especially since this speech was not divorced from the dreams of Egyptians. We witnessed a lot of achievements in all fields... education, labour, health services, culture... and these achievements were inspired by Nasser's speech.

Arts of different kinds were a mirror that reflected this period and the national songs were a key tool in the state policies that touched hearts.

This was the atmosphere that prevailed when I was born. My family provided me with another golden chance; they were more or less liberals. There was no discrimination in this family. My mother was a teacher and my father shared in all housekeeping duties and childcare. Both were socially involved and so I had no problems in engaging socially from the time I attended primary school. My mother helped us participate in the summer activities that were available at that time. She allowed my sister and myself to join our colleagues on summer trips and this proved to be a very useful experience.

It is against this background that I began to develop my dreams. My first choices were made in 1967 when Israel occupied our land without any effort. It was a big blow to the hopes of all Egyptians, including me. In spite of my young age I managed to join socially committed groups and, in 1968, I joined the Socialist Union's youth wing, the Socialist Union being the only political party at this time. This was my first foray into politics.

The most important activities I remember at this time were those of supporting the displaced people from the Suez Canal cities; visiting and providing psychological support to the soldiers in the firing line; resisting the sense of hopelessness and helplessness being expressed in our schools.

At the same time these activities obliged me to rethink several issues in Nasser's theory, mainly those concerning the responsibility for failure in 1967 and the nature of democracy. In 1970 my elder sister was abducted, with some of her friends, for about eight months because they were combating Roger's initiation. I suspected that the person in charge of the youth organization was behind my sister's detention.

After Nasser's death I left this organization, and a few months later I joined the university. There I met a small politically active group and made my second main political choice, that of opting for socialism, I was against the way that Sadaat dealt with our national and Arab conflict with Israel. My group and I engaged in advocacy work and campaigned against the Camp-David accords, and struggled for democracy.

In 1977 a national demonstration took place all over Egypt against certain economic measures that included rises in the price of many essential commodities. Surely enough, I was involved in this major activity.

I was arrested two months later and was kept in detention for fifteen months. Then I was arrested again only one month after my first release. This time, I was released after eight weeks.

At the end of the seventies, Sadaat played a very bad game. He allowed space for the Islamist movement to counter the socialists whose voice was the loudest at the time. This game resulted in his own death by the very same hand. But the Islamic traditionalists became more and more powerful.

I completed my university degree studies in 1983 and I worked for one year as a general practitioner in a very poor village, before joining a hospital in the anaesthetics department. In this village I was the only doctor available in the health centre, responsible for all the health issues from a-z and it proved to be a very interesting experience. And it was during this year that I first started working for the doctors' syndicate. The poor provision of health services and the doctors' low income were the reasons for my work with the syndicate.

In 1984 and 1987 I ran for the parliament elections. I did not aim to win a seat since the state members always obtain 99.99% in the Egyptian elections. This experience however provided me with a good opportunity to work with people and generate awareness about democracy, social justice, human rights.

At the end of 1993 Suzan Fayaad, my friend, told me that she, together with Aida Seif Al dawla and Abdullah Mansour, had established an NGO for the rehabilitation of torture survivors and asked me to join their organization. After a few days I decided to become the fourth doctor at the Nadim Centre. Work at the Nadim Centre has since been at the top of my agenda.

Can you tell us something about your experience of incarceration?

The State went berserk as a result of the 1977 public demonstrations. On 18/1/77, and for the first time in recent history, thousands of people began gathering in the main squares at 10.00 a.m.

People kept marching in the city centres and main squares until the end of the day. Despite their use of gas bombs and such other heavy handed methods such as firing at and beating people, the police failed to scatter the crowd. The next day the army was called upon to deal with the demonstrators.

As a result of the army opening fire on the people, more than forty persons died on this day. A state of emergency was announced with curfew imposed after four o'clock. At the same time, however, Sadaat revoked the unfair economic decisions. It was clear enough that all activists were to be detained on this day. I got back home to collect a small bag and many papers. At midnight the state security intelligence agents visited my home but I wasn't there. The schools and universities were closed from 20th of January till the 10th of March. On the 14th of March I went to the university to share in the commemoration event for a victim of these demonstrations and that was where I was arrested. I spent 24 hours in the state security offices. I was not exposed to physical torture. They tried to apply some psychological pressure and, when they found that there was no way they could obtain any information, they stopped. This was a first important lesson to register. If you remain strong and speak confidently, they begin to feel that they are weak. Yes they are weak in spite of their external power. They are strong males who impose their authority. They have these dark isolated custody cells and torture instruments and tools but they are weak.

We were about thirty female activists in this prison and most of us were released within a few months. At the end of the year I was alone in prison. At no time did I feel guilty. And I was not afraid of being a prisoner for a longer period of time. I know only too well that this is the price one has to pay for one's activity in non-democratic countries, and I accepted this price. The difficult thing is coping with the length of time. I tried to benefit from my stay. I had my university books and many other books from different fields and enjoyed the experience of being able to read so many books. I developed a good relationship with most of the female prisoners, some of whom I'll never forget. This provided me with another lesson. Poverty is the main criminal not these women. The same can be said of prolonged domestic violence . This was the cause of the imprisonment of two women who had killed their husbands.

In July 1977 the first terrorist operation occurred in Egypt. All the wives of those involved in the Islamic organization were arrested. The prison authorities applied the rules of prophylactic detention. Not a single wife resisted and fought for her rights. It was left to us, "the left radicals", to fight for their rights especially as many of them were carrying babies. I think this represented a new chapter in the story of trampling over prisoners' rights. After some time they accepted to engage in a normal relationship with us, and this provided us with a chance to understand the mentality of these traditionalists. It was surprising to discover that the majority were very poor and didn't choose this way of life. The leaders allow them to come to terms with their low social status with the vague promise that a second life awaits them. The leaders of this organization were responsible for their life; they chose the husband, prepared the apartment and covered the monthly expenses. The bylaws of the organization were horrible, as far as women's rights were concerned. The husband or the leader has the right to beat the female for what they regard as a mistake. They put her in a *falaka,* and there is a number of beatings for each mistake.

The mistakes the woman committed included those of raising her voice, laughing, and having her voice heard by other men. This serves to shed some light on the plight of these miserable women. Rich intelligent women were married to men of the same social stature and poor non-educated women were married to poor ones. And in the same way the leaders of the women's group happened to be the wives of the male leaders. So, once again, poverty, absence of social justice, and low social status were important factors behind these phenomena.

Helping victims of violence has been the focus of your activity since then and you have been working for the El Nadim Centre which carries out such work. Can you tell us something about the work of this centre?

Interview with Magda Adly

The El Nadim Centre for the Management and Rehabilitation of Victims of Violence is an independent Egyptian NGO that was established in August 1993 as a civil, and therefore non-profit, company. During the first year of its establishment El Nadim restricted its activity to the provision of psychological rehabilitation for victims of torture and the provision of medico-legal reports whenever this was necessary. At that time we had been working in other human rights organizations and found great difficulty in issuing reports for victims of torture from official medical institutions such as the university or government hospitals.

However, in our evaluation of the first year of our work, we realized that working with torture cannot be complete without making the issue public: publishing, campaigning and mobilization of different societal sectors against a practice that has gone completely out of hand over the past two decades. We adhered to this approach in all our later activities, whether those were related to torture, violence against women or other issues of democracy and freedom of civil society. I will mention some of El Nadim's activities. With regard to torture related activities, El Nadim provides psychological management and rehabilitation to victims of torture. Together with other NGOs and individuals, it also provides some form of social support and refers to legal aid resources. The access to victims of torture involves receiving them at the centre and reaching out for them in case of obstacles or fear of talking about their trauma. Clients, who are in need of investigations or management that is non-psychological in nature, are referred to a respective specialist. The Centre provides a psychological testimony to be added to the case files in legal aid centres. On two occasions EL Nadim testified in front of the prosecution regarding torture cases where compensation was being sought. Furthermore, El Nadim helped set up a Sudanese group against torture. All of the people involved were former clients at El Nadim.

Since 2000 El Nadim has been the reference for UNHCR in Egypt regarding applicants for refugee status on the grounds of torture. Other activities include campaigning on particular torture cases and on the issue of torture in general.

Since 1993 and until 2000 El Nadim has provided psychological, social and/or legal support to 2500 victims of torture, about two thirds of whom were males, one-third females and a small percentage being children. One third of them were Egyptian. In addition El Nadim is a founding member of AMAN and the Regional Network for Centres working against torture. It has members from Palestine, Lebanon, Morocco, Sudan, Bahrain, Iran and has Kurdish and Iraqi membership.

Within the framework of that network, EL Nadim has provided training in management skills and rehabilitation of torture victims as well as documentation of torture cases in Lebanon, Morocco and Sudan. It has helped in the foundation of a torture centre in the Sudan. It has also provided training for colleagues in South Africa. El Nadim is member of the Council of the International Rehabilitation Centre against Torture (IRCT) based in Denmark, the International Society for Health and Human Rights, Section of Torture and Psychiatry, World Psychiatric Association and the Amnesty Survey of Medical and Psychiatric Services for Victims of Human Rights Violation. The last mentioned has 70 organizations.

El Nadim is currently based in an office in the centre of Cairo. A team of 10 members work in two shifts at the Centre.

Can you outline the Centre's activities regarding violence perpetrated against women?

Since 1993 and until 2000 EL Nadim has provided psychological, social and rehabilitative support to 316 women. More than half of them are Egyptians, one third being torture victims and the remainder are victims of domestic violence and rape. In 2001 EL Nadim set up a women's programme through which women victims of violence are listened to and provided with counselling. The programme is primarily based at the El Nadim Centre but there are thirteen field extension centres: seven in Cairo, two in Lower Egypt and four in Upper Egypt.

In addition to the above, I must mention other important activities which we carry out at the Centre. These include the coordination of the first field study in Egypt—1994 and 1995—in which we assessed the prevalence of violence against women in the country and women's perceptions about and attitudes towards that violence. The research was presented at the Fourth World Conference on women in Beijing. Other activities include the drafting of the NGO Shadow report on the Convention against all Forms of Discrimination against Women that was presented to the UN in 2000.

We also participated in the FES organized project on advocacy for the implementation of CEDAW in Egypt. The project was organized over one year, from May 1999 until May 2000. It involved eleven dialogical sessions among civil society organisations, legislative and government bodies, and we produced a number of publications, among them a simplified version of the CEDAW convention written in common Egyptian dialect. We also held consciousness raising activities in several governorates all over the country regarding issues of violence against women in general and female genital mutilation in particular. The Centre also provided training to women grassroots activists on listening and counselling skills with specific reference to women victims of violence in Egypt, Lebanon and Tunisia. We also produced written guidelines on listening and counselling skills to be applied with respect to women victims of violence.

I should also mention that El Nadim has currently started a women's programme which entails the training of 10 volunteers to advocate and provide support to women victims of violence in Egypt. We have also been engaging in campaigning work on many issues in the field of violence against women. Nadim is currently engaged in two national campaigns concerning rape and one regional campaign for the introduction of legislation that criminalizes domestic violence.

What role is El Nadim playing in the context of developing a truly 'civil society culture' in Egypt?

Since its establishment in 1993 El Nadim has been registered as a civil not-for-profit-company to bypass the registration with the Egyptian Ministry of Social Affairs that exercises strong control over NGOs, their activities and their ability to network and interact with each other. In so doing, El Nadim has participated in the foundation of the Forum for the Promotion of Civil Society, which is an independent forum that involves 104 organizations and civil society associations. It has also organized and participated in several campaigns advocating the autonomy of civil society and has challenged several restrictive measures undertaken by the Egyptian government against NGOs. The last of those measures was the drafting of an alternative association law which aimed to put all voluntary and independent civil activities under the control of the government and included reprisals that amounted to several years imprisonment in addition to the dissolution of NGOs. El Nadim has participated in a national and international campaign against that law, has contributed to the distribution of legal and constitutional studies of its provisions and has participated in a one week hunger strike in protest. The law was ruled unconstitutional in June 2000.[1]

What kind of legislation would you like to see enacted in Egypt to combat domestic violence?

Combating domestic violence is one of the most difficult tasks anywhere. We are dealing with a phenomenon that is deeply embedded in public culture. Men, state and religious authorities and even women resist the attainment of complete equality, each for his or her own different reasons. Religion is one of the forces behind such resistance.

Changing public and legal attitudes necessitates the adoption of different and parallel approaches. Education should play a prominent part here, but the situation concerning gender relations, as promoted by the educational system, is a joke! One lesson deals with the sharing of responsibilities by all the family members and the text contains colored illustrations: "All of us are working," the child says: "I'm doing my homework, dad is reading the newspaper and mum is cooking." Another lesson underlines the important role of females in society " We can't live without women; they are very kind. When I was a child, my mother used to take care of me. During my adulthood, my wife is always supporting and taking care of me. Behind every successful man there lies a good woman. When I get older my daughter will help me."

These are just a few examples that illustrate how the inherited culture affects even those who have the responsibility to form Egyptian minds.

Drama, especially TV, also plays its part. 72 million—that's the Egyptian population—watch television, mostly films and tele-series. These provide messages similar to the ones contained in the educational materials. Moreover, national laws contain many discriminatory provisions and do not stipulate that domestic violence is a crime. Civil society has a crucial role to play in the strengthening of democracy. It has an important role to play not only in bringing about changes with respect to women's rights but also to ensure that all human rights conventions are implemented.

Despite the difficulties faced in combating violence against women, Nadim and other feminist NGOs have had a great impact as a result of their work. Until 1993, it was almost forbidden to speak about this issue. What went on in homes was considered confidential and no one had the right to interfere. This, in addition to other ideas that are of religious origin, was the basis of resistance in Egypt, as in all other countries. In 1993 we were presented with a great opportunity to tackle this taboo in Egypt. The preparatory international conference for the Beijing conference took place. During the twelve year period that followed this conference, violence against women became a normal issue in media coverage: newspapers, magazines, radio and TV. Many Master's degree studies focused on this subject. This led to national legislative changes. We first had a new law that criminalized FGM. The second was the introduction of an article whereby rapists are punished. The third change concerned the procedure in the implementation of the family law. A family court was established. Finally we saw the introduction of the nationality law concerning children with an Egyptian mother and a non-Egyptian father.

Besides these achievements, we saw violence against women being placed on the agenda of more and more NGOs. There are hot lines, many listening and counselling units for women who are victims of violence and hundreds of women access these units. This signifies increasing resistance to such violence.

Another service consists of the provision of shelters; there are now five shelters for women victims in four governorates. Access to these shelters suffered because of problems in the bylaws and the attitudes of persons in charge, but, after a strong resistance, women can now avail themselves of these places in cases of emergency. The impact of Nadim and other Human Rights organizations in the field of combating torture can be felt "mainly" in civil society and the media. Fifteen years ago there were only two organizations working in this field, one working in documentation and advocacy and the other, Nadim, that works in the areas of providing direct support to torture survivors, awareness raising, advocacy, campaigning, documentation of its work and training. Currently most non-governmental newspapers place this important issue on their agenda. Political parties now consider eradication of torture as an important part of the democratic changes they seek. Media and lawyer syndicates have committees dealing with civil liberties.

And one of the most important impacts can be felt through the attitude of the survivors themselves. They are now encouraged further to seek medical or legal support and campaign to boot.

As far as the State is concerned, nothing changed, except for establishing the national committee for human rights two years ago. This committee was not established through democratic means; President Mubarak nominated all its members, with only three being from the human rights NGOs. This committee has no authority. It is not allowed to investigate the cases of people in custody, nor provide legal aid. All it does is provide a yearly report with some recommendations.

But, torture is still a daily occurrence in all police stations, and in the premises of the national security intelligence. And we still have laws that protect the perpetrators.

What contributions are social movements making to the process of democratization of Egyptian society?

October 2000 is considered a landmark date for the democratic movement in Egypt, this being the date of the Palestine intefada. Nadim, together with many intellectuals, established the popular committee in solidarity with the Palestine intefada. One of the activities consisted of a demonstration. More and more Egyptians shared in these demos. This right was practically absent for many decades. The second landmark was the demonstration of a thousand people in the main square in Cairo a few hours after the occupation of Iraq took place.

Before 2000 there were movements for economic rights, but this political movement in support of the rights of Arab nations was, virtually, a novelty.

The activities of the Egyptian committee in solidarity with the intefada were an important experience; the committee carried out major activities without having been registered anywhere. Its legitimacy derived from the massive public support, and it provided a lesson for all.

Now there are many social movements—not registered according to the state laws—that are making their presence felt in Egypt. These include: The public movement for change "Freedom now"; The Egyptian movement for change "Kefaia"; Lawyers for change; Doctors for change; Journalists for change; Artists for change; Women for change; Youth for change; the 9th of March movement for university freedom; the Judges' Movement for freedom.

The Judges' Movement was one of the most effective this year. It placed the state in a tight corner. Judges were always non-partisan but, during the year of the "false" reform, they got involved in the democratic movement. Their movement has had an important impact on all sectors of society.

Notes

1. El Nadim is or has been involved in the following publications:
a. Code of Ethics: El Nadim has participated in a series of discussion groups regarding the development of a code of ethics for NGOs in general and human rights NGOs in particular. The initiative started after the governmental attack on civil companies in general and human rights organizations in particular. The declaration of principles has been drafted and is circulating among NGOs for their discussion and endorsement. El Nadim has endorsed the code of ethics and it is appearing in its three-year book as one of its references.
b. Torture report: El Nadim has published a report on torture inside and outside police stations, in the period 1993-1996. The report was based on the experience of the clients who came to the attention of El Nadim, and included a review of: the reasons for torture, the methods of torture and the physical and psychological consequences, reports on cases of those who died under torture, report on victims of state violence and some case studies of some of those victims. The report was written in Arabic, translated in English and widely distributed inside and outside Egypt.
c. *Three years of El Nadim*: This is El Nadim's first publication, and provides the history of the centre, an overview of its clients and the challenges it has faced. It also contains a compilation of the statements and appeals made by the center over the period 1993-1997.
d. "A Call from the Afterworld" is a booklet issued jointly by El Nadim and the Legal Aid Centre for Human Rights documenting the torture of an Egyptian farmer during his interrogation in a murder crime by Egyptian police in the governorate of EL Fayoum to the South of Cairo. The man was burnt with kerosene and left unconscious in front of El Fayoum Central hospital. El Nadim managed to transfer the victim via different hospitals into a university hospital in Cairo and, through pressure on the Ministry of health, granted him some of the expenses regarding his treatment. Unfortunately the man died because of the extent of his wounds and his brother is currently filing a case in court against the respective authorities. The documentation of this story was produced in over 6000 copies and has been distributed to all media contacts, political parties and all human rights meetings in Egypt.

e. *Torture in Egypt: Facts and Testimonies*, 2002 reprinted in 2004 (Arabic + English)
f. *Torture in Sudan: Facts and Testimonies*, 2003 (Arabic + English summary)
g. *Days of Torture: Women in Police Custody*, 2004 (Arabic)
h. *Doctors Against Torture:* 2005 (Arabic)
i. *Women Against Domestic Violence:* 2005 (Arabic)
j. *We Will Never Forget "about the State Violence with the Sudanese Refugee"*: 2006 (Arabic + English)
k. Many investigation reports:
   – Detention of 5000 in north Sini after Hilton taba bombs.
   – What happened in Sarando village?
   – 50 days after reform, 49 torture cases and death of 9 as a result of torture.
   "This report was investigated by HRW. The ministry of interior provided a report in response to the Nadim report. We will therefore publish a second report in reply to the Ministry of the Interior".
   – The human rights situation from June 2004-June 2005.

Popular Education and Social Change

Interview with Jane Thompson

Jane Thompson is a key figure in the radical debate on adult education and popular education in Britain. A prolific writer in the field and social activist, she has made an important contribution to socialist feminist politics over the years through her work at such institutions as the University of Southampton, Ruskin College and, more recently, the National Institute for Adult Continuing Education and Warwick University. In this interview she addresses some of the challenges faced by popular educators, socialism and most importantly radical feminism, with special reference to the situation in Britain. She also discusses Neoliberalism and its onslaught on public life and the bearing it has had on once vibrant social movements.

How would you define 'popular education' in this day and age?

The point of popular education is to connect purposeful educational engagement to the pursuit of social and political change—change towards more equality, more social justice and more participatory democracy. The sense that education has a partisan social and political contribution to make to the struggles of those who are poor, excluded, oppressed, reviled—in various ways in various societies—is not part of the usual debate to be had by adult educators these days. It probably never was. However, it has always been the inspiration and the purpose of those committed to radical and progressive social change. In the presence of global capitalism and of ideologies intended to advance the political and economic interests of the powerful at the expense of the poor, it is as urgent as it ever was to re-constitute and connect the principled and democratic impulse of popular education to those struggles and social movements which challenge all of this.

In practice, this means the kind of adult education which treats people as equals, as engaged citizens and social actors—rather than as unfortunates, or empty vessels, or variously malfunctioning misfits. It means a curriculum that reflects shared social and political interests and builds upon ways of knowing that take account of people's lived experience and their capacity to make sense of their lives in purposeful, complicated and critical ways. It assumes a pedagogy that is based on dialogue, critical thinking and problem solving rather than transmission or instruction. In terms of relevance and solidarity, it assumes a close and organic relationship between adult education and progressive social movements. It expects social learning to connect to social action and to resourcing the broader democratic struggle for increased political engagement.

Your contribution to popular education has largely been informed by your commitment to feminist-socialist politics. How important is it to constantly re-assert this politics for popular educators in an age when we are being swamped by either a technicist or a nihilistic and fragmentary postmodern discourse in adult education?

If you were to do a critical reading of my writing across the years, I hope you would have a sense of both continuity and change. I think some expressions of my politics have changed in line with shifting contexts and the greater recognition of ambiguity, contradiction and complexity about the ways in which we need to make sense of the world. I am actively engaged in the present and have an interest in creating the future. History is important to me, but mostly as a way of understanding what is happening now and imagining what could be different. Of course, fundamental principles—to do with equality between people, challenging vested interests, confronting discrimination and oppression and re-distributing material resources, including the resources of power, knowledge, information and the pursuit of happiness—remain abiding passions and are essentially non-negotiable when it comes to questions of change.

I recognise the commitment to socialism as a world view in the roots of my material and emotional upbringing. Although I never met my Scottish grandfather—he died when my mother was fifteen—his palpable presence in my childhood as a symbol of intelligence and resistance and struggle, in circumstances which ultimately defeated him, survives in my present feelings of anger and dissent about current injustices and oppressions—

global capitalism, human rights, genocide—and informs the degree of energy and persistence needed to hold to a political stance that goes against the grain of mainstream politics in Britain and against current thinking in adult education.

Feminist politics—and specifically radical feminism—has probably been more important to my thinking and practice than socialism. Feminism—as I understand it—exposes the significance of power structured relationships in systems of social and political oppression, recognises the socially constructed and contingent nature of what counts as knowledge, and is deeply committed to equality and commonality at the expense of privilege and individualism, humanism at the expense of technical rationalism and the recognition and respect for difference at the expense of sexual, racial and class division. Although feminism is now a broad church and survives differences of emphasis and re-interpretation, it has not been—in my view—as distorted as socialism has been by masculinist constructions of opportunity, reality and struggle.

Few women that I meet these days would call themselves radical feminists. It's a perspective that has been largely relegated to the history of feminist theory in academic texts and dismissed—usually inaccurately—as being constrained by biological essentialism and a belief in the cultural superiority of *all* women compared to *all* men. Radical feminism—in my experience—is a political analysis which focuses on patriarchy as a system of ideology and power which fuels oppression. Its manifestations have taken many different forms in different historical periods and within different cultures. But especially significant is the social construction of male and female sexuality in ways that privilege men and serve to control women. The ubiquity and social legitimation of male violence—against each other, but more significantly against women and children—are cornerstones of patriarchy. Thirty years on, I know these conditions are more complex than I once imagined but the focus of concern is not misplaced. The suggestion that sexuality is a political construct which has enormous repercussions in the ordering of gender in different cultures and different societies and that problems of violence—however differently and contextually they are manifested—are closely connected to the social construction of masculinity are not popular observations about the maldistribution of power and resources in the world. But constructions of sexual difference that keep women the poorest of the poor, the least educated of the least educated and the least powerful of the least powerful throughout the world, in which the apparatus of actual and institutionalised male violence has not gone away, still require radical feminist analysis and practice to expose and challenge the widespread accommodation made to patriarchal relations in the modern age.

Whenever your name is mentioned to us, reference is made to your open letter to 'whoever's left' in a 1993 issue of *Adults Learning*. There was a huge response to this letter, as indicated in *Words in Edgeways*. The majority of responses were in support of what you said. This must have filled you with hope that the left can claim the radical initiative in popular education. To what extent has this initiative been reclaimed, despite the drift in Labour politics brought about by New Labour?

I'm not sure how important this letter was. It's true that it keeps reappearing in the most unlikely contexts and is claimed as a kind of rallying cry. I think it is possibly useful because it is brief, explicit and political. But it seems a long time ago now that I wrote it. In 1993 I was just about to start teaching politics and women's studies at Ruskin College in Oxford—a place that should have been the hub of radical popular education in the UK but wasn't. In 1997 the Labour party returned to power after eighteen years in the political wilderness and after a huge shift to the right in British politics. Those of us on the left were hopeful. We imagined that we would be rid of Thatcherism. We supposed that such a landslide in favour of the new government would put socialism back on the political agenda. But it didn't.

The language in your question about 'the left' and 'reclaiming the radical initiative' sits quaintly with current ways of thinking and talking about adult education in Britain. Only those—of a certain age—who think of themselves as being 'on the left' ever use the concept of the left anymore. And 'radical' has become one of those words that is claimed by both the right and the left, as well as by Tony Blair in his references to third way politics being about radical policies coming from the centre ground. In terms of adult education, the discourse has been effectively de-politicised. The big contradiction—and irony—is that whilst party political support and resources for adult education—usually called lifelong learning—have rarely been greater, and whilst the preferred government agenda is totally consistent with an uncritical relationship to globalisation and the management of inequality rather than its elimination, the politics of this inter-connection is rarely debated by those employed to deliver its aspirations. Policy makers, providers of adult education and practitioners talk exclusively about systems, structures, standards, targets, measurements, outcomes. If you ask them why they are doing what they are doing, they say 'to secure learners,' 'to deliver learning,' 'to meet their targets,' 'to identify best practice,' 'to measure outcomes,' 'to monitor quality,' 'to encourage innovation.' Even the so-called social priorities concerned with 'combating social exclusion' in society generally and with 'widening participation' in adult education to include those who are socially excluded or socially disadvantaged, get translated into preoccupations with value for money, systems of delivery, monitoring processes, quality assurance and ticking off targets. It is as though the language of philosophy, social purpose, pedagogy and curriculum has been lost to this technical-rationalist nightmare. And with it any political awareness and critical debate about the organic connection between education, society and social change.

What other main challenges face popular education in this neo-liberal period?

The major casualty of neoliberalism, established by Thatcherism in Britain and consolidated by New Labour is the related demise of social movements formed around working class, trade union, feminist and Black politics. These are all social movements which have had close ties historically with popular education but which have never really recovered from the assault of neoliberal policies designed to weaken and discredit them. In addition, the advance of individualism and consumerism in western economies, fuelled by the collapse of communism and promoted by neoliberal governments as emblematic of freedom and democracy, has shifted the focus of attention from the collective and the public towards the individual and the private. As a consequence no one speaks in favour of working class solidarity anymore. Trade unions have been neutralised and professionalised. Feminism as a political movement has been effectively smashed. Black politics has been co-opted by multiculturalism, controlled by institutionalised racism and poverty, and in some respects, pushed towards reactionary forms of fundamentalism.

As an example, trade union education is now reasonably well funded but a pale shadow of its former self. Writing in 1988 John Field commented on the ways in which trade union education developed during the 1970s and 80s, cut off from many of the then radical developments in community-based adult education and from its own origins in the committed and politically alert work of the WEA and Labour College Movement. He criticised the loss of its radical edge or critical concern with the underlying economic causes of workplace issues in favour of more instrumental and technical preoccupations with bargaining skills and role education.

More recently this trend—with a few notable exceptions—has intensified and has even been exacerbated by increasing government investment since New Labour came to power. The government's Union Learning Fund, for example, is geared to union activities which support the government's objective of creating a learning society in ways that turn unions into learning organisations, rather than providing support for critical citizenship or ammunition with which to counter the bad effects of globalisation.

Today's trade unionists are much more likely to be white collar workers or employed in the service sector—including financial services—than in the manufacturing sector. Their trade unions are more likely to operate as professional associations or service organisations, concerned to supply learning opportunities, health insurance schemes, retailing discounts and sports facilities, etc. to their members in exchange for regular subscriptions, rather than critical political muscle in defence of their members' terms and conditions of employment or any sense of internationalism-from-below in the context of global capitalism. As with adult education more generally, the notion of workplace learning has been redefined in the interests of the state, with an emphasis on instrumental outcomes and competitive individualism, assuaged by accreditation and course progression. These are not developments which incline providers or learners to engage with questions or activities that interrogate social values or ethical and political learning in the context of their relationship to the global labour market.

You have been engaged in popular education in a variety of ways, including that of working within (should we say 'in and against'?) academic institutions. The University of Southampton and Ruskin College, Oxford are two academic institutions that come to mind. What are the limits and possibilities of engaging the academy in popular education?

I worked out of the University of Southampton between 1976 and 1989. When I joined the department of adult education I was—at thirty years old—the youngest member of staff and the only woman. The department was primarily concerned with extramural teaching in the liberal tradition. It was led by a man who had spent many years teaching in Africa and who would have been regarded as a progressive in his day. He had an understanding of popular education from his African experience and was keen to encourage community based education as an alternative to the more usual liberal arts approach with middle class students that was typical of extramural teaching at that time. However, I came to the work in the university as a feminist and a Marxist. I had been raised in a working class area in Hull. I had taught in a working class secondary school in a poor and run down part of town. I was involved in socialist and then feminist politics. When I came to Southampton I soon got involved in local campaigns and knew enough from my own experience about social class and women's lives to see all kinds of ways in which the resources of the university could be useful to people in the various struggles of their everyday lives. In retrospect, this was a good time to be working in adult education. Resources were relatively generous. The current obsessions (in Britain, anyway) to do with monitoring and measuring and accreditation were undiscovered. There was a quality of hopefulness in people's hearts that education could make a difference and was related to social as well as personal change. Of course, after 1979 things began to change. Spending on adult education was cut and rationalised as part of Thatcher's neo-liberal policies in relation to the state, and life became harder for working class people generally, especially women. As industries were restructured and unemployment rose, as local government and trades unions were emasculated, as the welfare state was dismantled, as single mothers in receipt of state benefits were demonised—there were lots of relevant issues to be explored and understood by working class students. It seemed to me as though the resources I had to offer as a teacher—involving consciousness raising, relevant and useful knowledge, critical thinking—and what I learned from the students and activists I worked with about learning from experience, resilience and courage, fed into the kinds of social and political action we all pursued in order to resist as best we could.

Although I look back to this period as a time when the political and educational work was its most relevant and powerful and rewarding, it was not an easy time for me. The liberal stance of the department of adult education and its director were sorely tested by the politics of socialism and feminism and by my Marxist, and subsequently, radical feminist analysis. Although I was writing about the work to which I was committed more than anyone else in the department at that time (*Adult Education for a Change* was published in 1980, *Learning Liberation* was published in 1983, *Learning the Hard Way* was published in 1989, for example) and although I was frequently invited to address conferences and to give lecture tours overseas—my position in the department was extremely marginalised. I was called to account for my ideas, inspected and reprimanded more than anyone else I have ever come across in a similar situation. I had to be defended by the union on one occasion and by a popular demonstration in my support on another. My personal life was scrutinised and challenged in ways that I can see in retrospect constituted serious harassment. I am still in contact with students from this time and know that what we did together was immensely important in the ways in which education should be life affirming and life changing. I can't say the same for my colleagues or the university.

Ruskin should have been more conducive. Throughout its hundred years' history it was identified as a college for working class activists. It had close association with the Labour Movement, with socialism and with liberation struggles overseas. The college had lent its support to strikes, had sheltered and taught members of the ANC in exile, had provided the venue for the first ever national women's liberation conference in the UK. It is a history that should have enabled a more imaginative and committed institution, when confronted with neoliberal policies—to articulate and provide a different model of working class adult education, based on popular education, as a real alternative to New Right, and in turn, New Labour's obsession with training for the global economy. But it did not.

However, I did not know any of this when I took up my appointment. Unlike my previous experience at Southampton University it felt easier—in one way —to declare myself a socialist, a feminist and a lesbian at Ruskin. The staff common room was full of old style lefties from the 1960s and 1970s, sheltering from the worst effects of Thatcherism in a place which, because it was relatively small, had not seen much disturbance to its academic privileges and traditional practices. But in 1993 Ruskin appeared more like a retreat than a hotbed for those whose political views had been shaped in more auspicious times but who had not been able to re-create themselves in relation to changing circumstances. Some had learned their politics from the New Left in various— and frequently opposed—splinter groups with Trotskyist, Marxist and Maoist tendencies. Some were more recognisably communist or socialist in sympathy. Some had developed their academic stance from universities teaching critical social science and philosophy in the late sixties—a somewhat masculinist, rationalist and adversarial tradition which has contributed enormously to critical thinking and the development of critical intelligence, but which can also be overly negative and arrogant in many ways. Some took their reference points from the old alliance between Ruskin and Oxford University which, in practice, has led to liberal rather than radical assumptions about working class education, and to academic elitism.

Raphael Samuel was still a force to be reckoned with in the College. As a Ruskin tutor for thirty years, founder of the History Workshop Movement and intellectual guru to many on the Left—including John Prescott, currently Deputy Prime Minister in the Blair government—he habitually addressed students, and those colleagues with whom he was on speaking terms, as "comrade," but beyond that, there was not a lot of evidence of community or solidarity deriving from shared values and beliefs in socialism. In practice it was possible to call yourself whatever you liked within the broad church of centre-left and progressive political movements, but it was a mistake to imagine that the apparent tolerance of left wing affiliations equalled much thought or understanding when it came to feminism. Raphael Samuel referred to himself as "reconstructed" in my presence but until the appointment of a woman to teach in 1994 there was not much evidence of feminist—or even women's history—in the curriculum for which he was responsible.

Like the history curriculum before 1994, most of what was taught in politics, economics, international relations and labour studies made no reference to women whatsoever, and was at least twenty years out of date in terms of its content, its pedagogy and its politics. The teaching of literature relied exclusively on deference to the western literary canon and included only one book by a woman and no black writers on its syllabus. Debates about the social construction of knowledge, interactive teaching methods and the negative and damaging consequences of, for example, sexism and racism in the curriculum, and in the wider college culture, had completely escaped the attention of most tutors. Ruskin had no anti-discrimination or equal opportunities policy, no harassment policy and no codes of practice attempting to promote high standards in professional relationships and college life. Raising some of these issues at Ruskin felt as difficult as they have ever done in patriarchal institutions I have known, despite the ostensible commitment to progressive and enlightened ideas about politics and education.

In these circumstances students were the saving grace. The historic mystique associated with the college continued to attract activists from trade unions, labour movements, community and user movements. It also attracted working class people living 'secret lives' as autodidacts, voracious readers and creative writers—people looking for the kinds of formal educational recognition which had previously been denied to them or rejected by them. Throughout the Thatcher years the numbers of students who were unwaged or unemployed, who were the survivors of economic restructuring in workplaces and communities, homelessness, drug and alcohol abuse, mental ill health, domestic violence and family breakdown, all significantly increased.

During the time I worked at Ruskin (1993-2000) a considerable number of changes were put in place. Women's studies, community studies, creative writing, sociology, social policy and law were introduced into the curriculum in ways which revived the notion of 'really useful knowledge' and relevance to students' lived experience. The politics of the new curriculum and curriculum content were hotly debated and forced traditionalists to review the masculinist, ethnocentric and elitist approaches typical of most Ruskin teaching at the time. New policies to promote equal opportunities, anti-racism, anti-sexism and anti-harassment were drawn up. For the first time in the college's history, women assumed positions of influence and prominence and the numbers of women students increased.

None of these changes could have been achieved without the active enthusiasm of students. In my experience they were invariably keen to pursue ideas and explanations that helped to make sense of their world and what they needed to know to change it for the better. They were, without exception, people with amazing and varied life experiences, whose contribution to the creation of knowledge and to alternative ways of knowing were always powerful and exciting. But their time in the college—a year at the most—was transitory. The continuing energy and imagination required to shift the culture of Ruskin from its preoccupation with a variety of myths about itself in relation to the past, to becoming a contemporary and purposeful critic of prevailing utilitarian and pragmatic approaches to learning—in order to recover and reconstitute the radical agenda in adult education—required a major sea change in the attitudes and enthusiasms of staff—staff who for the most part regarded change as an attack and whose capacity for inertia was staggering.

The crisis of commitment to working class and other oppressed constituencies that dogged the struggle to reinvent Ruskin was symptomatic of the wider crisis of the left in Britain at the time. Not until the emergence of New Labour in the 1990s did the former left discover any united and popular way out of the wilderness into which it had been consigned by the hegemony of neo-liberal social and economic forces. But of course, the creation of New Labour was largely dependent upon cutting any residual connections with the old left as a way of establishing its 'new' and modernising credentials.

The other main problem was the failure of the Ruskin culture and of those who gave meaning to it and perpetuated it to sustain informed and organic relationships with the very constituencies the college claimed to serve. Beyond the limited support and nostalgia about working class models of masculinity—as epitomised in the writing of George Orwell and DH Lawrence, for example—the majority of academics spent as little time as possible with students and tended to regard those who exhibited any or several of the social problems associated with being on the receiving end of poverty, racism and sexual oppression, at a time when social welfare was being structurally adjusted and the so-called underclass was being demonised, as being 'not the right kind' of Ruskin students.

Whilst the enthusiasm of students was contagious and the energy for change exhibited by some more recent members of staff at Ruskin were both crucial during this period, the power remained in some very traditional places. The old alliance with Oxford University was preserved by the system of external advisors and examiners which acted to restrain curriculum innovation and competing definitions of knowledge. The old boys' network of former students whose subsequent careers had taken them into influential positions in the trade union and labour movement and even the House of Lords still controlled the college's governing body and executive committee. When the opportunity arose to appoint a new principal who would consolidate the changes that a few of us had argued into place despite considerable sabotage, they chose instead an academic lightweight and political conservative who wanted to use Ruskin as a base from which to pursue his own private consultancy work with managers, to close down the opportunities for democratic debate and decision making and to adopt a pragmatic approach to course development. The general consensus among traditionalists on the staff and their allies in the governing body was that almost anyone would be better than 'another bloody woman'. The choice—although unusual, even by their own standards—turned out to have family and past connections with key members of the appointment's panel and could be relied upon not to understand and not to push home the changes which had been hard won in the five or six years prior to his appointment. As a result, the old guard were let off the hook and radicals—including myself—left to continue the struggle in more auspicious places.

Which particular progressive social movements and organisations in Britain provide the best context in which socially transformative popular education can be carried out?

When I think about social movements that provide a context for 'socially transformative popular education' in Britain today, there are a number of qualifications that need to be made. For example, the kind of social movements that connect people together in pursuit of shared concerns are not necessarily political. For example, the widespread (inter)national obsession with football. They are frequently reactionary in terms of purpose and right wing in terms of philosophy. For example, the National Front and the British National Party (two neo-Nazi movements, fuelled by racism, with membership drawn overwhelmingly from the ranks of young, working class men); the Countryside Alliance (a movement concerned to defend economic livelihoods in rural Britain, conventional social and class values and traditional rural sports and leisure practices—with membership that cuts across the wealthy and conservative farming class, small scale farmers and agricultural labourers); and the Animal Rights Movement (a disparate collection of predominantly middle class people, opposed to factory farming methods, cruelty to animals, scientific testing on animals for either commercial gain or medical research and with a militant wing prepared to use violence against those who they identify as profiting from animal cruelty).

Whilst environmental movements (for example, anti-roads protesters, campaigns opposed to genetically modified food, the anti-capitalist and anti-globalisation movements) are all associated with progressive politics and with the criticism of commercial interests and capitalist power in contemporary, international society, their membership tends to be socially privileged, well informed and well educated in ways that reflect the importance of knowledge and critical intelligence. In terms of popular education, there is much to be done by these movements to engage the understanding and participation of ordinary, materially poor and less educated constituencies around issues which have a big impact on their lives but which can seem—especially in terms of globalisation—to be completely outside of their control.

The other qualification, to which I alluded earlier, is the relative demise as active political movements of trade unionism, the women's movement, the black civil rights movement and the labour movement. However, the history of these movements has involved periods of inactivity and retrenchment as well as periods of activity and significance and I do not underestimate their continuing potential in the on-going struggle for progressive social change. So long as the political nature of the economy and the consequences of social class divisions, gender inequality and structural racism continue to inform the distribution of resources and power in society, the circumstances remain in place which generate conflicting interests, dialectical relationships, contested knowledge and dissenting politics. These in turn are the very conditions which create agency and should inform the curriculum and pedagogy of popular education.

Given the emphasis on 'widening participation' in learning, 'combating social exclusion' and promoting 'social cohesion' within current mainstream discourses about lifelong learning, and the ways in which these aspirations are routinely attached to community based learning, neighbourhood renewal in areas of multiple deprivation, work-based learning, literacy programmes, citizenship education and work with lone parents, 'excluded men' and minority ethnic communities—the opportunities are enormous for popular educational approaches and a re-politicised interpretation and understanding of how adult education connects to social issues and social change. I find myself continually drawing on the social and political analyses that have informed my work in the past to refer to the defining principles, characteristic relationships and social purposes that must inform the work we do in these present contexts. In many ways what I try to do and what I write about is no different from earlier teaching and writing I have done, except that the political context is different, the social context is different, the discourse is different and most of the people I speak to or work with are not used to framing who they are or what they do in the context of either political economy or socialism or feminism. The challenge, as I see it, is to make the 'old' case in 'new' ways that pay attention to the present and the future rather than the past.

Mention of Ruskin College brings to mind the 'great tradition' in British adult education which is constantly referred to in the literature and which you reviewed critically in your anthology of early essays, *Words in Edgeways (1997)*. In this review, you underlined this tradition's underlying 'ideology of individualism' and its selective nature (middle class, eurocentric, androcentric). Given that there is normally a collective

dimension to learning, within the context of popular education, is there anything worth salvaging or re-constituting from this 'tradition' to strengthen popular education for social change?

Again, this is a question for historians and students of adult education. I don't think the 'great tradition' *is* constantly referred to in the literature *any more*. I have written about it in the past when its impact was more significant. I was always rather critical of how it was played out in university extramural departments in Britain during the 1970s and 1980s but now there are more pressing and more troubling developments which need to be challenged and contested. On the other hand, in some of my more recent writing (*Women, Class and Education (2000)* and *Bread and Roses (2002)* , for example) I have found myself returning to RH Tawney and Raymond Williams— themselves heroes of the great tradition—for their socialist and critical references to what counts as knowledge and culture and solidarity with ordinary people: insights and commitments that were largely absent from extramural teaching in the liberal tradition in the 70s and 80s and which are still missing from the utilitarian ways in which adult learning gets discussed and written about today.

In our introduction to *Reclaiming Common Purpose (2000)*, Mae Shaw and I argued that 'the economy has become synonymous with the market and with ensuring favourable conditions for business in a competitive global economy: low taxation, low wages, low public expenditure and for many, of course, low expectations...policy is harnessed to the task of resourcing the economy, particularly education policy'. In this context, neoliberal assumptions about the economy and public expenditure have become increasingly taken for granted and the discussion has moved to matters of process, delivery, measurement and good practice. It is unusual in the mainstream literature about adult education these days, including the dubious trade in intellectual capital that takes place in refereed journals designed to establish academic reputations and to secure research funding, to find much discussion about social and political purpose or about adult education as a site of struggle.

It is true, however, that the predominance of liberalism (as distinct from radicalism or socialism) in adult education in the 70s and 80s, as a legacy of the great tradition and with its emphasis on individualism, did ease the way for neoliberalism in continuing education and the shift of emphasis to vocationalism, credentialism, instrumentalism and progression. It is not without coincidence that these preoccupations conveniently mirrored the ideological and political paradigm shift towards competition, personal enterprise, meritocracy and individual responsibility that is associated with Thatcherism and more recently with New Labour.

What important challenges have women brought to popular education in the specific contexts with which you have been directly involved?

The most important challenge women bring to popular education is the challenge to male politics and male class relations to do something about patriarchal constructions of masculinity as well as the inequality that characterises gendered power relations. This includes patriarchal assumptions about what counts as knowledge and experience and the recognition that men's behaviour in relation to women is frequently experienced as oppressive or sexist. It's a challenge that requires the men involved alongside women in popular education to seriously examine their behaviour and attitudes and for the balance of power to be changed. But I guess you don't mean this. I imagine you mean what are the challenges—in the sense of issues and conditions—that women want to confront with the help of popular education.

In my experience these are always about the consequences of inequality, especially in relation to gender, race, sexuality and social class. They may be articulated in relation to women's concern about their children or about their terms and conditions of employment in the workplace or about the social problems which affect them in their personal lives or about the conditions which prevail in the communities in which they live. They are very frequently to do with poverty or with male sexual violence.

The challenge for popular education is to relate the lived experiences and pressing concerns of women to the recognition of their existence, to some understanding of their relationship to wider social and political circumstances and to provide the kinds of awareness, knowledge and skills that can help to inform and strengthen the ways in which women act upon the world, both personally and collectively. Whether this takes place in the context of a social movement or in informal and nonformal learning activities with women does not matter so long as the curriculum and pedagogy take full account of the relationship between awareness, understanding and action, and do so in the spirit of solidarity and social justice for women.

One of the most important but difficult aspects of this commitment is to recognise and acknowledge the differences that exist between women which can often lead to conflict, in ways that encourage tolerance and a better understanding of their origins, but which also seek to build solidarity and the recognition of commonality across difference in the interests of all women's liberation.

Some years ago you moved from Ruskin to NIACE. Do you miss teaching? What are you writing?

Yes I moved to the National Institute for Adult Continuing Education (NIACE) in 2000. I do miss the regular contact with students that I had at Ruskin but I still do some teaching now and again as well as various workshops and conference presentations. Apart from three or four years in between Southampton University and Ruskin I have been a teacher since 1969—almost exclusively in the context of popular education. The NIACE job gives me the chance to work with a lot of adult and community education workers, to try to influence and question the ways in which current policies and practice happens, and to write in ways that seek to re-politicise current debates. I am enjoying this immensely.

So far I have initiated, edited and introduced a collection of essays written by radicals in university adult education called *Stretching the Academy: The Politics and Practice of Widening Participation in Higher Education*. I've worked with Mae Shaw from Scotland and Liam Bane from Ireland on a publication called *Reclaiming Common Purpose* about popular education and citizenship, which we distributed widely to adult and community education workers in the three countries. I recently finished a policy discussion paper which has been widely distributed to policy makers, providers, practitioners and activists about the relevance of the popular education tradition in adult education to the current government programme for neighbourhood renewal. The paper—called *Rerooting Lifelong Learning, Resourcing Neighbourhood Renewal*—raises lots of questions that are being currently used in a staff development context and in a consultative context with local community activists. A similar paper to be used by the Workers Education Association (WEA) and the Development Education Association (DEA) in the work they are doing with the Department for International Development (DfID) called *Global Perspectives in Lifelong Learning* raises issues about globalisation and sustainable development education in ways that I hope will help those organisations and the movements they support to advance the interests of globalisation from below. Currently I am working on a publication about cultural democracy and the potential within arts and cultural education for addressing political and cultural concerns. It's called *Bread and Roses*—for reasons that I imagine will be obvious to those who read this interview!

Curriculum as a Political Text

Interview with William Pinar

William Pinar *has recently moved to the University of British Columbia, where he directs the Centre for the Study of the Internationalization of Curriculum Studies. Pinar has lectured widely and published extensively on gender and racial politics, religion, curriculum theory and discourses, sexuality and queer theory. The father of a son named Gabriel, Pinar lives with his partner Jeff Turner in Surrey. This interview will zoom in on the concept of curriculum as a political text.*

How would you define your political standpoint?

I'm on the left, more Freudian than Marxian, very much influenced by the Greens, and by racial and gender theorists. The through-line among these influences is the centrality of subjectivity in political life. In the 2004 book, I called upon traditions of African American autobiography to teach this point; recently I completed a chapter on Fanon which underlines the same fact. Since 1968, I have dedicated myself to study and explicate subjectivity within the social through several traditions, including those listed in the first sentence above: my first book title included the terms "cultural revolution" and "heightened consciousness" (1974). For the next 20 years, I focused on autobiography, politics, and sexuality (Pinar 1994). In the second half of the 1990s I focused on the "crisis" of masculinity to extend our understanding of U.S. racial politics and violence (2001). During the first half of the present decade, I constructed a genealogy of "whiteness" in the West (2006a). In sustainability debates, I have long appreciated the eco-feminists who, by focusing on the gender of the assault on the earth, have directed our attention to that assault's subjective prerequisites and its subjective remedies (see Doerr 2004). Recalling the U.S. tradition in pragmatism, I argue there can be no social reconstruction without subjective reconstruction.

Where are you socially engaged beyond the field of academia?

I want to contest the assumption implied in this question, namely that it is important to be "socially engaged" outside academe, as if academe were not enough, or that "real" social change only happens outside the walls of the academy. While U.S. academicians are crestfallen by the capacity of the American fascists and neo-Confederates (Pinar 2006c) to sidestep their influence, no one ought not conclude definitively that teaching and research do not matter in macro-political terms. Certainly Mao thought they did.

The arrogance of the Marxian Left has been well documented (in curriculum studies see Pinar et al. 1995, chapter 5). The post-Marxist shift to cultural studies in curriculum studies (see Pinar 2006b, chapter 5) acknowledges the primacy of popular culture in processes of political self-formation; to the extent I am "socially engaged" outside the University it is in this sphere of cultural politics, specifically sexual politics.

Influenced especially by Butler, inspired by Simpson, I contest hegemonic masculinity by gay cruising, that is, by making clear to especially macho men that I regard them as sexual objects. Because hegemonic masculinity cannot be readily reduced to a sexual object—its political, political, economic, gendered status in North America contradicts such a reduction—cruising cannot function politically as does the straight-male commodification of women's bodies. What can be, in fact, politically progressive about cruising straight men is, in part, its potential to bring them down a notch. The firestorm set off in 1993 by U.S. President Clinton's policy on gays in the military underscores how destabilizing some straight men experience the presence of gay men (see Bersani 1995 for a brilliant and amusing commentary on this event). The politically progressive potential of that policy was not only unrealized, it stimulated political reaction, even violence, as subsequent murders of gay men in the military document. What is politically progressive about cruising straight men has to do with the look's potential to de-objectify and re-subjectify straight men (see Pinar 2006b, chapter 4). In many heteronormative men, subjectivity has been banished to body. Structuring their musculature is repressed emotion, including the residue of the masculinized repudiation of the pre-oedipal identification with the maternal body (see Chodorow 1978 for the classic account of pre-oedipal identification). That muscle also includes memory of the son's desire for the father. To bring homosexual attention to the surface of the (straight) male body threatens to de-crystallize that repression, and threatens its re-surfacing (see Pinar 2006a, 171).

Which issues are being confronted in this particular sector of activity (the one you have identified in the previous question)?

In cruising I confront racial and gendered (specifically queer) issues. In most public places in Louisiana (where I lived for 20 years, until August 2005)—from the gymnasium to restaurants to the neighborhood where we live—my African-American domestic partner (Jeff Turner) and I are confronted by racism and homophobia. While only sometimes physically threatening and often subtle, these confrontations are psychologically pointed and often quite violent in psychological terms. While Jeff—tall and muscular and younger than I by 13 years—performs versions of the threatening black man, I try to confine my responses to pedagogical interventions, rejoinders that question the assumptions embedded in the (almost always) white male assault on us. My "students" were rarely receptive, however.

Philip Jackson (1992) portrays Ralph Tyler's book, *Basic Principles of Curriculum and Instruction*, as a curriculum bible. Is Ralph Tyler still inspiring mainstream curriculum developers today?

Curriculum development—as schematized by Tyler—has disappeared as a sphere of professional and intellectual activity in the United States. As a scheme for structuring classroom practice—start with objectives, test to determine if they've been achieved—it remains uncontested in schools.

There is virtually no site-based curriculum development in the U.S. As textbooks provide and standardized tests structure the curriculum, public school teachers are forced to teach and students are forced to learn. The triumph of the "business" model in the U.S. has meant that teachers are unable to teach. Instead, they function as "managers of learning" (see Pinar 2004).

There remain, however attenuated, opportunities for curriculum development in intellectual, rather than, bureaucratic terms (see Pinar 2006b). As a curriculum developer today, I compose synoptic texts (such as Pinar 2001, 2006a, b) to enable public school teachers to reoccupy a vacated public domain, not as "consumers" of knowledge, but as active participants in complicated conversation that they themselves will lead in their own classrooms. In drawing widely but critically from various academic disciplines, from interdisciplinary areas, and from popular culture, the form of curriculum development I propose and demonstrate herein creates textbooks for teachers who can appreciate that our professional calling is the intellectual reconstruction of the public and private spheres. The audience is the teacher who understands her or his classroom as simultaneously civic squares and rooms of one's own. In such a third space (see Aoki 2005 [1990]; Wang 2004), students and teachers study academic knowledge not only for its own stake, but, as well, employ it to articulate their own self-formation in society at particular historical moments. In doing so, they are taught to articulate their own lived sense of the social sphere in the geophysical world. It is curriculum development that appreciates public education not as publicly funded academic vocationalism, but as the education of the public.

Can you identify curriculum paradigms that, today, are as influential as Tyler's model of curriculum development?

If you mean paradigms that are as influential as Tyler's in structuring school practice, the answer is no. If you mean influential intellectually in the academic field of curriculum studies in the United States, certainly there are paradigms (I prefer the term "sectors" of scholarship, although each tends to be paradigmatic in its totalizing tendencies) that are as influential. These we identified in *Understanding Curriculum* and are the 1) historical, 2) political, 3) racial, 4) gender, 5) phenomenological (no longer as influential), 6) poststructuralist (some loss of influence), 7) autobiographical-biographical, 8) aesthetic, 9) theological, 10) institutional (less influential due to the disappearance of curriculum development), and 11) international. In the sequel to *Understanding Curriculum* on which I am working now, I will add cultural and psychoanalytic studies as two sectors of scholarship that are influential today. Because the U.S. field is now balkanized and because it was totalized and made monolithic in Tyler's era, none of these contemporary curriculum discourses are as influential as was Tyler's Rationale.

Have reconceptualists made any significant inroads into mainstream curriculum reform in the US? Can you mention any concrete examples?

"Reconceptualists" is a historical category, referring to a theoretically disparate assemblage of anti-Tylerians whose scholarship functioned to reconceptualize U.S. curriculum studies during the 1970s (Pinar 2000; Pinar et al. 1995, chapter 4). Because school-based curriculum development has disappeared in the U.S., none of this work has made "significant inroads into mainstream curriculum reform." No doubt there have been influences in individual teacher's practices (see, for instance, Doer, 2004), but no systematic intervention has been politically possible.

In the book you co-authored, *Understanding Curriculum*, you trumpeted the collapse of the traditional field. Given the current obsession with standardization, continuous testing and league tables, how correct is your assessment today?

While it is true I approved of the intellectual collapse of the Tylerian model in U.S. curriculum studies, I was describing an intellectual shift in the field: from curriculum development to understanding curriculum. Given the triumph of standardization, of the "business model," in U.S. schools, now undergirded by legislation (No Child Left Behind), my assessment was absolutely accurate (see Pinar 2004; Gastambide-Fernandez and Sears 2004).

How would you answer to the most basic of curricular questions—what knowledge is of most worth?

It is a question to be answered individually within the context of national cultures, with their distinctive histories, cultural and political controversies, and economic agendas. This is evident in the international handbook of curriculum research (Pinar 2003).

The U.S. response to 9/11/01 suggests to me that knowledge of American narcissism is the knowledge of most worth today. The curriculum of a study of American narcissism would be interdisciplinary, focusing on the history of the nation: psychoanalytic accounts of its founding are suggestive here (see Pinar 2001, chapter 18; see, especially, Lasch 1978, 1984), as are studies in the role of Christianity in U.S. political identity, xenophobia, and imperialism (U.S. foreign policy specifically needs to be studied). The events in Abu Ghraib require attention to the cultures of racialized torture in the U.S., including nineteenth- and early twentieth-century lynching and interracial prison guard abuse today (Pinar 2001, chapters 16-17). The literature on globalization is also relevant here, obviously. This list of scholarly literatures that would comprise a study on American narcissism is, of course, hardly exhaustive.

In his book that calls for an anti-racist education, George Sefa Dei writes in terms of a multicentric curriculum that takes on board various social standpoints. Is this a viable proposition?

I am unfamiliar with this work. In the U.S. context, racism took very specific forms—such as lynching and interracial prison rape (see Pinar 2001)—that must be studied historically and in detail if an adequate anti-racist education is to be offered.

In the 2001 study, for instance, after reviewing the facts about lynching, I suggest an explanation for this uniquely American and, I argue, key instance of racial violence, reporting scholarship by historians on the so-called crisis of masculinity. In the South (see Pinar 2001, chapter 4), the Civil War forced white women to abandon their fixed if imaginary subject positions as "ladies" in order to do much of the supervisory and managerial labour absent husbands, fathers, and sons could not perform while off fighting the Yankees. This shift in southern white women's subject positions coupled with the crushingly complete military defeat of southern white men, a profoundly gendered as well as political and military event, set the stage for a beleaguered, regressed, frighteningly de-stabilized series of white male subject positions in the late nineteenth-century South, sensationalized in the formation of the KKK. Add to that more "gender trouble"—feminism in its various forms and settings, if muted and racialized in the South, shifts in the economy (industrialization swallows artisanal capitalism by 1900), in politics (in the 1890s Populism threatens what for many southern whites was a political miscegenation), in religion (even conservative Christian women made feminist gains; see chapter 5), in the law (as women gained elementary rights of divorce and property), and in the forms of homosociality (male-male "romantic" friendship ends as homoeroticism, surfaces socially and is named and tabooed), adding up to what a number of historians (not without controversy) have termed a general "crisis" of white masculinity in the 1890s—and we have the decade during which lynching was at its zenith.

Without study of the facts, and focused only on attitudes, anti-racist education risks, for whites, narcissism. Racism has always been all about "us" (Pinar 2006a).

How justified is the often-heard accusation, relevant to contemporary curricular debates, that the current pre-occupation with matters of identity and difference amounts to an insidious form of 'identity politics' that results in a fragmentation among potentially progressive forces struggling for a greater sense of social justice?

Given the misogyny, homophobia, and racism of past progressive forces in the U.S., concerns for identity and movements of identity politics have been necessary although indeed divisive. As an intellectual movement within education, identity politics is now, I suspect, close to exhaustion. Indeed, revising Spivak's phrase (but not the notion) of "strategic essentialism," I'd say there is evidence—among some African American scholarship (see, for instance, Nero 2005)—of a "strategically dysfunctional essentialism."

Given the intellectual and political collapse of Marxism, a new coalition of progressive forces will be required, one—obviously—not yet visible in the U.S.

Conscious of such controversies past and present, what issues face U.S. curriculum studies scholars in the future?

Our task is nothing less than the intellectual reconstruction of private and public spheres in education, a resuscitation of the progressive project, in which we understand that self-realization and democratization are inextricably intertwined. That is, in addition to providing competent individuals for the workplace and for higher education, we must renew our commitment to the democratization of American society, a socio-political and economic process that requires the psycho-social and intellectual education of the self-reflexive individual.

To focus upon the educational significance of schooling for the culture at large means returning academic knowledge to the individual him- or herself, teaching not only what is, for instance, historical knowledge, but also suggesting its possible consequences for the individual's self-formation, allowing that knowledge to shape the individual coming to social form. It means assuming the position of the private-and-public intellectual, especially now that this tradition is so attenuated and defamed. It is to suggest the significance of academic knowledge for the society at large. We might aspire to become, in Edward Said's (1996, 82) sense, intellectuals as "amateurs," not only "professionals" as academic vocationalism requires.

What does globalization portend for curriculum studies?

Like many others, I am suspicious of "globalization," worrying, for instance, that my call for an international association—realized as the International Association for the Advancement of Curriculum Studies (www.iaacs.org)—would be recoded as a call for standardization in curriculum studies worldwide. In anticipation of that concern and to underscore that curriculum studies are very much embedded within nations and regions, I chose the word "internationalization" to thematize the next phrase of the field's development (http://csics.educ.ubc.ca/). That term is still worrisome, insofar as it can appear to accept uncritically the historical and problematic concept of "nation," a concept David Held and his colleagues suggest, understatedly, "may need to be rethought and recast" (Held et al. 1999, 450). As Michael Hardt and Antonio Negri (2000, 49) remind us, "There was a time, not so long ago, when internationalism was a key component of proletarian struggles and progressive politics in general." May it become so again, especially so for us, engaged in our various locales in the project of understanding curriculum within and across national borders.

References

Aoki, Ted (2005 [1990]). Sonare and videre: A story, three echoes and a lingering note. In William F. Pinar and Rita L. Irwin (Eds.), *Curriculum in a New Key: The Collected Works of Ted T. Aoki* (367-376). Mahwah, NJ: Lawrence Erlbaum.

Bersani, Leo (1995). *Homos*. Cambridge, MA: Harvard University Press.

Butler, Judith (1990). *Gender trouble*. New York: Routledge.

Butler, Judith (1993). *Bodies that matter: On the discursive limits of "sex."* New York and London: Routledge.

Chodorow, Nancy J. (1978). *The reproduction of mothering*. Berkeley: University of California Press.

Doerr, Marilyn (2004). Currere *and environmental autobiography*. New York: Peter Lang.

Gastambide-Fernandez, Rubén A. and Sears, James T. (Eds.) (2004). *Curriculum work as a public moral enterprise*. Lanham, MD: Rowman & Littlefield.

Hardt, Michael and Negri, Antonio (2000). *Empire*. Cambridge, MA: Harvard University Press.

Held, David, McGrew, Athony, Goldblatt, David, Perraton, Jonathan (1999). *Global Transformations: Politics, Economics and Culture*. Stanford, CA: Stanford University Press.

Lasch, Christopher (1978). *The culture of narcissism: American life in an age of diminishing expectations*. New York: Norton.

Lasch, Christopher (1984). *The minimal self: Psychic survival in troubled times*. New York: Norton.

Nero, Charles I. (2005). Why are the gay ghettoes white? In E. Patrick Johnson and Mae G. Henderson (Eds.) *Black Queer Studies: A Critical Anthology* (228-245). Durham, NC: Duke University Press.

Pinar, William F. (ed.). (1974). *Heightened consciousness, cultural revolution, and curriculum theory*. Berkeley, CA: McCutchan.

Pinar, William F. (1994). *Autobiography, politics, and sexuality: Essays in curriculum theory 1972-1992*. New York: Peter Lang.

Pinar, William F. (Ed.) (2000). *Curriculum studies: The reconceptualization*. Troy, NY: Educator's International Press, Inc. [First published in 1975 as *Curriculum Theorizing: The Reconceptualists*. Berkeley, CA: McCutchan Publishing.]

Pinar, William F. (2001). *The gender of racial politics and violence in America: Lynching, prison rape, and the crisis of masculinity*. New York: Peter Lang.

Pinar, William F. (Ed.) (2003). *International handbook of curriculum research*. Mahwah, NJ: Lawrence Erlbaum.

Pinar, William F. (2004). *What is curriculum theory?* Mahwah, NJ: Lawrence Erlbaum.

Pinar, William F. (2006a). *Race, religion and curriculum of reparation*. New York: Palgrave Macmillan.
Pinar, William F. (2006b). *The synoptic text today and other essays: Curriculum development after the reconceptualization*. New York: Peter Lang.
Pinar, William F. (2006c). Independence. In J. Milam, S. Springgay, K. Sloan, and B. S. Carpenter (Eds.), *Curriculum for a Progressive, Provocative, Poetic and Public Pedagogy*. Troy, NY: Educator's International Press.
Pinar, William F. (in preparation). *Understanding curriculum: The next moment*. New York: Peter Lang.
Pinar, William F., Reynolds, William M., Slattery, Patrick, and Taubman, Peter M. (1995). *Understanding curriculum*. New York: Peter Lang.
Said, Edward W. (1996). *Representations of the intellectual*. New York: Vintage.
Simpson, Mark (1994). *Male impersonators: Men performing masculinity*. [Foreword by Alan Sinfield.] New York: Routledge.
Wang, Hongyu (2004). *The call from the stranger on a journey home: Curriculum in a third space*. New York: Peter Lang.

School Exclusion, Educational Engagement and Social Equity

Interview with Paul Cooper

Paul Cooper is a Chartered Psychologist and has been a Professor of Education at Leicester since January 2001. Before moving to Higher Education, he was a teacher of English in a Scottish comprehensive school and then taught in England in special facilities for children and young people with social, emotional and behavioural difficulties and a junior school. Since 1989 he has held academic posts in the universities of Birmingham, Oxford and Cambridge where he has developed research and teaching interests, along with an extensive list of publications, in the areas of social, emotional and behavioural difficulties in education, Attention Deficit/Hyperactivity Disorder, positive alternatives to school exclusion and effective teaching and learning in schools. For the last twenty years he has conducted in-service training in schools and, mainly through SEBDA (Social, Emotional and Behavioural Difficulties Association), advocated the concept of educational engagement as an antidote to school exclusion. In this interview, he will elaborate on the issues of school exclusion, neo-liberal discourse in education, special education, inclusive policies, educational engagement and parental voice.

What are the forces that promote real and symbolic exclusion from the learning process?

Educational exclusion is characterised by a failure to engage effectively in the educational process. Individuals who are thus excluded fail to derive benefits from educational experiences that are usually associated with positive social, emotional and cognitive development, and, as a result, are subject to impaired life chances, such as occupational opportunities and concomitant economic advancement. There are complex and multiple factors that can influence the exclusion process. One individual's route to becoming excluded, therefore, may be very different from another's. There are, however, commonalities and patterns that frequently recur in the life histories of excludees. These can be thought of in terms of socio-cultural and psychological factors.

Socio-cultural influences inevitably embrace political factors which, in turn, are rooted in the economic value of education as a commodity. High status educational opportunities, such as attendance at the most prestigious schools and universities are expensive and limited in availability, and, therefore, subject to fierce competition. In countries such as the UK and USA educational attainment for the majority of the population can be predicted on the basis of socio-economic status at birth. Children from relatively wealthy families are likely to have access to prestigious fee charging schools, which, in turn, are able to devote more resources to preparing students for entry to prestigious universities than less well endowed schools. In the UK, for example, approximately 7% of school students attend fee charging schools, whilst approximately 50% of undergraduate places at the country's two most prestigious universities (Oxford and Cambridge) are occupied by students coming from the fee paying school sector.

The power of material capital is also associated with 'cultural capital'. This refers to knowledge, values, attitudes and beliefs that are endorsed by prestigious educational institutions. Children born to parents who are not endowed with significant material wealth, but who possess significant cultural capital, are advantaged over others by being socialised in ways that enable them to outperform their less well prepared peers in state funded institutions. Arguably, it is for this reason that the dramatic expansion in the number of higher education institutions in the UK over the past half century appears to have benefited the middle rather than working classes, proportionately.

This perspective would suggest that students from certain kinds of backgrounds are disadvantaged from the start of their educational careers. It is no surprise, therefore, that children from these backgrounds tend to be over-represented in the exclusion figures.

A further socio-cultural dimension is that of ethnicity. In the UK students of African Caribbean origin are highly overrepresented in exclusion figures, whilst students from certain (though not all) Asian communities (especially Indian and Chinese) underrepresented. This fact can be related to the uneven distribution of cultural capital.

These macro factors interact with individual level influences in complex ways. The most common reason given for school exclusion is the oppositional and or aggressive behaviour of students. Interestingly, boys outnumber girls by a ratio of approximately 4:1. This can be explained, in part at least, in terms of socialisation practices which tend to produce gender differences in terms of behavioural patterns. These differences may also be related to deep rooted biological differences between the genders which affect maturational progress as well as behavioural styles. Crudely speaking, girls tend to be more socially adept than boys. Boys, on the other hand, are likely to be more physically active and impulsive than girls. As a result, girls are perhaps, by and large, better adapted than boys to the sedentary nature of classroom life, and less likely than boys to deal with peer group problems through physical, and, therefore obviously disruptive means.

Of course, it is only a relatively small proportion of students who actually experience formal exclusion from school, though there are many fine gradations of exclusion which are not all picked up in the recorded figures. Perhaps the most common form of 'invisible' exclusion is related to student disaffection, which can manifest itself in student disengagement from the learning process that is masked by superficial compliance behaviours. Students' accounts of how and why they become disaffected and disengaged often involve reference to what they see as dehumanising and disrespectful treatment at the hands of teachers. This can take the form of discriminatory behaviour, whereby teachers are seen to favour certain students over others, as well as unfair and inappropriate forms of discipline, which may involve humiliating punishment or disproportionate and/or inconsistent disciplinary measures implemented by teachers. Many students accept these inequities passively or with covert resentment; others respond with acts of retribution or reciprocation. It is members of the latter group who are more likely to be excluded.

Perhaps the single most common complaint of excluded students (or those most at risk of exclusion) is that their teachers often appear to show little interest in them as individuals. Rather, they tend to be subjected to crude stereotyping, by which their behaviour, regardless of the actual motivation behind it, is always interpreted as an expression of deviance. Over time this can have the effect of becoming a self-fulfilling prophecy, whereby the negatively labelled student, either out of a sense of resignation or as an act of rebellion, increasingly behaves in accordance with the negative label. Thus students who often have genuine, unrecognised learning difficulties, such as ADHD or dyslexia, which have been misinterpreted as laziness or oppositionality, adopt additional, sometimes intentional disruptive and oppositional patterns of behaviour. The sense of alienation from the formal 'official' culture of schooling, that naturally follows from these feelings of being mistreated, further leads, in some cases, to the development of deviant, anti-school subcultures that offer kudos and reinforcement for anti-school behaviour.

Can temporary or permanent exclusion from school ever be justified?

Far too many schools opt for exclusion as a way of ridding themselves of their responsibilities towards students who are experiencing difficulties of one kind or another. Having said this, there are times when the relationship between a student and school breaks down to such an extent that it is in the interests of both parties to end the relationship. The analogy here is with marital divorce, which is always regrettable, but is sometimes the only workable option after all reasonable efforts at mediation and reconciliation have failed. Even with the best will in the world, a school may be at a stage in its development in which it is not ready to make the changes necessary to make itself fully inclusive. It can take a long time for a school to change its culture and ethos. For some students the wait will be too long, and having a fresh start in a new, and more accommodating school can sometimes be the best option.

It also has to be recognised that there are a small number of students whose behaviour is such that they pose a threat to the safety of others. In an ideal world these students would receive appropriate intervention, sometimes without the need for their removal from the mainstream school. Sometimes, however, the act of exclusion is the trigger necessary for the student's difficulties to be highlighted and addressed.

Temporary exclusion can also, in some cases, be used for positive ends. It can provide a breathing space for both the school (staff and students) and the excludee, during which time there is a cooling of tempers and a chance for calm reflection. This enables the school staff to plan for the student's re-entry, and gives the student (and his or her family) time to consider how they would like to proceed. For this to work, however, the exclusion has to be planned and supported by the school and, where appropriate, other agencies. The student must have a programme of activity and the school must be committed to reintegrating the student.

In any event, exclusion should always be a last resort. For this reason it should be extremely rare.

What are the alternatives to school exclusion?

Students become alienated and disengaged from schools when they feel discounted and uncared for. It is salutary to remember that one of the highest compliments that students will give when talking about teachers and schools is that 'they treat you like a person'. On the face of it, this is not a lot to ask, and yet generations of school students the world over testify to the fact that this is a comparatively rare experience. The fact of the matter is that schooling is above all a social and emotional experience, and when any of us recall our schooldays it tends to be in relation to the feelings that we have about it. These feelings, in turn, are almost always intertwined with relationships we had during those years with our peers and teachers. I would go so far as to argue that the love and enthusiasm that some of us have developed for particular school subjects are often associated with the positive feelings we have for particular teachers. I think that the converse is also true: bad experiences with unsympathetic, uncaring or bullying teachers may have created barriers which prevented us engaging with certain subjects.

Having said this, there are longstanding features common to most schools and education systems that can help mitigate the effects of poor relationships between teachers and students. Students who are relatively academically gifted and who show an aptitude for certain subjects will tend to receive rewards and approval in the form of assignment grades, praise and school prizes. Such social and academic approval may well help them to tolerate shortcomings in their relationships with teachers. For less academically gifted students, however, it is the relationship with the teacher that is paramount. Not only does this form the access route through which they will (or will not) engage with the learning process, it is the key element in the school experience that determines for the student the extent to which schooling is an emotionally safe, worthwhile and rewarding experience.

Schools which are effective in engaging students who are at risk of exclusion recognise the importance of positive relationships between staff and students. They emphasise the importance of mutual respect between staff and students, and place a strong emphasis on the need for staff to take the lead in modelling respectful forms of interaction. In such schools all students are valued as persons above all else, regardless of their academic prowess. This means that staff take an interest in students as persons, and the school as an institution creates opportunities for students' individual interests and accomplishments (both academic and nonacademic) to be acknowledged and celebrated. Furthermore, all students in such schools are given opportunities to take responsibilities associated with the day to day running of the school, by being incorporated into decision making bodies and consultative committees.

This is not to say that academic aspects of schooling are neglected in these schools. Far from it. One of the ways in which staff show respect for their students is by taking their learning needs extremely seriously, regardless of their attainment history. This requires that staff are open and responsive to students' concerns when they encounter a barrier to learning. This responsiveness applies equally to curricular matters as it does to social and emotional issues. Schools which are effective in preventing exclusion are places where students always feel that they have a member of staff to go to when they are experiencing difficulties of any kind, who will listen in a non-judgemental way and offer constructive advice and support.

Can education systems that promote streaming/tracking, league tables, standardized tests and teacher-proof curricula serve all students equitably?

The rhetorical underpinnings of the English National Curriculum and what has come to be known as the 'standards agenda' are, in some respects, sound. It is desirable that all students should have access to a broad and balanced curriculum, and that measures should be taken to ensure that the best standards in teaching are made available to all students. As is often the case, however, there is a major gap between the rhetoric and the practice. The chief problem with these so-called reforms is the way in which they have come to be experienced as a straitjacket that has reduced the role of the teacher from that of an innovator and interpreter of curricular issues to that of an implementer of a prescribed curriculum. The art of effective teaching requires the teacher to develop a relationship with a learner that is based on respect for the knowledge, interests and aptitudes of the student. It is from this relationship that the curriculum should emerge, with the teacher taking the role of mentor and guide, rather than as a one dimensional transmitter of knowledge.

It is a truism that gifted teachers will always find ways of subverting and circumventing imposed curricula to achieve effective teaching and learning. It is regrettable, however, that gifted and dedicated teachers should feel themselves at odds with the prevailing policy context. What is needed is much more opportunity for teachers (and dare I say it, education academics) to be involved in policy development. Government policy needs to take as its starting point an appraisal of the vast wealth of talent within the teaching profession and to find ways of growing educational policy from this.

Of course, it might be argued by some commentators that there is considerably more scope for teacher and school autonomy than is widely perceived or currently practised. In England, for example, recently state funded schools have been given the chance to apply to the Secretary of State for Education for permission to be exempted from statutory obligations in order to engage in the development of innovatory practice. Furthermore, there are features of government policy, such as the SEN Code of Practice and the national numeracy and literacy strategies that are advisory rather than statutory and yet which are often treated by schools as if they were statutory. This is perhaps indicative of the cultural climate that has characterised the education sector in the UK since the late 1980s. At its most extreme, this is a climate of fear and aversion to risk. Schools and teachers fear being 'named and shamed' if they step outside the limits of government guidelines—even when they believe the guidelines to be flawed. This may account for the difficulties encountered by the UK education system in retaining young teachers in the profession and recruiting suitably qualified and experienced head teachers to primary and secondary schools. This is in spite of the increasing financial rewards associated with teaching as a profession in the UK. The consequences for the future of the teaching profession in the UK of a generation of teachers being socialised into a profession beset with such fears can only be guessed at, but it has to be said that the future does not look bright from this vantage point.

You have researched, written, lectured on and championed the cause of children with SEBD. How can these children be engaged positively within the education process?

In spite of the general air of gloom that is sometimes attached to the field of SEBD in this country, the UK has a long and distinguished history of innovative and successful work with children who fall into this category. Unfortunately, much of this work has taken place outside of the mainstream sector and has often failed to receive the recognition it deserves. As a result, insights from this work have not been incorporated into mainstream provision as fully as they might have been, to the cost of many children who might otherwise have benefited.

The middle years of the last century were something of a high point for individualistic, experimental approaches to meeting the needs of what were then called 'maladjusted' children. These were children with serious social, emotional and behavioural problems, some of whom would warrant psychiatric diagnoses and many of whom displayed delinquent tendencies. These were children who were not accepted in the mainstream schools of the day. The lucky ones of this group found their way into pioneering schools (often residential) that, although diverse and disparate in many respects, tended to share certain common characteristics. First, these schools tended to recognise that many of the difficulties experienced by their pupils were exacerbated by the formalism and impersonal nature of mainstream schools. Second, they recognised that effective engagement with these children was dependent on the forging of trusting, caring and supportive relationships with adults. Third, a crucial feature of the rehabilitation process was the development of a sense of responsibility in children. This often took the form of engaging students in various aspects of the running of the communities in which they were resident.

A simple, and yet profound feature of these institutions was the emphasis on the student as a person. Only if we treat our students as if they are people who need to be known and respected can we expect reciprocal treatment from them. The process of creating a reciprocal, respectful relationship involves the recognition of responsibilities and obligations on both sides. These simple ideas have enormous resonance today. And it has to be said, many of our mainstream schools are still a long way from even recognising the validity of these ideas, let alone implementing them. Having said this, there is evidence (at last) of some of these ideas creeping into some mainstream schools and of their being recognised by policy makers. The recent trumpeting of notions of emotional literacy and emotional intelligence reflects these values. The British government's 'Every Child Matters' (DfES, 2003) agenda, with its emphasis on the importance of emotional safety as a foundation stone of educational engagement, is also reflective of this view.

As has already been noted, however, there remains a serious tension between the needs of vulnerable students, such as those experiencing SEBD, and negative features of the overall policy and practice context, which largely sees such children as at best an inconvenience, and at worst an irrelevance. Part of the problem here is that, as far as the most powerful sections of our society are concerned, the education system as a whole is doing fine in relation to their own needs. It is for this reason, unfortunately, that exclusion is seen by many as being such an obviously desirable option. The irony of this view, however, is that these same voices despair at what they see as a decline in public order and civic safety. One of the challenges we face, therefore, is to convince the proponents of views such as these of the necessity to create an education system that is as responsive to the needs of those they would exclude, as it is to their own needs.

The key issue here is that of diversity of educational provision. In my view, the age of the 'mainstream' school is probably over. This is already reflected in the UK in the growth of specialist schools. These are so called mainstream schools that adopt a curricular specialism, such as sport, business studies, modern languages, or science and technology. These schools present themselves as offering advantages for students with particular curricular aptitudes. Having said this, these schools still reflect the institutional features of the educational factory. It is very difficult for such institutions to meet the needs of the emotionally vulnerable student. Many students (not only those designated as experiencing SEBD) might benefit from a period of study in small, socially intimate settings, which extend the kinds of opportunities created by small primary schools for more personalised relationships with staff, and the opportunity to be part of a small scale community. The practical, personal and educational advantages of such provisions are already demonstrable in the form of 'nurture groups', which are small classes (maximum of 12 students) located in mainstream primary schools, that provide a holistic curriculum combining academic and social/emotional learning opportunities.

Have you noticed any substantial changes in the way SEBD children are perceived, portrayed and dealt with by educators, education administrators, policy makers and UK society at large in the last ten years?

There is a paucity of empirical evidence on which to base an answer to this question. However, my personal view, as a consumer of the news and popular media, is that over my professional lifetime we have become an increasingly child-phobic society. There is a widely held perception, promulgated by the media, that parenting standards have declined and that children and young people are 'out of control'. Although this has been an age old complaint for generations, it has never had the degree of media support that it enjoys in the age of digital communication technology. Children and young people tend to be portrayed as either helpless victims of adult depravity, or as demons—the perpetrators of vile crimes. These apparently paradoxical perspectives appear to have the same consequence: they accentuate the distance between adults and children. The well intentioned adult who may at one time have struck up an innocent conversation with a child at a supermarket checkout or berated a child vandalising a bus shelter is more likely now to fain indifference for fear of negative consequences.

Having said this, I would argue that educational professionals are, by and large, more aware of the concept of SEBD than they were a decade ago. This is not to say that the concept is always accepted. There is still the sense among some educational professionals that the majority of children experiencing SEBD are un-deserving. This view tends to coincide with a dismissal of the kinds of approaches I have alluded to earlier, on the grounds that they are indulgent and misguided.

How strong is the parental voice in the context of SEBD?

Of all of the areas of SEN, SEBD is the least attractive of sympathy and understanding. As a consequence there are very few voices, from any sector, speaking up for this group. For parents the SEBD label is, more often than not either a badge of shame, or stimulus for fierce resistance. There are no parents' organisations (as far as I know) for children with SEBD. Part of the reason for this is that there is a strong trend in the news media to attribute childhood behavioural problems to poor parenting.

Interesting exceptions to this phenomenon are the relatively strong parental voices associated with such medically defined conditions as ADHD and Autistic Spectrum Disorders. These conditions clearly fall under the umbrella term of SEBD, but by virtue of the bio-medical paradigm place minimal emphasis on parenting in the aetiology of the conditions. This suggests that the widely disseminated argument that SEBD is the product of bad parenting is not only inaccurate (see above) but is also an additional burden on the parents of children experiencing these difficulties.

What is the prevalent model of inclusion in the UK?

Inclusive education in the UK is still very strongly associated with the notion of mainstreaming. The rhetoric does allow for the idea of the inclusive continuum, that incorporates special schools and other non-mainstream provision. In practice, however, these alternative forms of provision are still seen as second best. In spite of this, the drive towards creating mainstream schools that are committed to reducing the barriers to engagement by pupils with SEBD is not progressing discernably.

Can the global economy, informed by the hegemonic discourse of neo-liberalism, serve the interest of genuine inclusion?

The problem with the liberalist discourse resides in its idealism. We cannot correct the inequities of a class based education system simply by exhorting all 'mainstream' schools to become inclusive. For example, the Salamanca Statement on inclusive education is frankly disingenuous in its claim that students with SEN fare better in mainstream schools than they do in special schools. The fact of the matter is that there are good schools and bad schools. There are good mainstream schools and good special schools, just as there are bad mainstream schools and bad special schools. The problem with the emphasis that is placed on mainstreaming is that it gives rise to the assumption that a student is 'included' simply by being on the roll of a mainstream school. This is clearly an erroneous view.

As for the 'global economy', it is the reductionist view that education's primary purpose is to service the economy that is perhaps the greatest challenge to modern education systems. The chief responsibility of educators and educationists is now to educate their students (and politicians) about the civilising power of education. Global citizenship is important to the world economy, but it goes far beyond vocational preparation. It is most fundamentally concerned with issues of value and attitude.

It seems that special education and schools are making a strong comeback in the UK? Is our reading of the situation correct? Are you worried?

It is not the case that there is a resurgence in special schooling in the UK. Though it may be the case that there has been something of a deceleration in the closing of special schools. This is particularly so in the case of SEBD provision. The simple reason for this being that students with SEBD have been the most resistant to mainstream inclusion policies. This may well be a reflection of the systemic dysfunctions of the mainstream sector which, as I have already indicated, are endemic.

It does not worry me that students with SEBD still have access to specialist provision, provided that this provision is high quality, is dedicated to facilitating their return to appropriate mainstream education, and that arrangements are in place to ensure that they will be able to return to mainstream provision when they are ready.

What constitutes a good inclusive education policy? How far is the UK from your personal definition of a good inclusive education policy?

I do not like the term 'inclusive education', though I applaud the intentions behind it. I prefer the term 'educational engagement', because, it seems to me, it captures what proponents of 'inclusion' really want, which is, simply, effective education for all. I live in a society in which many of the most economically privileged make the deliberate decision to have their children educated outside of the state 'mainstream' sector. In terms of educational progression, this decision is vindicated by the fact that their children have a much enhanced prospect of obtaining places in higher education settings. Furthermore, less well heeled, but educationally informed parents are reported to go to extreme lengths to have their children placed in what they consider to be the more effective 'mainstream' schools. This leaves a rump of unattractive, stigmatised schools that are open to all. It is this group of 'mainstream' schools that tends to have more than its fair share of children with SEN and, inevitably, SEBD. Many of these schools are places where, in spite of the best efforts of dedicated staff, the majority of students are doomed to relative failure. To me this reflects the utter implausibility of the notion of the 'mainstream' school.

The alternative to the idea of inclusion in a mainstream school is the idea that all children have a right to optimum educational engagement. This means that they should have the opportunity to be placed in the educational setting most likely to meet their educational needs. It follows from this that as their needs change over time, so should the provision they access. There should be no stigma attached to attending a small scale unit, as opposed to a large scale comprehensive school.

Do the major political parties in the UK differ substantially in their policy/ies for inclusion?

As far as I am aware there is little difference between the two major UK political parties on this topic. This is partly because it is a relatively low priority issue for them. The one thing that they do seem to agree on is the desire to increase the powers of schools to exclude troublesome students. Both parties are locked in what many of us would see as an outmoded view of schools, which emphasises the importance of 'control' and 'discipline'. This is a view that sees punishment as the primary response to SEBD.

Theatre of the Oppressed: Italian Initiatives

Interview with Roberto Mazzini

T he Theatre of the Oppressed, attributed to Augusto Boal and which has strong affinities with the writings of Paulo Freire, has had great resonance in different parts of the world. Two years ago, we were invited to deliver a seminar and workshop on the pedagogy of Paulo Freire in Bologna, Emilia-Romagna, Italy. One of the organizations that sponsored the event is the Teatro Giolli. We caught up with one of their animators, Roberto Mazzini, from the Giolli Research Centre on the 'Theatre of the Oppressed' and Conscientization, Livorno (Leghorn), to discuss with him some of the potential which this type of theatre has for the generation of critical consciousness and social justice.

What does theatre mean to you?

A tool for work and pleasure that allows me to combine political choice with economic survival, an ethical commitment and a professional approach.

What contribution can theatre make to a humanisation process?

If we define "humanization" as an historical and personal process where we become aware of our being active subjects in the world, then theatre in general can help to discover our own inner self, our richness, our potential; it can lead us to imagine futures and explore the opportunity of being-in-the-world. Theatre also focuses our attention on social rituals enabling us to identify those that are oppressive and to create new ones that enhance a sense of community.

Furthermore, the theatre of Augusto Boal also serves as an instrument of self-awareness and of consciousness of the world; it centres on personal and social change at the corporal, emotive, intellectual, individual and collective (group) levels.

The Theatre of the Oppressed urges human beings, in solidarity with others, to react to oppression, to be active and proactive (in Freire's sense of denouncing and announcing) and to regard every situation as capable of being modified. It is therefore predicated on and reinforces the capacity for humans to "see themselves in action."

For Boal this is the essence of human beings who humanize themselves by deepening, using and developing this capacity.

As a holistic tool for change (mind, body and emotion), theatre can contribute in this manner to the movement for historical, social, political, human and collective change.

In what way does the Theatre of the Oppressed differ from conventional theatre?

As I have just remarked, the Theatre of the Oppressed directs our attention towards changing oppressive situations; first of all, it directs our attention towards our reading our daily life, in dialogue with others, to understand its limits and potentialities and to explore generative themes, oppressive rituals... then the identification of the key knots that prevent human liberation from occurring, that shackle a person's integral development; then the experimentation with possibilities for change within the theatrical context, a context that provides one with the chance to discover and strengthen oneself. Finally there is the process of extrapolation, transferring into daily life what has been learnt in the theatrical context. Classical theatre, including that which is political, is often based on catharsis, the purging of passions. The Theatre of the Oppressed is based on metaxis, belonging simulatenously to two worlds, theatre and reality. Both Brecht and Boal prevented catharsis from occurring, the former through the use of the 'alienation effect'and the latter through the 'spectactor's' action on stage.

In what way do Augusto Boal's *Theatre of the Oppressed* and Paulo Freire's *Pedagogy of the Oppressed* converge and differ?

I believe that they share a common cultural basis. Both of them speak of dialogue, oppression, generative themes, oppressive relations, humanizing persons, searching for truth without owning it, a maieutic system, problem posing...the goal is the same: help bring about human liberation, emerge from a situation of 'naive consciousness'and move towards 'critical, transitive and organizational consciousness'. The role of the director, in both cases, is the same. The director assumes the role of a maieutic person who does not judge but starts from the participants' knowledge of the world with a view to deepening and problematizing it. He or she does not judge or interpret but helps systematize this knowledge, establish connections and search for alternatives.

The methodology is also similar: from the concrete to the abstract, from the particular to the general. From that which is evident to that which is concealed. One difference is that Boal gives more attention to the corporal and ritual elements than to the word. The Theatre of the Oppressed strikes me as projecting the notion of a more integral human being, with less emphasis on the intellectual side and attention focused on a holistic reading of all the elements. One always learns to read the world, to give the word to the world, through dialogue. One however achieves this through dialogue in action and not just through pure and simple reflection. I believe that Boal's dialogue is a dialogue which is based on action. Moreover, the search for solutions occurs through the process of action followed by reflection, echoing the Freirean cycle of practice-theory-practice, however in a manner that accentuates the separation between the theatrical context and the more real context; these are conceived of as two distinct moments, more than in Freire's practice.

Finally, for Boal, theatre has an important gnosiological function that is, however, based on the senses. Boal calls theatrical space "aesthetic space" because, etymologically speaking, consciousness derives more from the senses than from the intellect; one learns by feeling, seeing, observing, listening, feeling emotions.

I am not aware that Freire expresses a similarly strong valorization of the theatre.

What type of response can the Theatre of the Oppressed provide in view of the various forms of oppression worldwide?

The response derives from the oppressed themselves. Boal's theatre allows them to search for alternatives in both the micro and macro contexts. A globalized oppression requires a global movement to confront it.

But the 'local-global relation' is worth exploring with regard to, for example, the theme of 'flexible work'. We are producing a performance dealing with typical Italian situations that are obviously dependent on the larger global context but also represent the manner in which globalization makes its presence felt in Italy. One engages in a good debate with the theatre when allying a global consciousness of the phenomenon with the concrete nature of the lived everyday situation, thus combining theory and practice and providing both an expansive view of the situation and a focus on the here and now. In the Forum Theatre, Boal speaks of the 'ascendance' that has to be pursued by the Jolly (who performs the maieutic role in the Theatre of the Oppressed) to lead the public, by means of questions, to move from the phenomenon to the law, from the particular to the general ideal type and the relations that govern it.

Can relatively privileged persons like us carry out theatre with oppressed persons and, if yes, how?

In my view...yes...in the sense of the Gramscian organic intellectual, that is to say a person who gives expression to a collective vision, operating in close connection with progressive social movements. According to the vision expressed in the Theatre of the Oppressed there is no such thing as the existence of two worlds, that of the oppressed and that of the oppressors. What we have is an intermeshing of oppressions where one comes across chains of oppression, with roles that change according to circumstance and power exerted at various levels. We are therefore all (or almost all) oppressors and oppressed, depending on roles, moments, circumstances, relations , contexts etc.

Every oppressed person is privileged with respect to others who have less power. The key consideration is whether the power we enjoy as director, a position of privilege in contrast to that of the participants (not unlike the privileged position the Freirean educator enjoys in constrast to that of the educatee in an educational setting), is used for the purpose of liberation or for manipulation. This is the challenge and it cannot be resolved once and for all. We should always be on our guard so that it would not be our turn to become oppressors. This explains why work is carried out in groups and direction occurs within the context of a team. This is why we need continuous research, self-analysis of power and self-criticism. These are powerful antidotes to our becoming oppressors, in our own way, of the oppressed with whom we work.

We must keep in mind that, throughout the contexts of everyday life, even we are, in turn, oppressed or oppressors.

How does one handle silence and inactivity in the contest of the Theatre of the Oppressed?

They are respected. Theatre of the Oppressed provides one with an opportunity to reflect on one's reality, both internal and external, but without forcing one to do so. The Jolly does not force the public to intervene neither does the Jolly force the members of the theatre workshop to participate. It is explicitly stated, in the educational contract, that one is not obliged to participate.

This having been said, one can come across situations when there is a stimulus for one to break the silence and stop being inactive. This applies to situations when silence and passivity are a form of defence, a manifestation of fear, etc., and it is considered more risky to continue in this manner than to make the required effort. But one has to act tactfully and intuitively. Silence and inactivity can also be symptomatic of other problems: problems with the director, with the group and with the type of proposed activity. It could, at times, be a matter of different cultures and so women do not speak in the presence of men, etc. Every situation must be viewed from different standpoints.

We are under the impression, from what we have seen in our recent work in Rome, Milan and Bologna, that there is a great social movements culture in Italy. We are not sure whether our impression is correct. How would you describe the relationship between the Theatre of the Oppressed and social movements?

There are social movements of different types even though they are not as strong as they were in the seventies. They are more sectorial and less connected among themselves. There are small nuclei of resistance that are interested in specific themes: committees against school reform (*N.B. resistance to the so-called Moratti school reform*), environmental committees, voluntary associations, NGOs concerned with North-South cooperation, centres for youth squatters, etc. The Theatre of the Oppressed has not been involved with these movements, mainly for political and cultural reasons. Theatre and politics are not directly united; when one thinks of theatre's involvement in politics one thinks only of an instrumental, ideological and propagandist use, agit-prop style. Or one thinks of theatre as representing a moment of entertainment and relaxation. People find it difficult to conceive of theatre as a vehicle for reflecting on action that has to be taken. Furthermore, the directive, authoritarian and hierarchical nature of Italian politics poses obstacles in the way of engaging in the type of dialogical approach, associated with Freire, that inspires Boal.

Can you indicate conrete ways by which the Theatre of the Oppressed has contributed to processes of social transformation?

Given that the most evident changes occur within individuals and small groups, it is difficult to indicate similar changes at the social level in view of the complex nature of the actors involved and the scarcity of resources that prevents projects from having a long life cycle.

I will however point to four different examples: A project such as the one carried out in Ravenna and called 'The City that Matters.' It involved the participation of three districts and a high school. By means of courses that contributed to the ongoing formation of a group of actors, workshops carried out at school and performances for the inhabitants, the project provided an opportunity for reflection on the hidden latent conflicts of the area (the territorio) especially with regard to immigration. It contributed to improving relations between some of the youths and their parents as well as teachers. The improvement did not come about through a moralistic 'let's wish ourselves well' but through a common strategy for reflection, which also entailed an emotional experience that allowed us to identify the knots and overcome mutual prejudices.

At Livorno and Rovigo we had the project: 'White Faces, Black Faces, Let's Provide Information'. Through theatre, this project dealt with the kind of information circulated by the media with respect to the immigrant. Through the Theatre-Newspaper (a series of old 'Theatre of the Oppressed' techniques) we sought to deconstruct the stereotypes that are reinforced by newspaper articles. This attracted the attention of certain journalists, as well as associations within the area, with regard to the problem of information and prejudice.

There was also the Modena project concerning generational district conflicts. Thanks to the Forum-theatre, it was possible to overcome and transform the situation of tension, including violent tension, between the groups into one of collaboration where the groups began to be dismembered and individuals disposed towards dialogue began to emerge. Finally, during the last scholastic year, our organisation produced a Forum-theatre centering around the theme of 'The School Firm: how the Moratti Reform Changes the School.' This was a proposed neo-liberal school reform. This Forum-Theatre toured several Italian towns, in collaboration with the 'Schools against Moratti' coordination movement. The play provided hundreds of parents and teachers with an opportunity to discuss how best to resist the reform and, at the time of this interview, we are still receiving requests to stage this play.

What impact has the Theatre of the Oppressed had on schools and teacher education institutions?

As far as Giolli is concerned, I would say 'very little', generally speaking. It is very difficult for teachers to follow courses of ongoing professional formation given their current contract situation. Continuing professional development courses are no longer obligatory. Their workload is perceived as being too heavy. It is difficult to obtain leave of absence to follow a refresher course. We have for years been carrying out a short module for prospective teachers at the Faculty of Educational Sciences at the University of Bologna. It is difficult to know what effect this has on the teacher, save for the positive experience and the possibility to actively reflect on the conflicts and the teacher's role itself.

Lorenzo Milani and the Barbiana Legacy

Interview with Edoardo Martinelli

The School of Barbiana, in the Mugello region of Tuscany, represents one of the most radical educational initiatives of the twentieth century. It was founded by a radical priest, Don Lorenzo Milani, whose works continue to be read for their insights regarding social justice, pastoral renewal and a democratic education. The major text to emerge from this school, authored by Don Milani and his students, is Lettera a una Professoressa *(Letter to a Teacher). Edoardo Martinelli is one of the eight boys who co-authored this text. He provided us with a lengthy interview in Italian which one of us translated into English.*[1]

What was your relationship with Don Lorenzo Milani and the School of Barbiana?

I got to know Lorenzo in the summer of 1964.

I ought to thank Maresco Ballini, one of the Prior's first pupils at the Popular School of San Donato di Calenzano, who, having been a trade unionist at Rho, put my family in touch with the School of Barbiana. All my brothers and sisters, who were of working age, were involved in the trade union.

It so happened that, during their honeymoon trip, my sister Maura and my brother-in-law Luigi took me to the Mugello for a planned visit.

The Prior asked me a lot of things, during an exchange we had, and he particularly made me dwell at length on my family. My parents were farmers who, when necessary, could transform themselves into hawkers. This was customary with the inhabitants of the Lunigiana, an area situated in the extreme North of Tuscany. It was also the reason why we emigrated to the North. At first, my father constructed a hut beneath the walls surrounding Rho's sports ground, just like other immigrants, and later he was allocated perhaps the first house in the 'Fanfani' social housing scheme.

I recall that Don Lorenzo was moved by my description of the space available in our house and my disclosure of the number of family members. We were 9 brothers and sisters. Then there were dad, mum and sometimes our grandma. We slept and studied as best we could. As I spoke he placed his head on mine and literally wept over me. I was taken aback and, I would dare say, was afraid. I did not remain there that day. His behaviour and the questions he posed made me reflect. He was so different from the other priests who frightened us with such questions as: "Impure acts? Alone? With others?"

When I got home, I relayed those questions to my mum and dad. This was the first time that I consciously engaged with the history of my family.

My mother was ashamed of her communist origins; the party in upper Lunigiana was founded in the home of my grandmother Virginia. My uncle Edoardo, killed by a *repubblichino,* was a Commander of the Garibaldi Borrini Brigade, very active in the antifascist struggle that took place in the area. According to Don Peppino, my mother was very religious; being communist was tantamount to being a criminal. This attitude was diametrically opposed to that of the Prior, who, when he served as Parish Priest at San Donato, did away with the crucifix at the popular school to allow young communists to participate in the school's activities.

I had not understood this difference in attitude then, though I had sensed something.

Of course I recount the episode with the benefit of hindsight. Let's say it appeared as if something within me had suddenly opened up. I did not immediately want to go back; I brooded for almost an entire year, then the difficulties I faced—my having failed at school—sent me back to the Giovi mountain.

Yes, I form part of that historical group connected with the letters, the letter to the judges and the letter to a teacher—the School of Barbiana's richest period, that which is commonly associated with the "humble technique of the collective writing and the failed Giannis—I Gianni bocciati". Mine is the standpoint of one who has had the privilege to have been a pupil of Don Milani, not through birth but through choice, and to have accompanied him daily till the very end. At first, I had to face the Prior and Barbiana out of necessity. Only later did I become an integral part of a community that welcomed me and allowed me to grow. How can I explain this relationship?

The Prior seemed to live solely in terms of community but then he would suddenly take you aside and place you in contact with your inner self. He listened and then touched chords…that always produced sounds that did not need to be reflected in particular appearances.

For him, faith was a gift. It could not be transferred. This is why the school had to be secular. The task of the educator or priest—the two were in perfect harmony in him—was only that of removing the obstacles. In his view, conveying the word (dare la parola) meant the fostering of the predisposition in the student, rendering the student autonomous, active and participative in political and social life.

He derived his authority from serving as an instrument to search, discover and gain awareness. Nobody spoke at the wrong time.

He allowed himself to be surrounded by exceptional collaborators. First and foremost there was Adele but there were also Eda, Gina, Barbara, Professor Ammannati, Giorgio Pelagatti, Mario Rosi, Luana, Ferrero....

At Barbiana, one lived within a context characterised by an interaction of human sentiments and passions that sublimated and enabled one to transcend the mediocrity of the lives of many. Learning and the school not only conveyed a sense of autonomy but allowed one to perceive the real meaning of freedom—participation. I felt as though I no longer lacked anything.

The friendships among us were profound. There was strong bonding between me and the Blonde and Mauro and the other children. Whenever I think of Barbiana I still feel a gush of energy.

That world no longer exists. Many have left us, alas. The world of Barbiana is now part of our inner life and my imagination.

This type of teaching can still be strongly felt even though I often ask myself, "How could a modern day youth live in such a coherent manner? A young person, who wishes to remain faithful to such teaching, would be isolated and unemployed to boot..." Today we have lobbies and they have, in fact, negatively substituted the old parochial or lay communities with a logic of control, belonging to the right and also the left.

And yet there is a growing desire among young people to adopt Milani as a model. Many maintain that in his way of life and his ideas one discovers the cultural and ethical bases for survival.

I wonder whether he could be the catalyst for a new movement—a return to the land, to the old peasant culture, one that is sober and not permissive. These values are no longer transmitted by the consumer society. But I am here wandering off the point, because it is as though I am speaking about the relationship that we pupils at Barbiana continue to have with him...because the issues he raised continue to stir within us.

What radical and credible alternative did the School of Barbiana offer to the kind of education provided through compulsory schooling in Italy during the 50s and 60s?

The schooling of that period—I would dare say that the same could well apply to contemporary schooling—was based on the strict transmission of ministerial programmes. These programmes were carried out 'to the letter' with the teacher being allowed little autonomy. Everything was planned to the extent that we students (there were several of us around, with different backgrounds) could anticipate the events, the questions and the title of the subjects to be tackled. We hardly came across anything that was unexpected and there were no situations that led to the adoption of pedagogical strategies that automatically connected with our interests, motivations and environments. The agenda was the same year in, year out. I recall that I struggled to cope at school and I hated almost every subject.

I could not perceive, at the time, the connection between learning and life. When I arrived at Barbiana, everything was different. The point of reference for the group's learning was life itself and this entailed an active research process. The learning setting itself was dynamic.

When I arrived for the first time, the children were analyzing two skeletons whose parts were rearranged on a table. The Prior explained to us that it was possible to determine whether they were male or female from the size of the hips, while the size of the head could indicate the period to which they belonged. He told us to bring the tape measure and the gauge. Some pupils grouped together and moved silently towards the office. Shouts were rare. I immediately realized that there existed strict and shared rules. We educators know that autonomy and liberty are not bourgeois elements. The Prior only allowed interruptions that served to enhance learning. Truth was objective and we had to search for it together without any competition among ourselves. He later explained to us that truth is historic and perhaps unattainable. He often asked: "Do you agree with what I said yesterday, what I am saying today and what I shall say tomorrow?"

The immediate motive, the key point of departure for his pedagogical activity, was provided by the fact that the floor of the society, which stood adjacent to the church, had caved in. Bones were discovered as a result. The more profound and long term motive, as he explained in the letter to the judges, with reference to his pedagogical practice, was to avail himself of this particular event to capture the pupils' interest and thus gradually lead them, once they had become so motivated, to tackle the core areas of the disciplines. A few bones were sufficient to enable one to learn how to use vocabulary and texts dealing with anatomy and physiology. These subjects were non-existent in the middle schools of the period. This is how we learnt to read, write and count.

The Prior had a Platonic concept of time. One attains knowledge by moving slowly and carefully. The immediate point of departure for learning was the reality, life or, better still, the everyday issues confronting the world of the poor. This constituted the immediate motive of the moment. The longer term purpose was that of enabling the pupil to acquire a baggage of knowledge that was necessary for him or her to grow and become capable of participating in social and political life. One had to be well equipped to attain such a level.

Let me provide an example. A few days ago I read that a bomb shook an old Sumerian library causing damage to a few carved slabs. This would have prompted him, that day, to start an interesting lesson on the ancient fishing civilisations. He would have posed connections between the wars of the time and those of today. He would have referred to past and present hierarchical and pyramidal social structures. He would have provided us with and forced us to search for the necessary elements to be able to engage in the country's debates. He would have made us construct conceptual charts and maps to attach to the school walls. They had to be intelligently done. Their impact had to be that of a bomb which lands, because of the absurdity of the war, in the right place. Such metaphors helped to explain things. The Prior frequently used metaphors. And this is where the real secret of Barbiana lay.

Alas, Barbiana is nowadays a museum. This is how the caretaker explained the charts attached to the wall: "We had so little money that we had to create our own material"—a terrible blow to the legacy of the Prior and a terrible form of mystification. It would have signified the ultimate defeat for an educator like Don Milani, whose primary goal was to demystify history, to find himself placed on an altar and witness such a distortion of his thought. Even worse, none other than the Hon. Fausto Bertinotti[2] was among those touched by these words. Amazingly, the explanation was provided by one of Lorenzo's first pupils, Michele Gesualdi. Luckily, we can still draw on the texts written by Lorenzo himself. They cannot be modified.

One could spend hours discussing the refined methods and techniques which Lorenzo Milani adopted. And yet, he responded to anyone who inquired about his pedagogical techniques and methods with the following words: "Don't ask me about methods and techniques but rather ask me how an educator should be to be able to teach."

As he directed the educational process around the table he prepared every day, he drew our attention to the formal aspects of life, to the Idea, the Archetype, the Essence of things, the Divinity and Etymology since the words spoken at Barbiana were living words. The Word, which constituted the primary vehicle for learning, was given great importance, not to indoctrinate or to inculcate ideologies, since his was not a school for isolated avant-garde thinking, but to open channels that had hitherto been closed. The whole process was intended to give voice to a culture that had remained silent. The goal was not to enable us to become socially mobile, according to the class logic that prevailed throughout society. On the contrary, he dreamt of a liberated farmer content with living a sober life.

Like Pier Paolo Pasolini, he hated the neoliberal society that he regarded as consumerist and a slave to fashion. He detected, in this society, the love of power, a sense of exclusion and negation of God. This explains his extreme views concerning social class: "to treat unequal beings equally is the ultimate injustice." He made us regard our sharing of resources as a form of co-participation in a common life with a view to creating a genuine community. The poor people of Barbiana loved their Prior so much that they remained with him till the very end. They woke up two hours earlier to arrive for work in Florence by 8 a.m. They spent four hours commuting to enable their children to attend his school. It was enough to stay awake during winter nights and chat with the older members of the community to gain an idea of their admiration and respect for him. Their eyes shone bright and their face lit up when they expressed these feelings. Less than a year after Lorenzo's death, the population of Barbiana decreased considerably.

The Prior was perceptive enough to realize, during the 60s boom, that one's needs had to be contained. He used to tell us: "There will be no end to the needs that this society will continue to manufacture." He was terrified by the emerging materialism. He noted the lack of persons who were sensitive to the real 'pleasures' of life. One had to learn the etymology of the word 'divertimento' (enjoyment) in the same way that one had to learn the multiplication tables! He used to tell us that it signified turning a corner, doing different things and, most importantly, he would tell us that we had to enjoy ourselves (in this sense) all our life. He took efficiency for granted regarding it as a feature of life: "there will always be someone who will transform sea water into a commodity."

If we read the letter to Pipetta, we will notice his state of grace in this "wet and smelly small house." We will also notice his ultimate vocation about which he never speaks—an impregnable faith that directly derived its inspiration from the 'Sermon on the Mount.'

His was a total refusal of any form of consumerist-materialism.

He did not live his sober life as a form of penance, abstinence or simply Christian living but as a way of embracing the values and pleasures that can be satisfied and learnt only through poverty.

It has often been said that the School of Barbiana came to an end with Lorenzo Milani's death at 43. Where can the spirit of this school be found these days?

Well, the spirit of that school can be found wherever there is a community composed of people who do not express avant-garde statements but whose hands are hardened by the effort of building their future together. Barbiana is not to be identified with living in discomfort. Many are grossly mistaken in identifying it with this situation. Barbiana represents the coming into consciousness. In this respect, it represents that collective 'us' that one associates with Freire.

I repeat: Lorenzo Milani did not want to liberate the farmer from his work but, on the contrary, he wanted to help create a liberated farmer, one who is participative.

Barbiana is not an exclusionary place, as some intellectuals would have us believe. Barbiana is a place that is characterised by inclusion where poverty is a matter of choice and takes on the form of a sober life because resources are limited. A genuine education for peace is at the core of this simple and Franciscan concept. The spirit of the Prior, which makes one struggle for life, is present everywhere, in nature and among children. We only have to unearth it. It is inside us. It is a gift from God: "...there is a law which is written well enough in their (*people's*) hearts. A large part of the human race calls it a law of God; the others call it a law of Conscience." [3]

Real love in place of the love of power!

Can you provide us with a portrait of Don Milani, since you lived close to the Prior until his death?

Everyone found the Prior striking because of his great intelligence. You would immediately notice, when he engaged in reflection, that he was not convinced a priori about the object of contemplation. Despite his enormous cultural baggage, he was devoid of any vain petite bourgeois or intellectual aspiration. While he adopted a very aggressive attitude towards the rich, he was full of tenderness for those who suffered abuse of power.

His sarcasm and sense of irony were unique. I vividly recall an episode that occurred in the room where he was to die two weeks later. We were all justifying Israel's involvement in the 6-Day-War. And yet, with one eye open and the other closed, he uttered in a faint voice: "It's the others who are the poor ones." This was greeted with an immediate silence—a reflection that defied the logic of the arguments produced thus far.

He was not concerned with who was militarily justified but continued to foreground the problem of social inequalities, the real cause of every conflict!

The pupil-master relations occurred within an initially 'neutral' space. I would not like to be misunderstood. There was obviously nothing really neutral about Don Milani. He believed in a committed educator, one who takes sides: "Better a fascist than indifferent!" He however felt the need to 'shuffle the cards', so to speak. He often said: "Let's stretch the concept to its extremes to understand it better!"

I'd like to briefly relate an anecdote evoking the sounds and noises of his school to give you an idea of how pleasant and amusing it could be. He once gave us an interesting lesson on sexuality. After having dwelt on genetics and the chromosomes, he told us "Today, children, we will give birth to a man." He used, for this purpose, the technique of the small sheet of paper, quite common in those days. Each one of us was to write down an attribute to be accorded to the yet unborn person. Some wanted the person to be blonde, others dark. Others wanted the person to be tall, others short. There were those who wanted the person to be a man; others opted for a woman, etc. As a result, we had small mounds each with papers selected according to the logical connections. He chose a small sheet from each mound and drew the 'newly born' on a large sheet of paper.

A teacher who happened to be present was startled and asked: "Father, how many hours do you dedicate to sexual education?" This led to a moment of silence. Strangers were not allowed to interrupt a lesson. Usually anyone who behaved that way was thrown out rather brusquely. On that occasion, however, the Prior, with a lovely smile, explained the criteria by which the time allowed for every single subject was established: "First we measured a man, then we measured his penis and then we established the necessary proportions."

If I were to draw the Prior's portrait by means of a few brush strokes, I would say that he was a mystic betrayed by passion. The contemplative life was not permissible in an epoch characterized by social injustice, when the cries of anguish called for concrete commitments and action. Let's not forget where he came from: born during the fascist period, suffered moral subjugation and racist laws... "I was thirteen at the time; it seems as if it were today. I jumped with joy for the empire."[4]

I recall that when a very good friend, Clara Urquhart, came to Barbiana for the first time and recounted her experiences in Labaréne (Gabon) with Dr. Schweitzer, there was a heated exchange: "The Africans are not inferior beings," he shouted, "we only need to give them the instruments by which they can express themselves." These were times in which the west, through its strategies, annihilated, one by one and even physically, the various leaders of the anti-colonial liberation movements, thus thwarting the birth of real nations having strong identities.

Yes he had the gift of foresight. We pupils rediscover the value of his teachings precisely because of the truthfulness of whatever he taught us. Bin Laden is, in fact, the product of this colonial mindset and interference. It's a logic of rejection, domination and violence, very much the case with the rich west in its relations with the poor. Bush and Bin Laden constitute the two faces of the same coin. The text of 'Università e pecore' (University and Sheep), one of the letters written to a friend, the Magistrate Meucci, enables one to gain some insight into the internal drama lived by Lorenzo. This autobiographical text reveals the personality of our teacher. This piece of reading would liberate young people from an exclusively virtual conception of the world.

Which pastoral and life experiences, as well as authors, influenced Don Milani's pedagogical thinking?

He certainly referred to the ancient thinkers, for example, Socrates, but he never cited the sources. He would never have started a lesson by saying: "Today let's tackle Aristotle's physics and metaphysics." And yet they were at the heart of his teaching, conditioning its formal, material and effective structure. Everything was however couched in the language of the mountain people of the Mugello and in a manner that abetted their process of emancipation. It seemed as though there was some providential design... Individuality and respect for the single person constituted a feature of the collective 'Us' at Barbiana. All his characters had names: Mauro, Gianni, Pierino...they were not impersonal. I find it difficult to identify influences... Certainly Camus, Saint-Exupéry, Plato... if one goes by the readings tackled with the pupils.

The Constitution and the Gospels were pivotal to his pedagogical strategy. However the newspaper and everyday news served as the integrating background sources for his school. The Saitta and Smith [5] were of value when they were confronted with each other to produce a dialectical learning experience and not because of their individual interpretation of history. I specifically cite these texts because they were among the sources used when the self-defence strategy in court was drawn up. They were read in a synoptic manner.

The mediations served to sublimate the personal factors. He taught us to respect diversity. He made us understand the importance of the DC/PC[6] dialectic. At the same time, he warned: "It would be terrible if one or the other should obtain a landslide victory."

Jesus and Gandhi were the real models but were not cited all too often. We however read their original texts. 'The Letter of the Hiroshima Pilot,' 'The Scourge of the Swastika' and Gramsci's 'Letters from Prison' were also compulsory reading. He had a deep love for those he hailed as the 'lay saints.'

What motivated your parents to send you to another school (the one at Barbiana) after you were flunked by the compulsory public school and what motivated you to withstand the several hours of 'full time' schooling at Barbiana? Is it because "school will always be better than cow shit"?

Our parents were initially solely concerned that we finally obtains the diploma. It was only much later that they, and not all of them, understood the importance of schooling. The youngsters who were born there certainly preferred going to school to working in the fields. So for what reason did someone like me, who came from the city, remain there? I'll explain.

'Full time schooling' is today a false objective. Some functionaries, such as Raffaele Iosa, recommended it as a solution during the time of Minister Luigi Berlinguer's term of office. They come out with this idea simply because they do not have, any longer, a concrete relationship with the pupil or, better still, awareness of the new dynamics characterizing the 'gruppo/classe' (class/group). Politicians run the risk of being alienated from everyday life because they belong to a type of profession. There are those who rightly consider our society a "controlling society."

I do not deny the importance of full time schooling. However I would nowadays prefer to talk about 'attention-time' or else 'motivation-time.' I am not interested in how many hours are spent at school.

Lorenzo worked at a time when there was neither free time nor the possibility to study. The children of the poor used to start work at 15, after their third year of middle school. One must remember that Barbiana was very much an emergency school. Having established this premise, I ought to remark that one often comes across misconceptions regarding the Barbiana School and misinterpretations of such accounts as the *Lettera a una Professoressa* (Letter to a Teacher). It is true that our school was open 365 days a year; however the best students spent months either abroad or engaging in life experiences that complemented schooling. Nowadays, in Italy, if you hold a job and cannot attend an educational institution, you would have no access to university—just to give you an example. We have gradually created more class differentiation than was the case in the past. I take the opportunity to talk about the time spent at school, in its broadest sense, in all its sequence and not just its chronological sequence. I recognise that I will have to repeat myself here.

For Plato—there seems to be an affinity between his ideas and Lorenzo Milani's—knowing signified looking at the past and proceeding slowly and carefully. In keeping with this logic, the process of teaching/learning involved leads us to a concept of time that is quite different from that which conditions the way we teach today. In the 'Letter to the Judges,' Lorenzo states: "So we took down our history books (simple textbooks at middle school level, not the monographs of specialists) and searched across the span of one hundred years of Italian history in search of a 'just war'."[7]

Let's consider the fact that the entire teaching activity taking place at Barbiana at the time was conditioned by one event—the communication by the military chaplains which we learnt about from the regional news, not even from the background article in *La Nazione*. This communication was brought to Barbiana by Professor Ammannati and some pupils from San Donato who were scandalized by the statement "...an insult to the fatherland and to its Fallen, as something alien to the Christian commandment of love..."[8] The priests, who made this statement, were referring to the conscientious objectors. It is true that one noticed an already tense situation in the Florentine ecclesiastical world because of the trial of Fr. Ernesto Balducci[9] and the removal of the Seminary's director. The Prior and Don Bruno Borghi had, however, already made their position on this matter known in a letter to all the priests in the Florentine diocese, priests who were wary of taking sides. Don Milani cut a lonely figure in the church of his time! One need only be reminded of the call to unconditional obedience issued by the poor Bishop of Florence, Ermenegildo Florit.

In this particular case, however, the **pupils' indignation** was accorded priority by Don Milani and triggered a genuine educational process centering around the issue of conscientious objection.

Those of us involved in the teaching profession would regard this indignation as a source of **motivation**.

It is the motivation we had which led us to learn and not the other way round. This situation is captured by Lorenzo in the following statement: "One can call oneself a teacher when one has no cultural interest just for one's own sake."

Let's return to the issue of the 'time spent at school' or rather, to the level of attention, perception and emotional engagement involved. Let's focus on the time allowed for reflection, a time that passes by rather slowly. And this is where Barbiana differs from the traditional school where there is not much time for thinking, as if thinking is confined to the four walls of the classroom and does not extend to the period spent afterwards discussing among friends or with parents at home.

At secondary level, we waste time providing children, who are maturing into adulthood, with amplifications of subjects that had been tackled at primary level (on the pretext, suggesting some kind of dementia, that there are dichotomies between the humanities and the sciences). This occurs to the detriment of one's acquisition of essential logical patterns, strategies and instruments that are indispensable for one's learning and 'learning how to learn.' Few are those who find the time or consider it necessary to help develop the class/group and cultivate its dynamics. This is considered a waste of time and a distraction from one's engagement in the 'real activities.'

It is clear that the Barbiana approach necessitates a slowing down of activities resulting from the need for learners to acquire a methodology, instruments of learning and a scheme of work. We should not worry unduly, however, since the attention span in a process of 'banking education' is so short that it effectively reduces the actual learning time spent at school to 25%. I would like to underscore a paradoxical situation brought to my attention by Rosanna Rota, a teacher from Verona. She finds merit in slowing down the learning process: "I realized that, doing away with our fetish of time on task, our work in the classroom actually develops faster. This is because human relations matter when it comes to learning. It also diminishes the children's anxiety about their performance. Also, when children are allowed more time to go deep into a topic, they develop a greater interest. And the children feel that, this way, they are valued more...I do not know clearly why, but it works!"

A real school reform can be predicated on the idea, adopted at Barbiana, that time devoted to learning should be continuous and prolonged. And by relating our reflections to everyday life, we liberated schooling from the kind of abstractions and isolation (living for itself) that characterized the Italian public school.

Let's return to the old masters so dear to the Prior's heart. Let's rediscover the vitality of the word when seen in its original meaning.

Plato would remind us that while Aion is the time of being which cannot be split since it encompasses past, present and future, Chronos signifies the time allotted to what is to come, a period of time that can be calculated. Finally **Schole**, from where all that pertains to the school derives, is the time one spends without any pressure whatsoever, not subject to the anxiety caused by the necessities of everyday life. This connotes taking one's time and moving slowly.

How have the Giannis, from the Barbiana School, been actively engaged in the Italian political and social fields, confronting the power of the Pierini?

I'd say, tongue in cheek, that I quite miss the Pierino of old. Today, everything has degenerated to the level of 'Gianni': "oggi tutto è ingiannato." Gone are the days referred to by Brecht in his proclamation: "Knowledge is Power." Today all one needs is functional knowledge. How else could one explain the lowering of standards among today's politicians? Politics does not stress the need to educate. On the contrary it places emphasis on interpreting and this is made possible through surveys, as would be the case to win any contest. The ancients (Aristotle) used to consider acting on behalf of the poor as democratic and were mentally and emotionally far removed from the fascist concept of the 51%. Recall the armed tank in the *Lettera a una Professoressa*. We used to refer to it with a smile. It was a time when the culture of the downtrodden was very strong in the West and was reflected in adequately organized structures: the unions and not the corporatist ones of today, let's be clear. Well, the economy with its linguistic autonomy—goods, exchange, profit, demand, property—created independent roots that embrace the entire world, including the world of the rich and the world of the poor. Its power, analysts tell us, is an internalized one and its ideas govern the world. We have confined the God of History and divinity, with all his manifestations, to a little corner, replacing him with Mammon.

Resistance can be put up only through learning, starting from below, because we have now understood that both the Pierinos and the Giannis are in the same boat. Only intelligence can enable us to overcome the danger of bloodshed that results from the struggle for the possession of wealth rather than for the attainment of a just and equitable way of life governed by 'poverty.'

We have derided the Arabs for cleaning their bums with water but now that a billion Chinese persons want to use toilet paper just like us, we realize that all the trees of the earth would not suffice to satisfy this need. Not only is our poor and vendor culture non-exportable but it places life itself at risk. At issue is no longer the need to confront power but the need to engage in a new way of living, producing and consuming.

In your opinion, did *Esperienze Pastorali* have any significant impact on Catholics, especially after Vatican Council II, despite the negative reaction it provoked among the upper echelons of the clergy when it was first published?

Nowadays there is talk of integration between religions and cultures. I have in mind Fr Balducci's concept of the 'global person.' We move beyond the questions raised by Lorenzo at Calenzano when he struggled to rid faith of ideology and to create a secular state or when he conceived of alternative relations between priest and people and distinguished between faith and politics. Nowadays it's the very concept of 'people' that is called into question and it is not a question of whether people are objects or subjects. There are priests around, counsellors to Silvio Berlusconi, who believe no longer in a Universal Church but in a small cultural and geographical church. In this regard, Lorenzo Milani was and remains a man of faith and not religion, one steeped in the tradition. He never manipulated or was only a mediator of that which was sacred. He helped create the Community in antithesis to the system that prevailed, taking Christianity back to its origins.

It is often argued that Lorenzo resolved the problem of divergences through obedience at the expense of participating in and adhering[10] to the Vatican Council II reform projects.

Like other worthy Catholics, La Pira, Facibeni, Bensi, Mazzolari, etc., the Prior sought to undermine the integralist project of Ottaviani, Lombardi and Gedda.[11] Let's say that the climate later—after Lorenzo's time—allowed greater freedom of expression and the accusation,[12] in itself, was a liberating moment with regard to the internal conflict that occurred over the primacy of one's conscience. I would say that the pastoral ideas of the San Donato parish priest reverberated throughout the entire Vatican Council II and he himself was aware of this before he died. It gave him great pleasure.

What is so amazing today is the prophetic nature of his message, one that transcends contexts and times. Yes, his was a prophetic dissent and not one of political contestation. It is for this reason that, as a teacher, he strove for freedom of thought and not for those formal freedoms he defined as "petite bourgeois."

Developing one's ability to think was the kernel of his apostolate. He felt that this would provoke the 'turmoil' necessary for people to become Christian or sovereign citizens.

Given his critical interpretation of history, evident in the letters to the judges and military chaplains, what would Don Milani tell us about imperialist wars in this period characterized by the infamous wars in Iraq?

He would only alter his use of words, using those that provide the key to our reading of today's world, words such as limit, expand, survive, etc. As a matter of fact: If the great migrations lead us to cultural expansion, pollution and the impoverishment of the earth compel us to limit consumption and production in order to survive.

War has brought about incoherence and lawlessness. Few make the effort to understand the conspiracies, motives and webs of the oil magnates in the so-called democratic front (Bush) and the terrorist front (Bin Laden). This is where Lorenzo the educator would place the emphasis. He would go about this task in the manner he went about the task then, invoking the sad violent historical experiences of the previous century, demystifying situations and reducing them to their bare essentials. He would remind us of the answer provided to an interviewer by Stangl, the commander of the extermination camp in Treblinka, Poland, where around 20,000 people were gassed and burnt in 24 hrs. "We needed the Jews' money...do you have any idea of what sum we are talking about? That's how steel was bought in Sweden."

A rereading of this interview sends shivers down one's spine since one feels that one is listening to the same kind of talk overheard in bars during the time of the bombardments in Afghanistan and Iraq when everything was bombarded with "intelligence," including women and children—a situation marked by the insensibility of the opulent west. Everything was legal and continues to be so provided that it serves to reduce the cost of our holidays spent driving around. I must remind you that all this boils down to profit and not passion or ideals— let's be clear.

Are there attempts to revive the School of Barbiana and aspects of the popular School of San Donato di Calenzano, maybe via a school reform movement?

There have been various attempts of late, mainly at the institutional level. The March of Barbiana is one of the latest. The Minister of Education was present for the last march that took place last May; our participation as pupils (former pupils) in this event is increasingly becoming passive. Three ministers succeeded each other in taking part: during Romano Prodi's first tenure of office as Prime Minister, during his second term of office and during the period of right wing government when it was Letizia Moratti [13] who participated. They all expressed themselves by focusing their attention on the School of Barbiana and on its Master. And yet, during these years, what changes have been made to the practice of teaching? None.

There is no grassroots movement because the left has always clamped down on movements. The only movement which made its presence felt, using the famous 'questionnaire,' was the teachers' movement that however only availed itself of the young people's drive to block the cycles' reform, a positive aspect of the Berlinguer[14] reform. I would dare say that the Prior of Barbiana never responded by declaring black as opposed to white and vice versa. What I mean to say is that not all that Berlinguer proposed, during his time, was to be dismissed.

Schools need to be regenerated. There is too much corporatism but it is the more capable teachers who remain silent. In truth one understands why since they continue to inhabit their own small world of good practice.

There is also a small group that goes to Barbiana every year, shouts "viva don Milani" and then returns home. Some are moved, others exploit these manifestations for their own political gain and games of power, but then who is really concerned about teaching? Who really wants to apply the method of Barbiana in a concrete manner?

Once an enlightened school leader asked me to try out the technique of collective writing in a third year elementary classroom. The technique is meant to subvert the logic of the established didactical approach. It does not entail writing together and producing collages of writings by children, as unfortunately was the case with the competition at Vicchio managed by political functionaries who were incompetent in matters of schooling and superficial. It entails a process whereby, through active research, the pupil is led towards the core of the subject. When we worked on the communication by the military chaplains and the interpretation of history from the standpoint of the Mugello mountain dweller, we amassed lots of parallel passages, resulting from interviews with parents, synoptic readings of Saitta and Smith, research in the State archives, consultations with historians and judges. The process of transition from the opportunity that presents itself—the 'motive of the moment'[15]—to the razor edge[16] process by which the master leads the pupil is a very complex one.

Now back to my story. I entered the classroom and immediately noticed that the children were not used to talking among themselves and to listening for a long time. I soon experienced some difficulty. Fortunately, I spotted a medieval castle, when looking out of the window. I immediately seized the opportunity, having found my Barbianesque picklock.

The children were very excited by this lesson that entailed their looking out of the window. There were those who disclosed that they had snacks in the square in front of the castle; there were others who knew little fragments of truth. Slowly an active research project concerning the castle and the medieval period began to emerge. Just when the children started working seriously on the project, a teacher approached me and whispered into my ear: "The programme on the Middle Ages is scheduled for next year." I need not go into details to recount the amount of time spent convincing the janitors to buy red color to design a time-line on the classroom walls. We had already carried out our measurements and identified the point, 1000 A.D., where to place the castle.

At the state school, one learns without dirtying one's hands or rendering one's clothes sweaty. There are inexplicable bureaucratic obstacles that stand in the way of realizing the Prior's ideas. In this age of consumption, a reform which costs nothing is of little interest to anyone let alone the corporate school.

The reform that Lorenzo Milani would propose would transform our consciousness, our way of approaching life. In short, it would make us rethink the role of the educator who would be a director of learning and provider of the instruments for learning.[17] Placing the accent on quality as opposed to quantity, we would look critically at our competencies as educators, the amount of effort we put into teaching and the time in which learning is expected to take place. Nature would call for a slow-moving, snail-paced pedagogy. Would it be possible to reduce stadium expenditure to provide better funding for schools? 30 pupils per classroom is too much. So, what are we going to do about it?

Notes

1. We would like to thank Mario Cardona for making this interview possible.
2. Leader of Rifondazione Comunista.
3. Letter to the judges, translation taken from James Tunstead Burtchaell (1988), *A Just War No Longer Exists*, Notre Dame, Indiana, University of Notre Dame Press, p. 67.
4. Tunstead Burtchaell, op. cit. p. 65. Translation from *Letter to the Judges*.
5. References to important history textbooks by means of their authors' surnames.
6. DC= Democracia Cristiana (Christian Democracy).
   PC= Partito Comunista (Communist Party).
7. Turnstead Burtchaell, op. cit. p. 56.
8. Ibid., p. 17.
9. See footnote 27 on page 121 in Burtchaell, op. cit.
10. Michele Ranchetti.
11. Cf Letter to Pistelli.
12. The accusation levelled at 'objectors of conscience'.
13. Minister of Education in the Berlusconi government.
14. Luigi Berlinguer, Minister of Education in the Massimo D'Alema government.
15. From the *Letter to the Judges:* when some pupils brought him the article published in *La Nazione*. See translation in Burtchaell, op.cit. p. 54.
16. From the *Letter to the Judges:* "A school is different from a courtroom. For you judges what counts is that the law be maintained. A school, by contrast, sits astride the past and the future, and must endeavour to make both of them present. It is a delicate art to lead the children along that razor's edge. We must form in them, on the one hand, a sense of lawfulness (in this our work resembles yours), and arouse in them, on the other hand, a desire for better laws: a political sense if you will (and in this our work differs from yours) ...thus a teacher, must, as best he can, play the prophet, and divine the 'signs of the times,' and inspect the eyes of the children to see the wonderful things that they will discern clearly tomorrow, but which we see only in a blur today." Translation from Burtchaell, op. cit. pp. 57-58.
17. *Letter to a Teacher*.

Literacy, Micro-States and Postcolonialism

Interview with Didacus Jules

Didacus Jules is a key figure in education in the Caribbean. Very much involved in the Grenadian literacy campaign in the 80s, he held a number of posts in the region which places him in an ideal situation to discuss a variety of issues pertinent to this part of the world and elsewhere. Included among these issues are those concerning the legacy of the Grenadian revolution, education and the micro-state condition, literacy in the Third World, the socialist experiments in the Caribbean, structural adjustment policies and postcolonial educational politics. He discusses these issues and many more in the following interview with us.

What are the major issues concerning education throughout the Caribbean?

The Caribbean faces great challenges as well as tremendous possibilities in its effort to modernize and improve its education systems. In many respects, Caribbean education has developed features of excellence arising principally from the post-colonial struggle and its impact on education. Following emancipation, education was posited by the colonial authorities as a means of developing a docile labour force and a compliant citizenship. As the struggle for independence developed and with the attainment of universal adult suffrage, education was widely seen by the masses as a means of further guaranteeing their liberation and by the leaders as an indispensable force for the modernization of society. As a consequence, there was a strong, nationalist social consensus on the importance of education and the need to make it a national developmental priority.

In the post-colonial and independence periods, Caribbean governments have had to contend with the full weight of responsibility for national development and have had to manage their own affairs. Significant investment was made in education with the initial focus being to facilitate the emergence of the nation state. As many of the newly independent Caribbean states opted to follow the developmental options of the West, the education project was inflected to this agenda. Education focused on basic literacy and skills training for the masses, the provision of some elite pathways for the formation of the new social elites. Compared to many Third World states, Caribbean education was more "progressive" in the sense that—given the small scale and size of the societies concerned—it was able to achieve universal primary education long before many other post-independence states.

Today the challenges faced by Caribbean education are complex and result from deficits of the modernizing project of the ruling post-colonial elites as well as the changing nature of education itself in the information age. In those Caribbean states in which the nationalist project was infused with some socialist tendencies, the educational project went beyond primary education to embrace a wider vision of literacy for the masses (expressed in strong literacy and adult education programmes), including a strong and earlier emphasis on post primary education (universal secondary education and tertiary education). In Guyana for example, the democratically elected Government of Cheddi Jagan started the University of Guyana in the later 1950s when universal primary education was still an aspiration for many other Caribbean states and the University of the West Indies was being established to serve the entire Anglophone Caribbean. In Jamaica during the socialist incarnation of the Michael Manley government, unprecedented attention was paid to adult literacy (the JAMAL program), to the expansion of secondary education and to an increased higher education opportunity. In Grenada, the revolution made adult education, universal secondary education and higher education fundamental priorities long before other Caribbean states.[1]

In short, despite the work of respected development theorists such as Sir Arthur Lewis who called for massive investment in human resource development as an imperative for national development, it was governments with a left-orientation that effectively prioritized education.

So today the Caribbean still has to overcome the challenge of achieving what many of us still consider to be "basic" educational goals—such as the eradication of illiteracy among the masses, universal secondary education, and the expansion of tertiary education. Additionally the region has to cope with the consequences and deficits of what have evolved as generally elitist educational systems. At the primary level, repetition rates are low and completion rates are close to 100%. However the World Bank Task Force found that—at the secondary level—"*25-30% of the students do not acquire the basic cognitive skills to benefit from education at that level. Some of this under-achievement is due to poor attendance, particularly in remote communities; some to failure of the school system to diagnose learning difficulties, and some to inadequacies in the teaching and learning process.*" Increasingly it is also being recognized that we have failed to pay sufficient attention to the affective dimension of education: our values (both civic and personal), our morality, our attitudes need to be reshaped to reflect a cultural orientation which balances competition with co-operation, individual ambition with national commitment, and local pride with global citizenship.

As I said earlier, one of the distinctive aspects of the World Bank Caribbean Vision 2020 is that it was principally shaped by Caribbean educators on the insistence of the Caribbean Ministers of Education, and it is to the credit of the World Bank that it accepted this. I had the honour of chairing the Task Force and the first order of business for the Task Force was to review all of the previous reports and diagnoses of Caribbean education to ensure that these were taken into account. We sincerely sought to produce a document that would be empowering for the region by emphasizing Caribbean priorities and by creating a framework that would enable multilaterals to be supportive of this agenda.

As two persons coming from what is often classified as a micro island-state we would be interested to hear from you, as a person who also has worked in and written about education policy making in micro states, what are the main educational challenges facing such countries?

I have already outlined earlier what I consider to be the main challenges from a technical point of view. Essentially the educational challenges are related to limitations of size and scale—micro-states have a real challenge mobilizing resources, both human and financial, to address their needs, and neither their demographics nor their geography allow them the economies of scale to make some of these investments "viable."

This is a question however that is often asked and I generally respond by saying that the headache of an ant is as massive and as bothersome to him as the headache of an elephant. Many have posited the somewhat idealized notion that "small is beautiful" and while that may be true in some respects, the truth is that there are both advantages and disadvantages to small size. It must also be pointed out that what Dewey called the "tyranny of the majority" tends to prevail in the perception of small states. Small does not translate into insignificant, and neither does it mean that there is nothing that countries with large populations and land masses can learn from the so-called micro-states.

In small states, one of the most perplexing dilemmas of policy formulation is the impact of personal relations/connections on the impartiality of policy. In my view, policy is policy and its raison d'etre is to ensure that no matter who you are, your rights, privileges and entitlements are preserved just as the responsibilities and obligations that the state imposes on the individual. In a small society, you cannot have rules apply to some and not to all. Yet this is often difficult in practice because there are few individuals who have the guts and the resilience to say no to someone because that person might be related to them or be a political constituent. The politicians are besieged by persons seeking personal favours and rewards for allegiance; civil servants have their own inter-personal politics in using the system to help friends and family and so on. At the end of the day, the impact of this type of mediation through personality tends to distort even the most objective policies and cause disenchantment among the general population.

In short I would say that the main educational challenges, besides what I have already outlined, facing micro-states include the following:

- The challenge of resource mobilization—given the small population base of most micro-states, the resources available especially for social development tend to be very limited and the capacity of the state is also limited by the size and scale of the economy. It therefore requires special skills in fund-raising, creative programming and an ability to ensure value for money to manage the educational agenda.
- The challenge of creative programming—small states cannot adopt many of the solutions developed by larger countries and apply them "off-the-shelf." Resource limitations (financial and human) make it necessary for really creative solutions to be examined that enable the micro-state to maximize the use of these resources and achieve more with less. For example, there is a common tendency to lament the human resource deficiencies of ministries of education in small states and invariably administrators call for "more staff" to undertake vital functions. I have often argued that the challenge and the solution is not necessarily ***more staff*** but ***more capacity***. Let me give an example. In debating the instructional strategy to be implemented in St. Lucia, a burning issue was the repeated need for more Curriculum Officers in the key subject areas to provide more site-based supervision and pedagogical guidance. Historically, the selection process of the ministry was such that there was no guarantee that persons appointed to these positions were necessarily the most pedagogically competent and the most energetic in their promotion of improved instruction. Even small increases in the staffing at that level would have a big impact on the education budget (in which almost 80% was being spent on salaries and wages). In that context,

I felt, one had to look for a solution that provided the capacity for improved instruction where it mattered most—at the school level—without creating new layers of bureaucracy or further disadvantaging the budget ratios. One possible solution was the formation of subject associations among teachers—led by secondary school teachers—which would be fully recognized and supported by the ministry but allowed to function with some degree of professional autonomy. These subject associations would take the lead in identifying training needs in their particular discipline; organize their own in-service seminars and workshops for improving instruction; expose members (through collective membership, attendance at international seminars, etc.) to cutting edge instructional discourse and practice in the discipline; and serve as a peer support network for subject improvement.

What are the lasting legacies of the socialist experiments in education witnessed during the 70s in the Caribbean?

As I indicated earlier, the ceiling of educational achievement in the Caribbean has been pushed most significantly by governments of a socialist tendency or left orientation. This occurred largely because for these governments, the concept of education for all from cradle to grave and education as an inalienable human right has been a sacred precept. As a result they sought to operationalize this principle through extending opportunity for all in all spheres of education from literacy to university.

Educators (especially those nurtured in a colonial context) can be the most conservative thinkers, and in many ways the legacy of the left in education in the Caribbean has been to break the barriers and to subject to questioning those things that had never been subject to critical scrutiny before. The most enduring legacy of the left is that it proved that it is possible to think outside of the box and that we can find indigenous solutions to our problems if we dare to question and to construct on the basis of our own historical rationality.

There are other dimensions of the legacy. Deeply embedded in the colonial legacy and paradigm is a profoundly elitist construct of education. Many postcolonial governments in the Caribbean never questioned this paradigm and took an approach that was concerned largely with "modernization" of their education systems. By modernization, they meant the broadening of opportunity to allow for the emergence of an educated middle class. The structures and even to some extent the content of colonial education were not dismantled. Structurally therefore the system expanded on elitist foundations. The legacy of the left was the proposition that none should be excluded, that all are capable of achievement and that education was not simply to serve the needs of the economy but was fundamentally a force for liberation and civilization. In many ways today's concepts of access and equity can be traced to this impulse towards education as a right of all.

Another aspect of the legacy in education is in the sphere of relevance. As indicated earlier, most post-colonial governments simply expanded on the educational construct inherited from the colonial masters. The socialist project in the Caribbean—whether it was Guyana in the 1950s or Jamaica in the 1970s or Grenada in the 1980s—raised serious questions about the relevance of education and the content of education. As a result one attempts a serious re-thinking of the curriculum. This took various forms:

- Historical perspective—the content of education experienced a paradigm shift from accepted and inherited perspectives to a people-centered focus. For example in history, efforts were made to restore self-respect and to view history from the historical and existential experience of the colonized—history as "our-story" and not "his-story" (gender biases included).
- Gender—the elimination of gender biases that sought to perpetuate the subordination of women through the educational socialization of children. This ranged from the removal of gender stereotypes in textbooks to removal of gender differentials in the teaching of subjects such as tech-voc subjects and home economics.
- Strong focus on the affective dimension—the socialist experiments sought to consciously fashion nationalist sentiment, an anti-imperialist world view, civic and community commitment and social commitment.
- A more holistic definition of education—invariably, these experiments were premised on a more holistic philosophy of education that incorporated sports, physical education and many formerly extra-curricular activities assumed co-curricular prominence.

Finally another important legacy of the Socialist project in education is what we call today "stakeholder involvement"—a different label for what was then called "popular participation." Many important initiatives in education involved substantial public consultation and discussion thus allowing the masses and parents in particular to make important inputs into policy and programme. Despite all of the anti-revolution rhetoric, these lessons have persisted, and it is the lessons of popular participation in education in Grenada, for example, that inspired the approach taken in St. Lucia in the design of the process for the formulation of the Education Sector Development Plan. The World Bank identified this process as a best practice on account of the extensive public participation in the process of shaping the plan.

Interview with Didacus Jules

You were very much involved in the literacy campaign in Grenada carried out by the Bishop government. What were the achievements of the literacy campaign and the contradictions which often characterize such campaigns carried out in revolutionary contexts?

The literacy campaign conducted by the Center for Popular Education (CPE) was an extraordinary education and political episode that is still fondly remembered by Grenadians most of whom participated in some way or other. The literacy campaign had the indisputable distinction of being the most popular programme of the Revolution—Grenadians of all class formations, of all religious persuasions, of all educational levels were motivated by this experience. In many respects the socio-political dimension of the literacy campaign was a bigger achievement than the purely educational impact (significant as that was). The Campaign provided an opportunity for Grenadians from all walks of life to work hard towards a common national developmental goal that was seen by all as highly desirable, a civic responsibility, an educational imperative, a Christian obligation. People felt that participation in such an activity was a response to a higher impulse—to do good to their neighbors, and make a tangible contribution to their communities and country. In short it captured the popular imagination because a country without illiteracy is a country cultivating the growth of intelligence.

From an education perspective, the literacy campaign posed a big challenge to the inherited pedagogies and raised many questions about the relevance and direction of education in general. In the first instance, so much was done in the training program to prepare the volunteer teachers to inculcate *respect* for the adult learner that this ideological difference between the posture of the CPE teacher and the traditional classroom teacher created new tensions for educational policy. Many professional teachers who were also literacy volunteers started calling for reform of classroom pedagogies as their experience in the campaign matured.

At another level, the textbooks and the content of the literacy campaign were all locally generated. And even more work was done in the preparation of a series of post-literacy consolidated textbooks (English, Maths, Integrated Science, Geography and History of Grenada) that were focused locally with a global outlook. CPE teachers started using these adult education texts in the classroom because they found them far more relevant than the traditional texts. What was even more interesting was the degree of integration across the subject areas and the linking of academic learning with community action. In the texts, for example, the theme of water is explored in reading and comprehension passages on the importance of water to human chemistry; it is continued in the science section discussing the composition of water and how it relates to life; in the geography section, it is explored as sources of water (rivers of Grenada and rainfall) and the production of water for human consumption. Throughout these lessons, learners are given practical exercises to do such as identify water problems in their community, invite the Water Corporation officials to discuss them with the class (inviting community presence) and find collective solutions to these problems.[2]

At a deeply ideological level, we tried to bring together two tendencies that were not necessarily mutually cohesive in the design of the literacy campaign. On the one hand there was the Freirean impulse that sought to take a dialogic approach, using literacy for social and self-critique and on the other hand, the use of a more prescriptive and dogmatic approach.

Paulo Freire was invited to Grenada to assist with the design of the campaign, and he facilitated several seminars with the main team planning the campaign as well as with volunteer facilitators. A purely Freirean approach requires highly trained facilitators with a high level of political consciousness—this condition is difficult to meet in a mass literacy campaign as one has generally to find a role for all who volunteer while at the same time ensuring that every learner is able to make acceptable progress.

What contribution have the ideas of the New Jewel Movement, and particularly its leader Maurice Bishop, made to post-colonial educational thinking in general?

In the period following the collapse of the Revolution, the United States made a concerted effort to obliterate any memory of the Revolution and to associate any reference to it with Reagan's notion of the "evil empire". Any wall paintings done during the revolution were painted over with pro-American slogans; the CPE texts were destroyed; selective releases of NJM documents were issued to reinforce American analyses of the Revolution, and an entire psy-ops operation was conducted to achieve this end.

In this context, many of the ideas of the New Jewel Movement and of Maurice Bishop have been buried or suppressed so it is difficult to speak of a contribution as many persons are not even aware of what these ideas were. Even in Grenada today, many persons of subsequent generations only have a perspective on the Revolution and on Bishop that has been fashioned by the US intervention. In many ways the contributions of these ideas have been effected through the work of persons who were integral to the Revolution and who continue to subscribe to its ideas about the Caribbean civilization, about justice and equity in the world and the vision of education as a civilizing force.

I sincerely believe that the Grenada experience represented the first major and comprehensive attempt to re-think and re-shape an education system in the Caribbean in the direction of Caribbean empowerment. The educational ideology of the Grenada Revolution has been explicated in my PhD thesis, and essentially it was undergirded by a profound sense of optimism in the capacity of the Caribbean and of small states to create a new civilization through the instrumentality of education reform. Philosophically all of the education reforms were predicated on the assumption that every child can learn and that by creating what has only recently come to be described as "a learning society," a small country could become a superpower in its own right.

Many of the reforms that subsequently came to be accepted and attempted in the rest of the region can trace their origin or antecedents to the Grenada reforms. In some cases, such as universal early childhood education, universal secondary education and in-service teacher training, the impact of the Grenada ideas were direct; in others the connection can be traced through the logic of the solution which, even after the passage of time, remained the best response to the issue.

Teachers are often accused of being, by and large, a conservative force, not prepared to live, in Henry Giroux's terms, dangerously. What role did teachers take during the Grenada revolution?

Giroux's comments must be historically contextualized—teachers in general play different roles in different historical contexts. In contemporary modern society, teachers tend to be conservative because their professional formation and practice has been largely conservative. De-skilling of teachers has made them more dependent on "cut and dried" solutions and they tend to stick to the known.

In post-colonial contexts particularly those of a revolutionary orientation, teachers constitute the cutting edge of the local intelligentsia and often by virtue of their greater education and international exposure (overseas training, experience of racism and exposure to alternative paradigms arising from working class struggles abroad) play a leading role in the movements for independence or change.

In the Grenada revolution, teachers played a leading role in the struggle leading to the triumph of the Revolution and in the process itself. Many of the leading NJM members were former teachers; several had gone abroad for training in other careers and had been exposed to many currents of third world thought.

The literacy campaign was an incubator for much community level leadership for teachers during the Revolution. There were many teachers who had not been politically active and who, by virtue of the exposure they received to working class Grenadians during the literacy campaign, came to understand their role as teachers in a more political or national developmentalist context and became active at community level in programmes and organizations for community upliftment. It is interesting that during the US invasion, such activists were consciously targeted by US forces who, in their forays in the villages, kept asking people to identify "the communist teachers."

While the majority of teachers played an active role of sorts in the Revolution, it should also be acknowledged that there was also a strong, even if minority, tendency within the teaching body that championed conservative and anti-revolution positions. While many of these lacked the political courage to stand openly against the revolution, they constituted the ideologues of the counter-revolution.

You have been the coordinator of the ICAE's task force for literacy. What would you regard as the achievements of this task force?

I helped establish the ICAE Task Force on Literacy and my engagement there was an eye opener in many ways. First I always assumed that since the NGO movement in the developed countries was generally progressive, some degree of fairness and fraternal relations would prevail. When the ICAE decided to establish the International Literacy Support Service, they felt that it should be located in a third world country, and we all assumed that the Caribbean would have been the logical place to host the initial programme since the region had the most developed literacy network.

The Caribbean Literacy Network comprised persons like Mike Brown (current Minister for Education in St. Vincent & the Grenadines), Pat Ellis, Pat Charles and many stalwarts of the literacy movement in the region. A unique feature of the Caribbean Network was the fact that it brought both old school and new school literacy practitioners together under one umbrella and the relations within the network were fraternal and very open to debate. As a result, the region had a strong record of innovation and advocacy.

The Caribbean's bid for hosting the ICAE international network was opposed by India who sought to use arguments of size as a basis for selection. In the end the Caribbean prevailed and the International Literacy Support Service (ILSS) was established in St. Lucia. The office was a small one but it was fully wired and we were able to communicate easily with all regions of the world. In the initial stages, the main priority was on the establishment or consolidation of literacy networks in all of the regions of the world and this was followed by networking activities between regions. One of the innovations that we spearheaded was the convening of Learners Conventions which brought together learners from within every region to discuss issues of literacy and empowerment. Such conventions were held in the Caribbean, Latin America and South Africa. The rationale behind these was that while practitioners and experts got to meet internationally and discuss literacy issues, the real constituents—adult learners themselves—were left out of the discourse. We felt that we needed to create fora in which learners could create their own discourse on the issues of relevance to them.

Generally the work of the Task Force helped to bring greater prominence to the work of Third World educators as a number of us played a prominent part in several international seminars and symposia including many held in developed countries (such as Canada) that had discovered that they had a problem of illiteracy also. This was definitely an area in which the developing countries had more answers than the developed world.

You have been serving as Permanent Secretary in the Ministry of Education in St. Lucia for quite some time. What efforts have been made to facilitate access to educational provision in the country?

When the Labour Administration took office in 1997, I was asked to become Permanent Secretary for Education & Human Resource Development and I agreed to serve for one term (5 years). It is now seven years and I am just winding up my term of office in this position.

I had the good fortune of having a Minister in the person of Mario Michel— a young lawyer with a strong history of progressive youth activism—to work with. He is a man of great principle and is very methodical in his approach to work. We became a formidable team and were able to focus on policy issues that needed clarification. As a result more has been accomplished in the last seven years than in any other comparative period in the history of education in St. Lucia. I make this assertion not as a boast but as a statement of fact, and I'm not seeking to ascribe that progress to the Minister and myself. I believe that the Minister's particular strength on policy, his tenacity and his courage in making difficult decisions have been major factors in the progress that has been recorded, but equally we inherited a well-defined sub-regional education reform agenda that has helped to give strategic coherence to the challenges faced in St. Lucia.

The countries of the Organization of Eastern Caribbean States (which includes all of the small Eastern Caribbean countries[3]) recognized the need in the mid-1980s to define a comprehensive education reform programme so that they could work harmoniously in re-shaping and modernizing their education systems. The OECS education reform strategy—published in a document entitled *Foundations for the Future*—was a remarkable accomplishment in itself as it provided a cohesive framework for undertaking this reform but left sufficient leeway for individual member states to take account of their own idiosyncrasies.

Although St. Lucia was a signatory to this education reform strategy, her record of implementation was very poor and with the new administration in 1997 came an opportunity to revisit that commitment. We set about developing an Education Sector Development Plan (which as I said earlier had been recognized by the World Bank as an international best practice). Teams of local experts and teachers were asked to review the historical record of the past 20 years and to undertake sub-sector diagnoses, making recommendations that would guide the future. When this task was completed, we held an internal seminar at the ministry with all senior education officials and critiqued this work. British experts were then sourced with the assistance of DFID to provide an international dimension to this effort. The British experts worked with the local teams to refine the draft plan and once this was done, we initiated a series of consultations island-wide with parents and with teachers. Twenty-seven zonal meetings were held and thousands of persons participated in these discussions. Many of the meetings with parents and communities were conducted in Kweyol (the local language) to ensure that every voice counted, and at the end of that process we published a document containing all of the recommendations and suggestions that had been made at these zonal consultations. It was important for people to see that we took their feedback seriously and thus were able to compare the final version of the Plan with the recommendations made at a popular level.

An important dimension of that sector development plan was the incorporation of the reform agenda of the OECS. We created a grid that showed all of the commitments that St. Lucia was obligated to as a result of international treaties on education and the rights of the child, commitments to various reform initiatives arising from the Summit of the Americas, from the ruling party's manifesto, from the OECS education reform and so on and incorporated these into the Sector Plan. By so doing we ensured that once we worked diligently to implement the plan we would simultaneously be implementing these commitments.

All of the major accomplishments of the past seven years have come from this fundamental effort. We have improved performance levels at the primary school through a series of measures that include the introduction of a diagnostic minimum standards examination which lays the basis for remediation. We have opened new special education centers, have started systematic training of special education teachers, have created district support mechanisms for special education opportunity island-wide. We have put new systems for school repair and maintenance that are more empowering of principals, have undertaken systematic refurbishment of the most dilapidated of the school plants, and have defined new infrastructural standards for primary and secondary schools. Education administration has been revamped with the provision of management training for all principals and vice principals in the system using an in-service mode, and we have made the Ministry itself a major focus of organizational transformation, on the premise that we should not assume that the problems of education emanate from the schools—often they emanate from the bureaucracy, and it is very important to empower schools by changing the role and functioning of the Ministry. We expressed this organizational change thrust in a very simple vision and mission statement. Our two strategic goals we said were "to change the Ministry from a command center to a service center; and to make the school and the classroom the center of focus of the education system."

A logical outcome of this was the need to ensure that we removed as much red tape from all systems and procedures of the ministry and that everything was re-directed to the end of **serving the schools**. This was a very radical posture because even within the parameters of the OECS Education Reform Strategy, there was not too much emphasis on reforming the ministry itself. We stressed staff training and development in areas such as customer service, computer literacy and competence-based training in areas related to people's day to day responsibilities. A striking feature of this training was that it involved staff at all levels—the computer training for example involved everyone from messenger to minister (at no cost to staff) to the level of Microsoft Certified User.

I have painted this picture to contextualize the work done and show the coherence of policy that underpinned these efforts. The main thrust in terms of access involved two important areas of educational deficit in St. Lucia. The first was adult education—and to accomplish this we completely re-designed the adult literacy program to offer what we called the National Enrichment & Learning Programme (NELP). NELP offered a range of training from basic academic upgrading (from literacy to early secondary) in literacy and numeracy; skills training and professional development; and personal enrichment (which involved courses taken for leisure or learning for fun). The diversity of courses offered has made a big difference to the old stereotypes about adult education and even qualified professionals are now registering for programmes that they have an interest in. Through NELP we are increasing access to adults and providing new opportunities for continuing education.

The second major thrust is the move towards universal secondary education. In 1997 we were at about 50% access to secondary education; in the past seven years we have moved to about 70% and within the next two years (with the construction of two new secondary schools and the conversion of senior primary schools) we will attain universal secondary access. What is also notable about this effort is that it involves the improvement and reform of secondary education itself. We are setting new standards for performance, re-designing the secondary curriculum, providing more diversity of offering so that students of different aptitudes can map their careers, integrating extra-curricula activities and student clubs as integral to the new thrust, incorporating technical and vocational subjects and utilizing information and computer technologies into the teaching-learning process.

I can assert that these efforts constitute the most comprehensive and strategic efforts ever made to improve the St. Lucian education system and the testimony of this is that we have emerged as the leading country with respect to education reform in the region.

Confronting the legacies of colonialism in countries such as St. Lucia and ours (Malta) is not easy. What progress has been registered in your country in this regard?

One of the unique things about St. Lucia as a small island state is the historical fact that successive governments have invested heavily in education. From the time of adult suffrage, education has been highly valued by the St. Lucian masses, and education has played a major role in the formation of a middle class in the country to the extent that education is widely accepted to be an important means of overcoming poverty.

Notwithstanding this, the legacy of colonialism was expressed in several ways. Because of the linguistic situation of the country—a French creole is the native language of the rural masses; yet English is the official language and the language of privilege—persons from a predominantly rural background were often disadvantaged in the period up to the 1960s. After that access to education improved, but the absence of a progressive language policy ensured that this colonial legacy still prevailed.

Regrettably, there is still much to be done on the language policy front, but a great deal of research and experimentation has been done in the last ten years on the teaching of English as a second language and the reading and writing of Kweyol. A Kweyol New Testament has been published by the Summer Institute of Linguistics, and the Ministry of Education has worked with a range of activists to produce a Kweyol dictionary (with SIL), and Kweyol literacy textbooks (with An The Nou and Michael Walker).

Another aspect of the colonial legacy is the pervasive elitism that has characterized the St. Lucian education system. Many persons equated elitism with high standards but this is a false equation. Elitism is about limiting opportunity so that only a selected few can gain access or reach the levels of accomplishment held up as the pinnacle. The Common Entrance Examination is a good example of this—an examination that passed or failed students not as much on academic criteria but on the availability of places at secondary level. In many respects the Common Entrance was simply a sorting device that allowed only the required numbers to get through. As we move closer to universal secondary education we will be reforming this exam so that it is replaced by a system of continuous assessment that will take account of academic performance, extracurricular participation, project work, etc.

The remediation efforts taking place in the system have benefited from the Minimum Standards Test (MST) that is administered at strategic points at primary and secondary levels. The MST enables teachers and parents to identify a child's specific weaknesses in relation to what is considered to be the minimum standard required to function at the particular grade level.

The major blow against the colonial legacy has been the effort to increase access generally. Of greatest significance are the efforts that I have already mentioned with respect to adult and continuing education and the thrust towards universal secondary education. Additionally, tremendous advances have been made in higher education—we have been very aggressive in sourcing tertiary education opportunities for St. Lucian students worldwide but the single largest contribution to this effort has been the Bilateral Scholarship Program with the Republic of Cuba. A recent analysis prepared for the Cabinet of Ministers on this scholarship programme revealed that it has been instrumental in forming professionals in critical areas such as medicine, engineering, and agriculture. By 2005-6 (when the new General Hospital will have been constructed by the Government of St. Lucia), we anticipate that over 50 St. Lucians will have returned from Cuba as qualified medical doctors.

The final area in which the colonial legacy resides is in the area of relevance of education. Unfortunately this is an area in which not enough progress has been made. Much of the struggle in this area involves the affective dimension of education. It is about the formation of social mentalities and identities. After 25 years of national independence we still do not have a definitive published history of St. Lucia. The existing history was written by a Catholic priest who came out of the colonial tradition. We have only just discussed with the University of the West Indies the urgency for such a work.

What have been the effects of structural adjustment programmes on the educational systems of St. Lucia and the Caribbean more generally?

Fortunately structural adjustment has been limited to a few countries of the Caribbean, and so its devastating impact on education has been contained to those unfortunate few. Jamaica, Guyana and now Dominica have been the most notable cases. In every structural adjustment project, the social services including education have been subject to drastic cutbacks in expenditure—of both a recurrent and a capital kind. As the early experiences, Jamaica and Guyana were particularly brutal. Since then, the financial multilaterals have become a little more sensitive to the impact of structural adjustment on poverty and have been less insistent on some of the more draconian measures.

The classical scenario for education under structural adjustment has been closure of schools with small populations, reduction in the numbers of teachers (in order to reduce the monthly salary bill of government), cutbacks in resources available for the daily running of the schools, neglect of areas such as special education, technical and vocational education and a re-focussing of the school on "essential/basic" areas.

I have often argued, however, that the country in the Caribbean that has had the most brutal experience of structural adjustment is Cuba—and in their case, it is called the Blockade. In spite of this Cuba has persevered and succeeded in achieving great social gains in education, health and other areas. It would be highly instructive for Caribbean economists and educators to study this experience to discover how so much could be done using so little under such overwhelming circumstances. If we can appropriate this secret, our national development will be assured.

Notes

1. It is only in recent times that the countries of the Organization of Eastern Caribbean States (OECS) have articulated a common education reform agenda and even more recently (2002) that universal secondary education has become a policy priority.
2. This process of textbook preparation is discussed at length in a paper by Jules, Didacus in Apple, Michael *The Politics of the Textbook*, New York and London, Routledge.
3. The members of the OECS include: Anguilla, Antigua & Barbuda, British Virgin Islands, Cayman Islands, Dominica, Grenada, St. Kitts-Nevis, St. Lucia, St. Vincent & the Grenadines.

A World That Can Be—Democracy, Education and Participatory Budgets

Interview with Sergio Baierle

Sergio Baierle is one of the founders of CIDADE, an NGO that carries out research and capacity building with respect to the Participatory Budget (PB) in Porto Alegre, Rio Grande do Sul, Brazil. The Participatory Budget, as will be explained throughout this interview, is heralded as an example of 'deliberative democracy' which entails a process of citizenship education and participation. In this interview, Sergio Baierle discusses this project as well as such other relevant topics as the World Social Forum with its message that another world is possible, the role of the PT in Brazilian society at the municipal, state and federal levels, Lula's performance as President of Brazil, and the impact of neoliberalism on Brazilian politics. The interview was carried out half way through President Lula's first term of office.

Porto Alegre has, in recent years, been the focus of attention of progressive people, all over the world, searching for resources of hope in an age characterized by widespread cynicism concerning possible alternatives to neoliberalism. How justified is this focus on Porto Alegre and the Workers' Party (PT) initiatives there?

There are many reasons why Porto Alegre has become a world reference for the left. One of them seems fundamental to me: the radical way in which the participatory proposition was undertaken in the context of a global scenario characterized by precarious employment and the dismantling of the welfare state. In Porto Alegre, social questions, as felt and as defended by citizens through direct participation and new forms of representation, became the central policy of local government, strongly shocking those who traditionally took over municipal policies (private public transportation companies, contractors, real estate incorporators, retailers and proprietors of mass communications).

Professor Boaventura de Souza Santos rightly classified this moment of global affirmation for neoliberalism at the end of the 80s and the beginning of the 90s as a process of growing social fascism, a form of domination and social exclusion without the need for a totalitarian State. The 90s were characterized by the coexistence of liberal democracy and the dismantling of social solidarity.

From the moment when this counter-tendency represented by the Porto Alegre experience revealed itself capable of winning succeeding re-elections, it became generally perceived that a leftist project was politically feasible, despite never being able to avail itself of the support of the local major media, and notwithstanding the enraged reactions from those sectors that traditionally dominate the local economy.

Winning the State governorship in 1998 and the Federal Government with Lula's election in 2002 seemed to indicate the establishment of a new hegemony in the country. However, Lula's government has only represented the appearance of this possibility, immersing the social movements in the worst crisis since they emerged on the political scene in the early 80s during the military dictatorship.

Besides this, the conservative sectors also recycled themselves and started to incorporate the discourse on the value of citizenship in defending social inclusion. Practically no party nowadays avoids centering its electoral discourse on the solution of social questions. It is a long time since electoral campaigns represented heavy criticism of civil servants, for instance, or proposed the privatization of public companies. During the recent defeat of the Labour Party in Porto Alegre, this year, in 2004, the opposition candidate centered his discourse on what was good (Participative Budget and the World Social Forum) and on changes, for example, to the health services. This new social conciliation strategy had already been victorious in the elections for the State of Rio Grande do Sul in 2002. The idea was sold that those propositions that had been socially built up by the Porto Alegre Labor Party were held to be good as long as they were stripped of their radicalism, their call to social division. In short, the popular classes are entitled to a better life as long as they do not transform this right into a class war. The discourse in favour of conciliation and social concert was taken to heart by the local middle classes and the petite bourgeoisie, who saw some municipal policies (cycles of education systems, tenders linked to social offsets, investment in popular housing) as a risk to their strategies for reproduction and social ascendancy.

At the same time the local government itself was running into political and economic limits to advance in the democratic radicalization project. As of the fourth mandate of the popular administration (2001-2004) there was no additional way of increasing local incomes, for several reasons, amongst which the renewed concentration of public resources in the federal government and the tax losses in the exporting states. Conversely, the local government had incorporated more and more subjects as possibilities for demands within the participative budget, generating a populist temptation to include more projects within the budget without the effective capacity to carry them out.

On the other hand, to advance with democratic radicalization would mean breaking with the operational bureaucratic structure under which local power functioned (the black box of budget execution, public tender system, increased space for organized communities in the management of social policies). Wear and tear appeared in the relationship with civil servants (interruption of salary increases for inflation every 2 months, pressure on service quality), in the relationship with suppliers (constant demurrage of payments, demand of social offsets), in the relationship with society as a whole (focusing on the poorest of the poor, no concrete solutions for the problems of attending at the hospitals that had agreements with the Unified Health System [SUS], difficulty in reacting to pressure for municipal involvement in public safety), as well as in the growing difficulties in capitalizing on what had been achieved (the option for large investments with international resources such as the Third Perimeter Avenue, crossing the city from North to South, sucked up resources that were already scarce and even so were not enough to counter the growing disenchantment by the middle sectors).

In the last few years the city has seen a rebirth of middle-class movements, such as movements in support of access to the sun in districts where the verticalization of buildings has been seen to grow through the sales of building indexes (built soil), or the movement of residents of the Menino Deus district against building a Sambódromo (a Samba Plaza for Carnival), against the realization of political rallies in what had already become a traditional rally site for the Labour Party.

In short, one could answer that, yes, there were good reasons for the international left to concentrate its attention on Porto Alegre, but we must warn that recently the enthusiasm had overcome the capacity for critical discernment.

What promise does the World Social Forum hold for the conception and creation of a world not as it is but as it should and can be?

Though it is strongly supported by some progressive governments, and largely maintained by some international foundations, the World Social Forum is characterized by the conglomeration of civil society organizations and social movement activists. Even considering that the Labor Party had a fundamental role in developing the Forum, it is not a meeting of political parties within the framework of the old internationals, nor is it a meeting of governments as the Bandung Conference of the 50s.

The promise of the World Social Forum is precisely in its capacity to: merge social forces that have been excluded from the neoliberal governance; and offer these forces political visibility and permit the exchange of experiences and the learning of new possibilities of reacting to the dogma of the absence of new alternatives which the international financial system imposes. However, even though it is innovating, the new political-organizational format of the civil society is itself one of the questions to be solved in the reconstruction of projects for social transformation.

The great political quality articulators of the World Social Forum are the NGOs and their networks. Even if they establish themselves as legitimate role players around public interest themes, they are not elected actors. They are part of the civil society but cannot have the pretence of altering civil society. But this is exactly what has been taking place in certain circumstances.

If, on the one hand, one can say the World Social Forum was successful in that it opened some doors to dialogue, for instance, with the institutions that articulate neoliberal consensus such as the World Bank, on the other hand the idea of inviting NGOs to join in these new spaces for dialogue, as though they were representing civil society, is problematic. NGOs have no way of assuring commitments involving societies they supposedly represent. Frequently, they depend on international donors for survival and have a low resistance to being seduced by these donors' thematic agendas.

Consciously or unconsciously they frequently end up reinforcing fiscal straitjackets, in tune with neoliberal monetarism, within their own countries. For instance, in Brazil a large number of the NGOs supported the Fiscal Responsibility Law, the main objective of which was the integration of municipal and state government levels to the national effort of generating primary surplus (i.e., increasing the volume of public resources committed to the service of the public debt to enable an increased margin of remuneration of this service, to the contrary of what neoclassic economists argue).

How really transformative, in terms of a social justice agenda, are the educational reforms that have been introduced by the PT administration in Porto Alegre since 1989?

One of the main boons of the participative experience in Porto Alegre is that an entire participation system was built up starting off from the Participative Budget, involving practically every public policy area, from urban planning to economic development. It was not different in the area of education. In the first popular front administration (1989-1992) the work within this area was too restricted to pedagogical discussion (the then Secretary for Education defended the constructivist proposition and tried to create reference points at some schools in order to progressively enthuse teachers and pupils of the school network). In fact, the concept of democratization did not affect the administration. It was limited to assuring places in the public school system.

After 1993, with the consolidation of the Participative Budget of the city, education began to change structurally. Based on the democratization of access, management and knowledge, elections for school directors were established, with proportional votes (50% parents and pupils, 50% teachers and employees). School councils were created, composed of all the segments of the school community (students, parents, employees and teachers). School councils were vested with the power to decide and inspect the school management (which was set up after the decision to decentralize the school maintenance cash resources and after the creation of the Participative Budget for schools—for projects set up by the school communities for the schools).

Teaching quality was ensured through various instruments, allowing schools to migrate to the new system and prepare the cadres of teachers. Learning laboratories were created for students who lagged behind others within the same age group, and resource integration schoolrooms were set up for those with special needs.

Besides this, the programme for the Education of Young People and Adults—EJA—was created to allow young people and adults to return to formal schooling. With the creation and enlargement of Groups, through the Participative Budget, it was possible to extend the programme to every part of the town. In order to fight illiteracy, which in 1980 was at the 6.7% level, the Movimento de Alfabetização—MOVA—was created with the cooperation of popular educators. It was operated through agreements for funding between civil entities and the Municipal Secretariat for Education.

To ensure the democratization of knowledge, schools developed new pedagogic and curricular experiences. Constructivism, based on generative themes, starting from the students' realities and their fundamental questions, was foregrounded. Theoretically, a break with the concept of knowledge as a sealed unit, unconnected with the peoples' realities, was achieved.

Of course, this entire process had its limitations. First, in order that there may be a correct dimension of the impacts of municipal policies for education we must first stress that the municipal basic learning schools represent a mere 12% of the basic schooling in Porto Alegre, though the municipal schools represent 24% of placements at this level of teaching. It must also be shown that the municipal schools are those that are mostly established in the poorer regions of the city, where income per family is not more than $350 a month.

NETWORKS	Schools 2003		Students 2003	
MUNICIPAL	47	12%	50.701	24%
STATE	234	62%	120.834	57%
FEDERAL	2	1%	911	0%
PRIVATE	97	25%	40.363	19%
TOTAL	380	100%	212.809	100%

Source: Porto Alegre City Hall Education Department, 2004.

Secondly, the Citizen School project, in transforming the operation and direction of education practices in municipal schools, caused ideological resistances to change. The culture of considering schools as places where elites are selected rather than places where solidarity is built up is still very strong. In the last elections the opposition candidates frequently used the argument that in the citizen schools many children do not learn and, in fact, their level of learning is not even measured, since end-of-year exams have been abolished. Here, once again, what is being shown is social discrimination regarding lower-class children who frequently enter school at a later point in life without the same family life and culture enjoyed by middle-class children. These are phase differences that can, with time, be overcome with adequate pedagogic strategies. As to evaluation, this effectively becomes more complex and preventative since it is translated into a permanent evaluation and re-evaluation of work as carried out in the classroom. If anyone has to repeat a year it is not the student but rather the teacher!

The PT has been in government in a number of municipalities and states throughout Brazil. It is now in government at the Federal level. How would you assess the PT's performance in all these sectors to date, bearing in mind the party's commitment to a socialist politics?

Whether the national PT is still a party that is committed to socialism is something that has yet to be shown. Besides, the Lula government has not opted for a government with a strong PT character. Instead, it is striving for the creation of a great alliance with the most varied sectors of national politics with a view to returning to pure and simple economic growth. From this point onward the central axis of the government is a search for governance. Up to recently this search for governance was presented as a conjuncture based on the economic difficulties the country faced early in its mandate. But by now, when almost half the mandate has been reached, and considering the maintenance of a continuity with the policies of the previous government of Fernando Henrique Cardoso, it is more difficult to maintain that macroeconomic conservativism is just a tactical move and that further on we will have a strategic turnaround. On the contrary, what appears each time truer is the irreversibility of conservatism, as though new doors were closed at each concession to the international financial system.

Over the years, the PT leader and current Brazilian president, Luiz Inacio da Silva(Lula), has captured the imagination of progressive people worldwide. Now, that he has been president for well over a year, has he been delivering on his promises, or is there the danger that one is expecting too much from him, given the pressures exerted by IMF and investors, as well as the question of the external debt?

President Lula may feel pressured by the international financial organizations, but, sincerely, he at no moment has the appearance of a person tortured by the difficulties in implementing his original propositions. The parties he throws for friends, enemies and foreign visitors always seem to find him serene and confident about the work of his economic team.

Can you name any significant changes effected by the Lula government in response to collective voices for more democracy in education?

So far there is nothing to be lauded within this context. Initially, the minister for this area was Professor Cristovão Buarque, who ended up out of synch with the government and was replaced by the attorney Tarso Genro. Alleging democratization, the present minister proposed increasing the number of bursaries for students who cannot pay private universities, as an offset to the fact that these entities have not paid social security for many years, considering themselves as philanthropic entities. In practice it is the transformation of an irregularity into a fiscal exemption programme, transferring public resources to private groups, without any control over the management of these resources other than the granting of free places.

The reform of public universities is also under discussion. In essence the reform is not different from measures traditionally proposed by the World

Bank and other international agencies. The fact that a space has been granted to discuss proposals does not alter the limits within which the government has operated.

Paulo Freire, a founding member of the PT, is on record as having said "Today, if the Workers' Party approaches the popular movements from which it was born, without trying to take them over, the party will grow; if it turns away from the popular movements, in my opinion, the party will wear down." (exchange with UNAM scholars in the book *Paulo Freire on Higher Education*, SUNY, 1994, p. 40) In light of Paulo Freire's statement, can you provide some insights regarding the current relations between the PT and Brazil's major social movements?

Once again, Paulo Freire was absolutely right. If at a first moment the social movements sided with the Lula government and actively waited for more than a year to see a strategic turnabout, or at least a declaration that the government was suffering from economic "constraints," more recently the mobilizations are no longer to organize congresses and choose members to take part in federal councils but rather to directly protest against the extreme slowness and a certain disregard for proposals by civil society.

What was seen during the discussion of the Pluriannual Government Plan was unbelievable. After counting on the cooperation of a wide articulation of entities in every state to organize meetings and present propositions to the government, we witnessed the final document being practically discarded in the formulation of the final Government Plan. Meanwhile, the government still had the audacity of presenting it as the result of a dialogue with society. And this is what has taken place with the majority of areas of social interest, with some exceptions in the area of housing and urban development and the area of agrarian reform, although concrete results in these areas are so far either extremely limited, as in the case of agrarian reform, or still tied to the banking logic which manages existing resources in the case of urban policies.

The strategic option of the Lula Government was not for a government based on popular participation but rather for traditional forms of governance, with the maintenance of so-called coalition presidentialism, through which the government controls votes in Congress through the release of funds for individual projects by members of the legislature. In this model there is not the slightest space for a proposed participative budget at a national level, which, in fact, was explicitly refused by the government from the word go.

How do the major social movements in Brazil view PT administrations? Is it a case of their perceiving themselves as being tactically inside and strategically outside the State system?

First we have to distinguish which PT administration we are discussing. During a certain period we could discuss a PT way of governing, which was based on the idea of social justice (tax, distributive and political), seeking the promotion of a priority inversion in favour of the popular classes, to make the ones who make most use of urban income pay more taxes, to ensure that urban property accomplished its social function, to ensure a real power base to those who never had a voice in managing the State through the Budget and to encourage participative planning around local public policies. Even in some PT municipalities, frankly, neoliberal ideas such as privatizations are accepted, as occurred in Ribeirão Preto at the time when the present Minister of Finance was the mayor.

Therefore, it is difficult to generalize on the relationship between the social movements and the PT administrations. In the case of Porto Alegre in a way the social movements are in power, to such a point that, today, after the loss at the polls in October 2004 the larger question is not if the popular organizations are sufficiently strong to face the present political juncture but rather how to maintain the present level of articulation without using governmental co-management space in local politics. The organized popular sectors appropriated certain spaces to such a point that they ended up by relegating their own autonomous organizational space to a secondary level.

You are one of the founders of CIDADE, an NGO that carries out research and capacity building with respect to the Participatory Budget (PB) in Porto Alegre. How viable as an exercise in deliberative democracy and 'active citizenship,' to use a current buzzword in the latter case, is the PB initiative?

The Participative Budget is, in a way, the expression of a crisis in local legislative bodies. In my opinion, it is the structural incapacity of these bodies to add and give consequence to the demands of the less favoured sectors, open a space for the emergence of a fourth power, which is this plebeian public sphere built from the Participative Budget. Why is it so? Because in Brazil local executives have much more power than local legislatures, because by nature budgetary laws are merely authorizations, i.e., the mayor may or may not execute what is in the budget, and, after the Fiscal Responsibility Law it may legally be better if he does not fully execute the entire budget, ensure fiscal surplus, etc. Besides, votes in Brazil are cast for individual candidates and only if the elector has no candidate may he choose to vote only for the party. This generates a tendency for the politicians to place themselves above their parties, change party according to momentary convenience and organize their mandates as council persons in a very individualistic way, frequently refusing party orientation, which tends to make municipal councils a private business exchange. Besides, votes are not district based, the candidates being voted all over town which means those politicians with better media exposure are more easily elected (footballers, TV actors, sports journalists, ex-governors, ex-mayors, all sorts of famous people) The large majority of elected people therefore come from downtown areas, have few direct links with the outskirts and tend to use the mandate to leverage their personal power projects.

In a city such as Porto Alegre, where popular sectors, in order to access urban infrastructure, had to become strongly organized to demand the solution of their problems from the government, since the 50s, the emergence of the Participative Budget represented the opening of a river lock that for decades had dammed the political participation of the lower classes. Before the Participative Budget the popular movements were forced into a client relationship with public powers to obtain responses to their demands. Subsequently, they became political subjects and came to hold the power to decide what was better for their regions and for the local public policies within the city.

It is of course not a romantic and contradiction-free process to begin with because the conservative sectors began to regard the experience in an increasingly preoccupied way. From initial indifference they moved to attempts at deconstitution, and more recently, as in the recent elections, they began to defend popular participation, as long as this occurred without the PT.

To what extent can this PB experience be 'reinvented,' internationally, given that there has been talk concerning the development of PB in other countries such as South Africa or Canada?

The PB is a process and a structure. As a process it cannot be transferred since it comprises our particular history and cannot be cloned. As a structure, although it was built historically and collectively, the Participative Budget can be reinvented elsewhere. Today, in Brazil, even conservative party administrations are implementing forms of Participative Budgets. The World Bank itself has incorporated the idea of PBs as one of its main cores for local development, i.e., if up to a short time ago the neoliberal policies seemed to consider themselves above more direct social articulations, present neoliberal consensus carries a social project that incorporates the conversion of projects originally presented by the left, through increased scope of space for philanthropic action of great corporations and the search for active consent. That is why the most important discussion may not regard the possibility of replication, which tends to grow, but we must ask: What is it good for? Where do we want to arrive?

Critical Environmental Education 'Justice in Trade' and the No-Global Movement

Interview with Vincent Caruana

V incent Caruana is a deeply committed social activist from Malta who is very much involved in the international environmental movement and the movement for 'justice in trade.' In this interview, he discusses such issues as critical environmental education, the notion of 'sustainable development,' 'justice in trade,' the issue of 'development', learning from the South and the relationship between religions and the environment. He also speaks about his formation as an educator and the impact of critical pedagogy on this formation. He combines his social activism with his teaching of environmental education in the Faculty of Education at the University of Malta.

When did you make the personal shift from the conventionally pedagogical to the deeply political?

During my university years—while I was studying to become a teacher—I used to volunteer once a week with an NGO working with children living in an urban zone with a particular concentration of social problems. I could see at first hand the failures of the then current educational system—in spite of the inspiring commitment of some individual educators working at the primary school which most of these children used to attend. Overcoming the failures within the system required a step beyond what committed individuals could do within the realms of the classroom.

During my final years at university I was exposed to critical pedagogy and this exposure helped me to understand and put into words what I had already observed but which hitherto I had not been able to express. I started to understand how the classroom, and the Maltese education system based on streaming at an early age, both echoed and reinforced a social structure which privileged particular groupings to the exclusion of others. I found the whole debate regarding a shift in power from "teacher" to "teacher and student together" very inspiring, and the aims of educating for social justice and the creation of a more just and democratic society through working to model those same principles in the classroom very stimulating.

At the same time I was afraid to take critical pedagogy too seriously because I felt that the sometimes highly specialised language used by some critical pedagogues in their publications could result in limiting communication to a small group of specialists who could understand that language. I had always taken pride in being a person who could communicate at many different levels and with many different people and who liked the language used in campaigns. So critical pedagogy remained somewhat of a "passion in the background"— guiding me in my thoughts but never taking me over completely to identify in totality with the eminent academics developing and furthering it. Some years later I met a brilliant academic—Prof. Tonino Perna from the University of Messina who in spite of his academic wit was an activist and the brains behind so many sustainability ideas in the South of Italy and beyond. I felt I had found a person and a role model who was seamlessly combining academic excellence with radical activism.

Does critical environmental education differ from other approaches to environmental education?

The ability to think critically is very important if individuals are to live, work and play meaningfully in our current and changing environment dominated by market forces and an economic model of globalisation that favours profit before nature and people. If critical skills are about defining and clarifying a problem with the inclusion of all stakeholders, evaluating information related to the problem and solving problems and drawing conclusions, they have been part and parcel of what has been identified as central to environmental education since the 70s. Critical thinking skills have always been an essential component of environmental education. Unfortunately the type of education that maintains the *status quo* and that is happy to churn out "information about the environment" has often posed as environmental education but this was never the spirit of the subject. Similarly programmes that neglect local concerns and the significant life experiences that children bring to classrooms and adults to the workshops have often posed as environmental education. In other words only when the critical dimension is present can we talk of real environmental education.

Recent developments within (critical) environmental education see the field as a collaborative effort among local communities, schools and other actors who reveal their interest in solving local environmental issues, creating new spaces for encouraging synergistic interactions between the formal sector and local knowledge systems. This is an exciting development that acknowledges the grassroots and empowers them in bringing about the necessary identified changes through the critical construction of knowledge for social transformation and collaborative problem solving. Within this framework, investigations are driven more by the nature of the unfolding of the issue rather than by the prior commitment to teaching a body of knowledge and skills.

To be more effective (critical) environmental education needs to interact and dialogue more with the other so-called "adjectival educations" such as citizenship education, development education and peace education. In other words it needs to actively search for the ecological dimension to citizenship issues, social justice issues and peace issues and raise them as part of the struggle. The current boycott of Coca-Cola (www.killercoke.org) is in protest of Coke's murder of indigenous working class organisers in Colombia but there is also an ecological dimension to this struggle—Coke's support for the mass-herbicide poisoning of the entire countryside with Monsanto's Round Up. The current boycott regarding produce from Israel and illegal Israeli settlements in the West Bank and Gaza is about ending the military occupation of Gaza and the West Bank but there is also an ecological dimension to this struggle—the poisonous cloud of pollution (containing high levels of poisonous lead, mercury and PCBs) spread over a third of Lebanon (an area that is home to half its people) from a fire in a bombed fuel tank that burned for 12 days. The same bombing released about four million gallons of oil into the sea, in the largest-ever spill in the eastern Mediterranean. The unprecedented response of concerned citizens to the tsunami disaster is about reconstruction, but it is also about re-thinking coastal zone management and respecting the laws of nature. In other words students of environmental education must be given more opportunities to challenge disciplinary borders and to appropriate knowledge as part of a broader effort of ethical responsibility.

Can critical environmental education be carried out throughout the school curriculum?

The worrying trend to position schools in the service of the economy—and the recent WTO debates where education is seen as a service under the General Agreement on Trade in Services (GATS)—will make it much more difficult to carry out (critical) environmental education throughout the school curriculum.

This "marketization of education" can only serve to further narrow class, race or gender interests to the exclusion and detriment of the poorer people. When education no longer remains a public service but becomes a commodity, values such as equal opportunities, social justice and respect for the environment will find themselves marginalized. Strengthening quality public education needs to become part of the debate of carrying out (critical) environmental education throughout the school curriculum.

Of course "another education is possible"—where the desired result is ecological literacy and the empowerment of students and teachers to bring about social transformation and change on the basis of democratic and socially just ways. Here *how* we educate is the key. An interesting continuing professional development programme SEEPS (Sustainability in European Primary Schools) has shown that the most action-focused environmental education occurs in schools that promote and maintain sustainable practices through the participation of pupils in whole-school approaches, where children as present citizens deliberate, formulate and practise sustainable lifestyles.

Developing active citizens often involves environmental education programmes where schools work together with communities to develop a new critical awareness of the roles that communities play in influencing the course of environmental issues, making explicit the values and interests of the various participants. Examples abound, ranging from planting traditional varieties of grains and wild herbs in cooperation with parents and local farmers, to students taking over the school canteen and changing it to a fair trade canteen supporting a development or community project, to recipe contests involving mother-daughter teams cooking dishes that might represent the wise use of wild vegetables such as dishes with special nutritional values, dishes that help to cope with extreme seasons and calamities, or dishes with medicinal values. One role of the (critical) environmental educator is to make such efforts more known, bridging the gap between knowledge creators and policy makers.

How can critical environmental education take us beyond cynicism and accepting the present as determinant of what is possible?

There are grounds for cynicism. **The gap between the world's rich and poor has never been wider.** Malnutrition, AIDS, conflict and illiteracy are a daily reality for millions. Some island nations face complete obliteration from climate change and rising sea levels. Multinational corporations trade around the world, causing harm to communities and the environment, violating the rights of workers and exploiting children. This takes place at a point in history when we have all the resources, knowledge and opportunity to end this shameful situation. The first step in going beyond cynicism is to acknowledge it. The next step is to realise that it is not destiny, chance or bad luck that keeps people trapped in such situations but human factors such as an unjust global trade system, an irrational reliance on fossil fuels, an unsustainable debt burden and useless aid.

This brings us to ask a very basic question: "Education for whose development?" If development is conceived mainly as economic growth then we will witness a type of "technocratic" environmental education marked by an almost blind faith in the capacities and qualities of science rather than considering political and sociological factors. If development is conceived mainly as a process of building a society of subjects rather than objects—with the human being at the centre—then we will witness a type of environmental education that is a dialogical process of development of each and every person's and community's potential within the carrying capacity of the earth.

To be a "technocratic" environmental educator who functions within the paradigms of development as growth and education as preparing students for a market economy is a guarantee of robbing him or her of the enthusiasm to advance with the job creatively. To be an environmental educator working within the paradigm of nature and people at the centre is to start understanding the schooling structures that do not allow education in general and environmental education in particular to ensue, and when and where appropriate to choose to resist those structures. Hope lies in asking and answering the question "who makes the decisions about what and how to learn?" Hope lies in asking and answering the question "for whose development are my education endeavours?"

On a different note cynicism is also the result of using wrong methodologies. In Malta the authorities sent out leaflets to all households asking them to separate waste at the source without providing the necessary infrastructure for a successful differentiated waste strategy. The result was that citizens saw no openings for real change and now approach the subject of waste with a fair dose of apathy and cynicism. As in other cases unlearning is harder than learning and any renewed efforts for popularising separation at the source will need to deal with one added obstacle. The professional environmental educator needs to understand processes of change so that any call to action is the result of tapping the capacity of citizens for awe and awakening their sense of possibility.

Is the concept of sustainable development a viable model in the context of a hegemonic capitalist arrangement that emphasises maximum profit and private accumulation?

Environmental educators today claim that they have a major role in educating for eustainable development. However sustainable development is one of the most overused, misused and abused concepts in recent times—

officially supported both by speculators who pillage the land and by radical environmentalists. What is it that as (critical) environmental educators we want to educate for? And what is possible within the context of a hegemonic capitalist arrangement that maximises profit before people and nature? I will not attempt to produce my own definition of sustainable development because I will just be adding one to the thousands of definitions that already exist. I will just say that I prefer to look at sustainable development as an on-going process of experimentation and social learning—where a long-term perspective is a necessary condition for success.

Perceptions of the word "environment" differ from one society to another, and for the poorest people it is above all a question of survival related to access to drinking water and health care, possessing the means of production necessary to cultivate one's land and ensure food self-sufficiency and being involved in the management of natural resources. A critical perspective will therefore question what are the factors that control access to clean water, that limit access to medicines and health care, that are destroying subsistence economies that have guaranteed food sufficiency for ages, and that transfer the management and ownership of natural resources to the powerful few? Within this context sustainable development will be a process whereby a community reacquires and uses its resources, in conformity with its cultural values, to solve individual and collective problems by generating, step by step over a long period of time, a new behaviour and lifestyle. It is the experimentation that is taking place in numerous communities around the world to reacquire control over their resources, and the accompanying social learning that takes place, that is of particular interest to me. These initiatives—that can loosely be grouped under the term "social economy"—are providing viable models of sustainable development in spite of the dominant hegemonic capitalist arrangement. One example lies in experimentations related to the right to food—which was enshrined in the UN's 1948 Universal Declaration of Human Rights and, subsequently, in 2004 the UN's Food and Agriculture Organization Council adopted voluntary guidelines for the progressive realization of the right to adequate food. While few countries have taken steps to legally establish the right to food, those that did can report significant results. When Adriana Aranha declared healthy food a right of citizenship in Belo Horizonte, Brazil, the infant death rate fell by 56% over the first decade. The experimentations in implementation included twenty-five fair-priced produce stands supplied by local farmers, open-air restaurants serving 12,000 subsidized meals, and radio broadcasts leading shoppers to the lowest-priced essentials.

It might take some time for states to be able to declare poverty illegal—although some Civil Society Organisations are already campaigning in this direction. The strength of such an approach would lie in the fact that illegality implies some form of mechanism to enforce that law and some form of redress for injured parties. But to be effective it would need to be strengthened by the promotion of democratic concepts such as real participation, group decision-making and gender equity. Through teaching these concepts among the landless peasants in Brazil and organising families to fight for their rights, the Landless Workers' Movement (MST) have created new settlements with new farms and businesses, new schools, lifted family wages and cut the infant death rate. This consciousness raising leads to the creation of citizens who believe that a better life is possible and that within them, both individually and collectively, lies the power to make change. The biggest success that the hegemonic capitalist arrangement can achieve is the labelling of citizens who believe in change as naive—the biggest failure is when ordinary citizens (reclaim) their dignity, walk with their head up, and start building their own sustainable futures. The thousands of citizens working on fair trade, micro-credit, the Participatory Budget, the radical Local Agendas 21, eco-villages, and local exchange systems are just some of these ordinary citizens!

How does the struggle for ecological justice intersect with class, gender and ethnicity? Would you agree that class and other interests are interfering with the effectiveness of the ecological movement?

During a 1976 Conference of the United Automobile Workers one black woman shouted: "Until you talk about me having food, shelter, and clothes, I'm not listening to any appeals from environmentalists." This appeal is indicative of the false separation we have created between food, shelter, and clothes issues, and environmental degradation. One reason might be that environmental education as it has been practised in the formal and non-formal education systems has often followed a too instrumental and technical approach. Another might be that mainstream environmental education was framed with the under-participation of people of colour. The strengths of the environmental justice movement—founded in the USA to highlight the fact that waste sites were disproportionately located in low-income and people of colour areas—lie in reconnecting what we have separated and in affirming the fundamental right to the political, economic, cultural and environmental self-determination of all peoples.

An environmental injustice occurs every time members of a disadvantaged group—whether related to class, gender, colour or ethnicity—suffer disproportionately from environmental risks or hazards and from violations of fundamental human rights as a result of environmental factors. An environmental injustice occurs every time a disadvantaged group is denied access to natural resources, information or participation in decision making related to the environment. The environmental justice movement commits itself to the promotion of environmental justice and economic alternatives that contribute to the development of environmentally safe livelihoods, and to secure the political, economic and cultural liberation denied through colonization, oppression and neo-colonization. Although the movement has its roots in the USA, its principles resonate throughout the world wherever some form of environmental injustice or racism is present. The movement is a challenge for environmental education to work from the ground up, together with the grassroots workers, organizers and activists, and to recognize traditional knowledge.

Is "No Global" still an effective counter-hegemonic movement?

Globalisation in its current form compromises both people and the environment. One counter movement is the World Social Forum—an open meeting place for reflective thinking, democratic debate of ideas, formulation of proposals, free exchange of experiences, and interlinking for effective action, by groups and movements of civil society that are opposed to neo-liberalism, to the domination of the world by capital, and to any form of imperialism. Activists within the Forum are committed to building a planetary society directed towards fruitful relationships among humankind and between it and the earth. This forum, as well as the various demonstrations against the WTO, the World Bank and the IMF, the G8 and other expressions of neo-liberal globalisation, are often loosely labelled as the "no global" movement. Unfortunately powerful interests use the term in a dismissive way, sidelining the fact that the World Social Forum and linked initiatives are the result of a genuine concern regarding the suffering experienced by ordinary citizens in both rich and poor countries due to the inequitable social and economic realities, the growing militarization, the degradation of the environment and the continuing human rights violations.

Can these initiatives be considered as an effective counter-hegemonic movement? There is no clear answer to such a question, but perhaps the strength of this movement lies in providing a useful opportunity for different civil society actors to find common ground, engage in joint strategising, and plan joint activities for the future. One very visible result of such a strategy was the launching of the Global Call to Action Against Poverty (GCAP) in Porto Alegre with the key message that if the right decisions are made at critical global meetings such as G8 and WTO the world can see an end to poverty. This led to the setting up of national platforms or coordinating bodies in more than 100 countries—made up of a diverse range of community groups, coalitions, trade unions, organisations, individuals, faith groups and campaigners—all committed to the fight against poverty. Subsequently as part of the GCAP Campaign, between the 15th and 16th of October 2006, 23 and a half million people in more than 100 countries around the world have set a new Guinness World Record for the largest number of people to stand up against poverty. The website whiteband.org reported that cricket fans in India, school children in Gaza and the West Bank, crowds at a concert in a slum in Zimbabwe and in Times Square in New York all joined for the world record attempt. This is yet another clear sign that the voices of citizens are growing louder in demanding their governments to do more against poverty, for equality and in meeting and exceeding the Millennium Development Goals.

The loosely termed "No Global" movement has also been a major actor in opposing the wars declared by the United States and its allies against 'terrorism.' In doing so activists within the movement oppose the current militarization that daily adds to the numbers of innocent dead, causing immense suffering, political instability, economic insecurity, refugees, minor and gross violations of human rights, increases in racism and diminishing civil liberties. This movement does not try to privilege the suffering of one person over the suffering of another. In making a statement that there are no significant differences among avoidable deaths—whether an American dying in the tragedy of the World Trade Center, a child in Bangladesh dying as a result of violations by multinationals of the World Health Assembly marketing requirements for baby foods, an African dying in the current conflict in Dafur or a Palestinian child killed by Israeli mortar while at school—the movement seeks to engage in a critical and compassionate search for peace in an era of violence and war. While the movement has not managed to stop the invasion of Iraq or the occupation of Palestine it remains a valid actor in articulating an alternative vision of a non-violent world based on cultures and institutions of non-violence. In denouncing combating terror with terror and torture with torture the movement seeks to delegitimise the violence in the West and in this sense offers an effective counter-hegemonic framework to read the world.

You are greatly involved in the international movement that promotes justice in trade. What are the basic tenets of this movement and what is the status of this movement internationally? What has been your involvement in this movement to date?

The International Federation for Alternative Trade (IFAT) defines fair trade as a trading partnership, based on dialogue, transparency and respect, that seeks greater equity in international trade. It contributes to sustainable development by offering better trading conditions to, and securing the rights of, marginalized producers and workers—especially in the South. According to IFAT fair trade is more than just trading: it proves that greater justice in world trade is possible. It highlights the need for change in the rules and practice of conventional trade and shows how a successful business can also put people first.

During the latter half of the nineties, together with a group of friends, I set about creating the first fair trade initiative in Malta. We formed a cooperative—because we considered that the democratic principles adopted by cooperatives best expressed our values—and by 1997 we had opened the first fair trade shop named *l-Arka* (the Ark) to symbolise hope. The fascinating thing about fair trade is that apart from creating opportunities for economically disadvantaged producers, it combines many other positive values such as properly valuing women's work and actively encouraging better environmental practices and the application of responsible methods of production. One problem in mainstream trade is its anonymity—in my education work I often ask students to tell me all they know about the jeans they are wearing and the best I get is limited to the size and style. In seeking to overcome the anonymity in trade and show a face behind the product, fair trade reminds us that trade is fundamentally a human transaction between two needs that meet.

From the beginning the Maltese fair trade cooperative aimed to raise the awareness of consumers on the problems caused by conventional trade and to campaign to change its rules. The sale of products always went alongside with information on the production chain, producers and their conditions of living, and two yearly national fairs mobilise consumers to participate in activities for more global justice. Recently the cooperative applied for and obtained the Fair Trade Organisation (FTO) mark—a quality mark that guarantees to consumers that standards are being implemented regarding working conditions, wages, child labour and the environment. These standards are verified by self-assessment, mutual reviews and external verification. The mark demonstrates that the Maltese cooperative is actively committed to continual improvement.

Today the fair trade movement has developed into a widespread movement with recognition on a political and mainstream business level, and in Europe alone sales of fair trade products have grown by 20% since 2000. The movement has been given an official boost recently through a European Parliament resolution supporting fair trade and recognising that the fair trade system has proved to be effective in poverty reduction and sustainable development. One very interesting point in this July 2006 resolution is the proposal to integrate fair trade criteria into public tenders and purchasing policies—thus complementing and completing the already existing Green Procurement Policy recommendations. In fact Civil Society Organisations have already been active in promoting the concept of Fair Trade Towns or Cities—an award given to municipalities or regions committed to the promotion of fair trade labelled goods and to the inclusion of fair trade criteria in their tendering processes.

Fair trade seems to be the best practical tool we have thus far for consumers to impact on sustainable development and poverty reduction through their purchasing. It is not perfect, and debates within the movement often focus on problems linked to long distance trade and on the inherent tensions between the will to nurture locally produced and locally consumed goods and the need to support small-scale businesses in the global South. The creativity inherent in grassroots Civil Society Organisations ensures that they will keep on experimenting with new models, building on those ideas that have proven to be successful. One such new initiative (Just Change) is seeking to do this—in the words of one of its founders, Stan Thekaekara, it seeks to take fair trade one step further through providing alternative trading structures and mechanisms. Just Change tries to directly link poor communities and encourages them to trade among themselves to ensure that as much money as possible flows between these economies, thus strengthening them. Just Change is a radical project because it recognises not just the social and political power of organised communities but also their economic power. Schools have also been experimenting with fair trade, either through one-off activities such as an organised fair trade breakfast on International Fair Trade day or through longer term whole school approaches where students themselves form cooperatives and take over the school canteen, stocking it with fair trade, local and organic produce. Through a project of ACTIONAID UK primary schools students can also learn about the concepts behind Just Change.

What can the West learn from the activities of indigenous and Southern movements?

The West has often maintained the presumption of exporting democracy—to the extent of fighting senseless wars to promote democracy—even if poll after poll often shows us that citizens have low confidence in politicians and in political institutions. Perhaps a more balanced approach would be to celebrate the advances of democracy while recognising the need to reinvent democracy, including through learning from indigenous and Southern movements. In fact the South has produced a number of tools that can help the West address the challenge of furthering democracy and developing an active citizenship.

One such tool is the Participatory Budget—an ongoing process where citizens have a regular venue to be engaged in between elections to address issues that concern them.

Since the municipal level is often the closest to citizens' needs and wants, it is an ideal level to revitalize civic engagement and participation. It finds its origins in Porto Alegre in 1989 and has since been refined, deepened and expanded to many other cities in Latin America, Africa, Asia, Europe and Canada. Through the Participatory Budget social and political exclusion is challenged as low income and traditionally excluded political actors find new opportunities to participate in policy decision making. The process is sustained through training and workshops since education for participation is necessary for the "democratisation" of democracy. The process sometimes involves—as in the case of **Barra Mansa, Brazil**—a children's Participatory Budget Council to ensure that the municipal council addresses children' needs and priorities. In some localities– such as in Cotacachi, Ecuador—transparency and participation, through a Committee of Social Controllership, are extended to the implementation and management phases of works and projects that have been approved by the municipal participatory budget.

Another example of good practice from the South finds its origins in Bangladesh with the founding of the Grameen Bank in 1976 by the economist Professor Muhammad Yunus. The Nobel Peace Prize of 2006 has just been awarded to him and his micro-credit bank "for their efforts to create economic and social development from below" showing that "even the poorest of the poor can work to bring about their own development." Through the Grameen Bank Mohammed Yunus has also changed the structure of social production focusing on 'man as the breadwinner' to accommodate a substantial and permanent role for women as income-earners. This is done by ensuring access to small amounts of capital to women to engage or build on their small-scale livelihood activities. As in other "social economy" experiments micro-credit provides a space for the liberation of the potential of humanity—including equality and autonomy for women. The risk for micro-credit is the co-option by big businesses that tend to adopt a more capitalist outlook.

One of the most inspiring Southern authors on democracy is surely the Indian physicist and grassroots activist Vandana Shiva. She has created the Earth Democracy movement based on local living democracy with local communities, organised on principles of inclusion and diversity, and ecological and social responsibility having the highest authority on decisions related to the environment and natural resources and the sustenance and livelihoods of people. For Shiva Earth Democracy connects people in circles of care, cooperation and compassion instead of dividing them through competition and conflict. It globalises compassion, not greed, and peace, not war.

At a time when more and more power risks being transferred from parliaments, regional and local governments, and local communities to corporations and other big economic interests the experiments in living democracy from the South strike a new chord. They are a timely reminder that democracy is not about elections and casting votes every five years or so but about the food we eat, the clothes we wear, the water we drink and the air we breathe.

You are actively involved in the ongoing debate on religion and ecological issues. What is your position on this matter?

Even regarding issues pertaining to religion we have a lot to learn from the global South. Brazil's Catholic bishops have openly espoused a theology that actively defends the rights of the oppressed by taking 'an option for the poor.' One of the founders of liberation theology, Leonardo Boff, had once pointed out that 'Jesus was a political prisoner, who died on the Cross, not an old man who died in bed.' Unfortunately the influence of liberation theology has been diminished through the appointment by the pope of conservative bishops throughout Brazil. I am starting with this example because I think it summarises my position—namely, that religion is often caught up between the interests of the institutions, which frequently require the support of other established powers, and the faith that inspires social and ecological justice. As one who identifies himself as an "educator for change" I can sympathise with the basic tenets of liberation theology, which wants change now and not accommodation.

Of course all the great religions of the world have a lot to offer to long-term solutions to environmental problems—and as long as religions participate as partners "in search" in these discussions and not as definitive agents of moral authority—their presence and their closeness with the grassroots could strongly enhance any participatory process for the environment. I was elated when recently in Oxford I saw a Christian church with a big notice "This is a fair trade church." I regularly read the journal of the Buddhist Forum for Peace, Culture and Education and admit to being fascinated by the importance they give to ecology issues and ethical responsibility. When I participate in Euro-Mediterranean encounters, the passion and commitment of Islamic NGOs to environmental and social sustainability are outstandingly visible.

And I know that the clash of civilisations is more of a clash of the perversions of civilisations rather than a real clash because I have experienced friendships that go beyond artificial divides promoted by political and military agendas. Religion can give rise to a profound sense of justice, compassion and stewardship, but the power games often played in association with religion can lead to hostility, untruth and revenge.

Trade Union Education in an Age of Globalization

Interview with John Fisher

John Fisher is an adult educator who has worked for the Transport and General Workers Union in the area of trade union education and workers' education more generally. Since the interview was carried out, Dr Fisher published his book on the history of education in the T&G with the title of Bread on the Waters. *In this wide ranging interview which centres around five basic questions but which drew forth lengthy responses, he deals with the history of trade union education in Britain with special reference to the T&G, the prospects for trade union education in an age of globalization, the relationship between trade union education and higher education institutes in Britain and a host of other issues.*

Kindly tell us something about your educational work within the Transport and General Workers Union in the UK.

The Transport and General Workers Union has 850,000 members and is the third largest union in the UK. Its membership is mainly unskilled and semi-skilled, and the T&G is the largest union in the car industry, passenger, road and air transport, docks and waterways, chemicals and food and drink processing. It is also very important in public services, the voluntary sector, construction and engineering and is the only UK union in agriculture.

The union has a very extensive education programme, mainly aimed at its activists: shop stewards, safety reps and union learning reps. There are normally about 10,000 T&G students each year. In all our regions (except Scotland, which has a different education system), T&G courses are operated in partnership with an "accredited partner," a college or university, so that T&G students gain free learning credits from T&G courses, and in some regions can access higher education up to certificate, diploma and degree level through the union. However, the bulk of the courses are "role education," aimed at supporting the members in their union activities, as well as generally widening their horizons politically.

You are about to publish your book on TGWU education. What are the defining moments in the history of education provided by TGWU?

The T&G was established in 1922 and began its own education programme in 1939. The first phase was aimed at assisting members to understand the history and structure of their union, almost without reference to their workplace. The second stage, beginning in 1950, focused on the shop steward and workplace activites and collective bargaining. This is still the core of the programme. In the 1970s the focus shifted to the regions, with an education officer being appointed in each of the union's eight regions, and also a purpose-built and fully-equipped education centre was built.

In the 1980s, the union introduced a greater emphasis on diversity, with women's courses and courses for black and ethnic members, and also developed explicitly political education. In the 1990s, "lifelong learning" became more important, and the current system of accredited partnerships was introduced. Most other unions use the confederation (TUC) for their education, but most of the T&G's education is carried out independently and under the full control of the T&G.

Apart from the short-lived *ABCA* programme during the Second World War,[1] trade union education (if we include the work of the WEA and Labour Colleges) was the most important mass adult education programme carried out for specifically working-class people during the last century, and the T&G had, and has, the largest of these programmes amongst affiliates to the TUC, and for the greater part of the century had a larger programme than that of the TUC itself. For those reasons alone, the programme is interesting in the light of the debate around adult education, day-release, human resources management and employee development and, latterly, lifelong learning. Most of all, though, it is a story of *activism*; of the motivation of thousands of students and hundreds of tutors, often for little or no financial gain, who believed that education played a central role in developing themselves, the union and the labour movement as a whole. What moved them was commitment to an ideal and the need to gain as much knowledge and as many skills as possible in order to move nearer to their goal, and among the tutors and organisers more often than not their motivation was a combination of a belief in the value of learning found in all good educators, coupled with a wider commitment to the labour movement.

How would you describe the state of trade union education and the broader area of workers' education in Britain, and its status within British universities, in this day and age?

How does one look at the current state of trade union education, and linking trade union education to the wider issues of adult education? This is a crucial question for the T&G, and relates first of all to the definition of "trade union education."

There are inevitably contradictions which surround trade union education. In some quarters, it is suggested that trade union education is a mechanism for social integration under capitalism, and essentially strengthens trade union bureaucrats at the expense of rank and file members, and some of the more extreme criticisms of the TUC programme as being the tool of the government's attempt to regularise industrial relations steer close to this.[2] In the early Thatcher period in the UK, for example, questions were raised as to the value of the TUC's previous collaboration with the Callaghan government and the effect of this in sanitising TUC education and preparing the ground for the Tories.

Overall, such a view would only be tenable if one took the view that because trade unions exist *within* capitalism, therefore they act as maintainers of the system, and not even Marx and Lenin took such a one-dimensional view, and recognised that trade unions were essentially contradictory. They do of course help to regularise industrial relations and sometimes "police" agreements, but they also organise the working class and are the main vehicle for opposition and working-class political education.

The T&G is only one union within the trade union movement, usually occupying about one-seventh of all trade union members. Its education programme, though of more significance within the organisation than that of most unions, is part of a wider tradition of trade union education and needs definition, especially for those who have not encountered it before, or who are unclear as to its purpose. Such attempts are rare, and as Holford points out "no theory of trade union education has emerged. It is truly remarkable that no book-length study has been published... apart from official and semi-official reports."[3] One of these reports was written in 1959 for the WEA by Hugh Clegg and Rex Adams. Its main conclusion was that "the central purpose of trade union education must be to provide education suited to the needs and the abilities of active or potentially active trade unionists."[4] No one would dispute this, but it cannot be held to be a comprehensive definition. In September 1950 an article by William Morgan, then Assistant Labour Information Officer in the US Economic Co-operation Administration, attempted to characterise it as follows:

> Trade union education today has three main strands. Firstly, there is education for specifically trade union purposes—a study of union histories and procedures, and other topics most necessary to hold union posts. Then there is general education of a liberal kind—usually in the social studies. As a bad third there comes semi-technical training in problems of particular industries in joint consultation, and training for management.[5]

In a period when modern trade union education was still in its infancy, this was a good attempt at a definition, covering as it does the core of internal role education with a link to wider lifelong learning on the one hand and workplace industrial relations on the other. It should be noted that this definition plays down education as skills training, whether in the initial basic skills usually taught in schools, or vocational skills of whatever kind. On the other hand, the skills of advocacy, representation and the wider range of inter-personal and transferable skills are very much implicit in the definition. A similar definition was given by Jim Fyrth in 1980:

> Trade unions are vehicles for learning. Unions are in the business of defining and analysing problems and seeking solutions."[6] He went on to define trade union educational objectives as "Internal Education," supplying activists, "Industrial Education," based on dealing with workplace problems, and "Social and Political Education" looking at economics, politics and so on.[7] These broad definitions were echoed some years later by Hopkins who defined what he called "Workers' Education" as "that sector of adult education which caters for adults in their capacity as workers and especially as members of workers' organisations." [8]

He went on to identify five major components:

1. Basic general skills
2. "Role skills" for trade union activity
3. Economic, social and political background studies
4. Technical and vocational training
5. Cultural, scientific and general education.

Whilst such definitions set the scene in which trade union education operates, they do not answer questions regarding elements of purpose and activity in trade union education which might outweigh other elements, nor do they allow for different emphases in the actual process of education, which are important in determining the policy within the education providers.

Government inquiries into adult education stressed different aspects of trade union education in their definitions. The *Interim Report of the Committee on Adult Education* or "1919 Report," established as part of the post-war process of reconstruction, emphasised the benefits to the individual and to the wider society. In a passage most likely drafted by RH Tawney and Basil Yeaxlee, the report noted that

> workers demand opportunities for education in the hope that the power which it brings will enable them to understand and help in the solution of the common problems of human society. In many cases, therefore, their efforts to obtain education are specifically directed towards rendering themselves better fitted for the responsibilities of membership of political, social and industrial organisations. [9]

Fifty-five years later, the 1973 Russell Report, *Adult Education: A Plan for Development,* emphasised role education, especially training and development for individuals in their roles as shop stewards and other trade union positions. This was in response to pressure from TUC leaders who were looking for legal and financial support for trade union education on the basis of its contribution to more harmonious industrial relations:

> In a period when industrial relations are becoming increasingly complex, it is of vital importance that the large numbers involved on both sides of industry should be given the opportunity to study the problems and acquire the necessary techniques. [10]

That trade union education contains a range of elements from the philosophical through to the practical skills of industrial relations has not really been in doubt, but the most important disputes have been about the different emphases within this range, and, implicitly or explicitly, the political purpose and consequences of trade union education.

Among those engaged in teaching and organising within the trade union education movement, there has been an intensive debate about the purpose and direction of trade union education. The earliest debate was between the champions of WETUC and the NCLC, contrasting individual betterment and cultural awareness with the strengthening of collectivism through "independent working-class education." It was argued by the Labour College Movement that the working class should control its own education, free from the capitalist state, and that its rival the WEA, by accepting state funding, was compromised and was a "sheep in wolf's clothing," weakening the movement through the dissemination of bourgeois ideology and the seduction of potential working-class leaders into the academic world. The WEA, on the other hand, characterised the Labour College Movement as propagandist rather than educational.

Although this controversy was current many years ago, in the 1920s and 1930s, it is still important in the current situation. The main focus of the Labour Government has been to encourage the role of trade unions in carrying through a "learning and skills" agenda—essentially an exercise in which trade unions are used to enhance the skills and employability of their members. Millions of pounds have been given to the unions through agencies such as the Union Learning Fund, and this has created a distortion in trade union education, where skills and workplace-linked personal development programmes have come to the fore, and political education and "counter-culture" have receded into the background. This is unresolved, and in some trade unions not even recognised, but of course relates to the role trade unions play in any capitalist society.

The seeds of this current dilemma go back not only to the WETUC/NCLC controversy, but to the debate surrounding the response to Thatcherism in the 1980s, primarily in the pages of *The Industrial Tutor,* journal of the Society of Industrial Tutors, and *Trade Union Studies Journal,* produced by the WEA.[11] This controversy touched on a number of issues of the time; corporatism and state-funding at a time when the overtly hostile Thatcher government had arrived, paid release and joint training with employers, but mostly concerned itself with the ostensibly technical issue of active learning methods. At some stages it resembled a theological debate around seemingly obscure matters; the initiated, however, recognised the issues as codes for fundamental questions of doctrine.

The real issue was the alleged removal of political content from trade union education by the TUC. In its 1968 policy statement, *Training Shop Stewards,* the TUC had defined such training in a way which distinguished training from education:

> Training means systematic instruction, study and practice that will help to equip union members to be competent as representatives of their union in the workplace. Obviously this excludes consideration of their educational needs, as citizens or even potential general secretaries, or cabinet ministers. The boundaries to the training task, are, therefore, set by the richly varied duties and responsibilities of the workplace representatives themselves.[12]

The issue went back to the establishment of the TUC scheme in 1964, when JPM Millar, General Secretary of the NCLC, bitterly accused the TUC of removing political content through the elimination of a number of politically related courses which had been offered by the NCLC, and the focussing on narrow collective bargaining skills. Millar commented that "the less the members know about Socialism, the more the TUC like it."[13] The election of the Thatcher government, with millions of trade unionists' votes, and the splits within the TUC over "respectable" trade unionism and accommodation with this government brought the issue to a head. Key policy documents of the 1960s and 1970s had stressed the role of trade union education in "inculcating the notion of constitutionalism and the need to respect agreements" in the minds of shop stewards,[14] and the Royal Commission under Lord Donovan itself had specifically attached this function to trade union education:

> The need for shop steward training is immense... Additional resources are undoubtedly required. They should be used...with a view to using training of stewards as part of a planned move to more orderly industrial relations based on comprehensive and formal factory or company agreements. This is where shop steward training will be able to make its biggest contribution.[15]

At this time, the TUC was strengthening its links with FE colleges and insisting that courses follow a ten-day release format, and essentially only concern themselves with basic shop stewards' and safety reps' training. Also, active learning methods were encouraged, with the tutor as "facilitator," rather than lecturer or leader in the traditional adult education style. It was claimed that these methods were more democratic as they were more participative, and many references were made to the value of active learning rather than "rote learning" in schools. John McIlroy and others argued that the focus on student-centred learning methods obscured the "wider questions of content, curriculum, what is to be learned and the nature of the power system within organised education which determines these questions."[16] He quoted the Marxist educationalist Douglas Holly:

> We must, of course, distinguish between...genuinely progressive methodology and *progressivism*. Progressivism can be defined as the mysticism of method, the belief that the only thing that matters in learning is the technique, or at best the social relationship between learner and teacher in the narrow. Progressivists delight in enquiry as an end in itself and rejoice when the classroom atmosphere is happy no matter what bunkum is being taught.[17]

The argument was that the focus on method went along with an extremely restrictive definition of what trade unionists wanted or needed, one essentially related to workplace industrial relations:

> TUC education appears to accept that there *is* a trade union knowledge "out there," but a knowledge based on an extremely limited view of shop stewards. Yet what many trade unionists want today is social, political, economic knowledge—rooted in the workplace, yes, but qualitatively transcending it as well.... And now we are reaching the real problems. What *is* the "end" of trade union education for the educators and the students? Is it the provision of the preconditions for social change, as many of us believe, or is it, as the Code of Practice prescribes, "improved industrial relations"? Until we address ourselves to these questions, then whether a tutor talks for three minutes or three hours in the classroom s/he may be talking to little effect.[18]

The implication, of course, was that the TUC was ensnared by the acceptance of state funding (a throwback to the NCLC/WETUC controversy) and did not want to jeopardise its continuation, even from the Thatcher Government: "Until 1979 the state operated with the carrot of rights. After 1979 the carrot was maintenance, the stick the threat of withdrawal of support."[19] McIlroy summed up his view:

> The ideology that informed trade union education and industrial relations training was based upon Labourism's split between industrial and political. It emphasised a "unitary," hierarchical, "common-sense" conception of trade unionism with unproblematic goals, blurring differences of objective or interest between leadership and members and asserting politics as outside the realm of "workplace industrial relations..." The presentation of workplace skills training as neutral failed to acknowledge that exclusion of a critical examination of politics and power in unions, industry and society, taking the wider context as given, was liable to legitimise existing authority relations and the politics of the *status quo*. Or that industrial relations training carried a view of trade unionism as centred on workplace collective bargaining at the expense of a view of trade unionism as a social movement with a political mission. And a conception of lay activists as a subaltern stratum was at the expense of conceiving lay activists as a critical, empowered, cadre. The economistic ideology of skills training reduced real divisions of purpose and policy to a simplistic, conservative technicism.[20]

There was also criticism of the TUC approach from those who were supportive of active learning methods in principle but who felt that the TUC was not using them as part of an overall progressive approach. One such was Dan Vulliamy of Hull University, a long-standing associate of TGWU education, who identified a paradox in the TUC approach:

> British trade union education, particularly as defined by the TUC Education Department, focuses on what British trade unionism is best at and overwhelmingly ignores its weaknesses. The result of the paradox is that the front line against continued workplace reorganisation, plant closures and redundancies, imposition of new working methods and tighter discipline, hostile government legislation and other policies is manned by shop stewards who are now the best note-takers in the world, can calculate statutory redundancy entitlements in seconds and are all too aware that most forms of effective resistance have just been outlawed, but have no idea what to do when management takes unilateral action or bypasses the union with direct appeals to members, are largely unaware of alternative political and economic strategies which can be implemented at local and wider levels, and have often accepted the ideological barrage of Government and media about the inequities of the closed shop, the illegitimacy of effective industrial action and the responsibility for the mess of Communists, women, blacks and part-timers........in certain respects the contribution of trade union education in recent years has been worse than inappropriate, by fetishising collective bargaining as the sole method and joint regulation as the sole purpose of trade unionism, and by encouraging a reliance on legal methods and written agreements in preference to more traditional trade union methods.[21]

Vulliamy argued that participative and small-group learning methods were an important step forward in trade union education, but that their main function had been to highlight the inadequacy of workplace organisation currently existing.

The response to these charges came on two levels. On the one hand, leading members of the TUC Education Department justified the TUC's approach on the grounds of its being the appropriate policy for the time and claimed that the emphasis on participative methods was of value in itself. They also claimed that McIlroy and his supporters over-emphasised the focus on skills, and that TUC education was more broadly based. Thus, according to Alan Grant, the head of TUC education:

> The three legs of the educational school are "attitudes," "skills" and "knowledge", and even the most basic course should operate on all three fronts.... However, the acquisition of skills and the questioning of what passes for "common sense" cannot take place in a vacuum. The context must be formally based upon employee/employer relationships at work. This context is established through the students' experience as the starting point, but must go on to extend knowledge to areas and issues beyond the students' experience. The view that the sum total of students' experience provides sufficient knowledge and information for a course and should itself set the limits of the syllabus, is... not the TUC view, but a parody of it. The most important person in this process is the tutor and I have very little patience with tutors who feel that their effectiveness increases with their invisibility. [22]

These comments kept the argument within the area of method and did not meet the demand for education dealing with economic and political issues demanded by McIlroy.

A more theoretically substantial response came from practitioners who argued that the use of active learning methods was itself a political and developmental process, taking their theoretical cue from Paulo Freire[23] and their practical one from their own experience as trade union tutors. Radical tutors such as Tom Nesbit, Simon Henderson and Doug Miller argued that a "dialectic pedagogy" based around active learning engaged workers in building a collective consciousness which was itself a necessary learning process in trade union development. They criticised McIlroy and others as viewing the Labour College Movement through rose-coloured glasses, arguing that it was based on a passivity of process and only reached an already motivated elite. They argued that mass trade union education based on day-release was far more significant in the development of activism in trade unions:

> In our experience, one of the ways union members and representatives become active is by learning how to learn. We believe that by concentrating on the content (the "what-is-to-be-learnt") to the exclusion of "how the content is to be learnt" (methods), assumes a false division between the two. Knowledge is 'created' by the

process of learning-defining and clarifying a problem, questioning, observing, generalising, verifying and applying—not by memorising someone else's questions... We believe that people are most interested in the issues which affect them and that the best time to learn anything is when it is most immediately useful to us. By encouraging people to become actively involved in those issues, the cause of unionism is advanced.[24]

At this stage, these writers even argued that courses for trade unionists specifically concerned with training in active learning methods had significant political value. Later, Tom Nesbit refined this view into a more comprehensive definition which tried to link political objectives and learning methods together:

Although no education programme can resolve deep-seated economic changes, it can, however, help identify the causes of such changes, encourage an understanding of options, and challenge the apathy that overwhelms many in the face of crisis. Labour education can also encourage workers to rediscover the wider perspectives essential to development of real alternatives and policies, while simultaneously equipping workers with the skills and organisation to implement them.[25]

These contradictions are unresolved today. Trade unions are not political parties, but they have an important role in bringing political education and awareness to the working class. They are not transformational bodies, indeed they are integrated into capitalism in varying degrees, but they are also critical of aspects of their societies and play an important role in raising the issues of alternative social and political strategies.

Management seems to have developed its own agenda for 'worker participation' at the place of work. How can unions respond to this without 'selling out'?

In his book *The Third Contract*, set in a mainly Australian context, Michael Newman tried to deal with the separation between trade union education and other forms of adult education and to examine the relationship between the educator and the requirements of union policy.[26] He argued that there are three "contracts" involved in trade union education. The first is between the union and the trainer: "the union will set the objectives for its training programme and these are likely to be organisational ones to do with equipping members and officials with the necessary skills and knowledge to make the union function more effectively."[27] The second contract is between the trainer and the participants, which will need to be in accord with the union's policies and objectives. However, he argues that there is a third contract:

between the participants in the course and the union they belong to, and is summed up in the saying: 'the members *are* the union'...The trainer is not party to this contract, but can influence it...we need to ensure that the members know that the union is theirs, that the officials are their servants, and that the structure they are a part of has been constructed to serve their interests as workers and members. And we need to ensure that they have the necessary skills and the motivation to act on this knowledge....The third contract is essential to the continued success of a union. If the interaction between a union as a sum of its members and a union as an organisation is vigorously and continuously democratic, then the union will be able to resist domestication by employers, governments and its own peak bodies and, when necessary, will be able to engage in radical action. Defining, redefining, establishing and continually re-establishing this third contract must be the overriding purpose of all our training. [28]

Education, then, can be an internal force for liberation and development within trade unions. The extent to which employer "participation schemes" draw the union into a pro-managerial, corporatist role is not only a question of the wider role of trade unionism in any particular society but is also an internal matter, linked to how the union sees its members and how the members see their union, and of course the extent of membership democracy within a union. In the T&G, we see an important role for education to be maintaining and extending democracy and membership participation within the organisation, allowing the experiences and the views of the members to bring themselves to bear in countering particular management strategies.

What challenges do trade union education and workers' education face in an age characterised by the intensification of globalisation?

Responding to the globalisation of production and of society is a crucial issue for trade union education today. It is often said, especially by Socialists, that without education, trade union consciousness will remain parochial at the level of "factory gate" or "office door." With no explicit political content, and with the scope of inquiry self-limited by active and discovery learning methods, it would in theory be possible to engage in trade union education and come out with no wider perspective than when one went in. However, what evidence there is suggests that whatever methods are used, the effect of education is to broaden horizons beyond a person's immediate experience. This should, of course, be no surprise and should be applicable to all genuine education. Perhaps the essence of the problem in trade union education is the motives of the union and the tutors, rather than the methods. Do they *want* their students to learn about the history of the movement and its national and international objectives? Do they see themselves as part of a *movement* at all? Whatever their motives, almost all trade union students will bring to the classroom some experience of the increasing globalisation of society.

As with many other aspects of trade union education, there are some fundamental contradictions which must be understood, faced and accepted. Education programmes should enhance the ability of trade unionists to extend their organisation, to bargain more effectively and strengthen their systems of job protection, and achieve better wages and conditions. These are then used by employers as justification for moving production elsewhere in the world, to places with lower wages and fewer rights. Union policies support the international solidarity between workers, but the immediate demand of any given group of trade unionists will be support in defending their factory or community from being closed down and exported to workers overseas. Contradiction is a fundamental part of trade union life in a capitalist society, and education is no exception.

In the T&G, we have been trying for the past few years to raise the awareness of our members to the issues of globalisation, development and international trade union action. We have a dedicated website with education resources on globalisation (accessed via the activist's resources link on the home page, www.tgwu.org.uk). We have tried to follow the principles of recognising that we must start where trade unionists generally are—protectionist and worried about their own situation, and fearful of globalisation. We then try to overcome their awe of the global economy and get them to understand more about international trade unionism and especially successful campaigns of solidarity and support. During this process, they begin to understand that neither short-term protectionism nor "the race to the bottom" give them any sort of future and that solidarity, co-operation and issues like core labour standards are crucial to their future. We also encourage them to use their bargaining power over corporations in the "developed" world to assist the growth of trade unionism and workers' rights in the "developing world" on the basis of solidarity between workers and also self-interest.

We believe that is the right approach, but these types of educational projects are in their infancy. We have now established a course in the mainstream T&G education programme called "Winning in the Global Workplace" to develop some of these ideas. We work very closely with the Global Union Federations and educational bodies like IFWEA. Training our members in the use of e-mail and the Internet is also included in these courses, although we do have ICT training centres around the union which give free training for members in all aspects of ICT.

In the present period of globalisation and the unremitting attack on established working conditions and practices by the advocates of neo-liberalism, of the absence of any counter-model to free-market capitalism, of the undermining of the social institutions of the EU and the rise of China on the basis of the super-exploitation of workers, I see no function in the trade unions being more important than education. Traditional trade union strategies will not work in the new conditions, as the employers have too many cards to play, yet workers have no clear picture of what they want and how they might get there. I believe we are at the very bottom of the ladder of ideas in coping with the new challenges; we need to recreate a belief that there are Socialist alternatives to capitalism, that individualism and petty nationalism will never give the power to challenge globalisation, and that the old slogans of solidarity and international unity between workers are the only way forward. These lofty goals need to be raised and discussed through education in one of the few places where working class people feel at home—in their trade unions.

Notes

1. ABCA, the Army Bureau of Current Affairs, was introduced as a programme of using education methods to instil war aims but was taken over by progressive tutors and students alike, and in the first half of the war at least, was turned into a debating society looking at social policies for the post-war world—and criticising what had gone on pre-war. It was said to have played a role in the Labour victory of 1945. See S P Mackenzie, *Politics and Military Morale:* Oxford, Clarendon Press, 1992: P Addison, *The Road to 1945: London*, Quartet, 1975.
2. Perhaps the nearest is John McIlroy, "Adult Education and the Role of Client: the TUC Education Scheme 1929-1980," *Studies in the Education of Adults,* No. 2, 1985.
3. J Holford, *Union Education in Britain: A TUC Activity:* University of Nottingham, 1994, page 250.
4. H A Clegg and Rex Adams, *Trade Union Education:* London, WEA, 1959 page 9.
5. *Ibid,* page 6.
6. Jim Fyrth, "Industrial Studies in an Industrial Society", in E Coker and G Stuttard (eds.), *Industrial Studies 3:* London, Arrow, 1980, page 162.
7. *Ibid,* page 163.
8. PGH Hopkins, *Workers' Education: An International Perspective:* Milton Keynes, OU Press, 1985, page 2.
9. *Interim Report of the Committee on Adult Education Industrial and Social Conditions in Relation to Adult Education:* London, HMSO, 1918, page 3.
10. Dept. of Education and Science, *Adult Education: A Plan for Development:* London, HMSO, 1973 page 89.
11. The debate was extensive. See P Caldwell, "State Funding of Trade Union Education," *Trade Union Studies Journal,* No. 3, 1981: D Gowan, "Student-Centred Approaches Revisited," *Trade Union Studies Journal,* No. 7, 1983: C Gravell, "Trade Union Education; Will State Funding lead to State Control?" *Trade Union Studies Journal,* No. 8, 1984: C Edwards, et al., "Student-Centred Learning and Trade Union Education: a Preliminary Examination, *The Industrial Tutor,* Vol. 3, No. 8, 1983: D Miller, "Student-Centred Learning in Trade Union Education; Some Further Considerations," *Trade Union Studies Journal,* No. 8, 1983: T Nesbit and S Henderson, "Methods and Politics in Trade Union Education," *Trade Union Studies Journal,* No. 8, 1983: J McIlroy and B Spencer, "Methods and Policies in Trade Union Education; a Rejoinder," *The Industrial Tutor,* Vol. 3, No. 10, 1985, pages 49-58: J McIlroy, "Goodbye Mr Chips?," *The Industrial Tutor,*

Vol. 4, No. 2, 1986, pages 3-23: J McIlroy, "Education for the Labour Movement: UK Experience Past and Present," *Labor Studies Journal*, Vol. 4, No. 3, Winter, 1980: J McIlroy, "Independent Working-Class Education," in R Fieldhouse et al., *A History of Modern British Adult Education:* Leicester, NIACE, 1996, pages 264-289.

12. TUC, *Training Shop Stewards:* 1968, page 9.
13. *The Guardian*, 1.9.1978. Quoted by McIlroy, "Education for the Labour Movement: UK Experience Past and Present,": *op, cit.* page 212.
14. WEJ McCarthy, *The Role of Shop Stewards in British Industrial Relations:* Research Paper No. 1, *Royal Commission on Trade Unions and Employers' Associations:* HMSO, 1967, page 76.
15. *Royal Commission on Trade Unions and Employers' Associations:* HMSO, 1967, Cmnd. 3623, para 712, pages 190-191.
16. McIlroy, "Student-Centred Learning and Trade Union Education: a Preliminary Examination," *op, cit.*, page 47.
17. D Holly, "Politics of Learning", *Radical Education 7*, Winter, 1976 page 6. Emphasis in original.
18. McIlroy, "Student-Centred Learning and Trade Union Education: a Preliminary Examination" *op, cit.*, page 52-53. Emphasis in original.
19. McIlroy, "Independent Working-Class Education," *op, cit.*, page 281.
20. McIlroy, "Independent Working-Class Education," *op, cit.*, page 283.
21. Dan Vulliamy: "The Politics of Trade Union Education," draft paper, page 4. A version was published in JA Jowitt & RKS Taylor (Eds.), *The Politics of Adult Education*: Bradford Centre, 1985.
22. A Grant, "Trade Union Education, a TUC Perspective," *The Industrial Tutor*, Vol. 5, No. 1, Spring 1980, page 12.
23. See P Freire, *Cultural Action for Freedom:* Penguin, 1972. For a useful survey, see P Jarvis (ed.) *Twentieth Century Thinkers in Adult Education:* London, Croom Helm, 1987.
24. T Nesbit and S Henderson, "Methods and Politics in Trade Union Education," *op cit*, page 5.
25. T Nesbit, "Labor Education," *Adult Learning*, 2(6), 1991, page 16.
26. M Newman, *The Third Contract:* Darlinghurst, NSW, 1993.
27. *Ibid*, page 269.
28. *Ibid*, pages 38, 270 and 272.

From Madness to Consciousness: Redemption through Politics, Art and Love

Interview with Antonia Darder

*A*ntonia Darder is professor of Educational Policy Studies and Latino/a Studies at the University of Illinois, Urbana-Champaign. Her current work focuses on comparative studies of racism, class and society. Her teaching examines cultural issues in education with an emphasis on identity, language, and popular culture, as well as the foundations of critical pedagogy, Latino studies, and social justice theory. Over the years, Professor Darder has also been active in a variety of Latino/Chicano grassroots efforts tied to educational rights, worker's rights, bilingual education, women's issues, and immigrant rights. Her interview touches on some of her personal and community-oriented struggles.

> *In time of crisis, we summon up our strength. Then, if we are lucky, we are able to call every resource, every forgotten image that can leap to our quickening, every memory that can make us know our power.*
>
> *Muriel Rukeyser*[1]

Excavating one's life experiences could be a very painful endeavour. Why did you decide to answer our questions?

I was not born to a family where questions of social struggle or deep critical reflections fuelled the din of dinner conversations. Instead, I was a child born of the "underclass." It is not a place that can easily or honestly be romanticized —not if one has known the anguish and torment of its shadows. Or lived the mounting tensions of an everyday where surveillance in a million different forms is commonplace. It is a prison of another sort, camouflaged behind the white sheet of political scriptures proclaiming "all men are created equal" and "justice and liberty for all." It is a place of tremendous fear and despair, where daily survival is at best dubious. A place that we may be tempted to recall as more benign, so that we need not return to the pain, even as memory. In this no-person-land, chaos and anguish are the direct outcome of contentious social, political, and economic forces that exert their brutal pressure upon the impoverished. While all along, as William Ryan so rightly attested, employing self-righteous moralism to blame the poor for their absence of wealth, power and knowledge. Yet, it cannot be forgotten that the madness that ensues from the oppressed and forgotten as Frantz Fanon so eloquently argued is nothing more than the normal psychological response of people driven to the edge.

I pronounce these words not as one who has been a good reader of theory, or one blessed with compassion to empathize, but rather a woman who has known the edge of American life. So it is, that my story is about a long struggle to decolonize my mind and liberate my body from the internalized maladies of childhood. But it is about much more. It is an unlikely tale about a displaced woman's tenacious confrontation with the contradictions of U.S. liberalism and capitalist greed. Indeed, my rage clamoured first to enter, then to shatter, and finally to dissolve all inkling of oppression that crossed my path. Naively, I often forgot the power of loyal institutional gatekeepers, men and women of every colour and persuasion, who safeguard the doors of the empire, refusing to surrender the unrighteous power wielded over the lives of so many.

This response is a first attempt to mine the recesses of a life filled with so much conflict, pain and disappointment—but still much love. How much do I expose? What do you want to know? What do I have the courage to say, despite the humiliating critics perched on the wall of disdain? Can I step fully into the jagged and gritty humanity of a woman who loves, hates, cries, envies, despairs, fights, hopes in the everyday? How exactly do I begin to make sense of my life and my evolution as an activist scholar? How did I move from madness to consciousness?

It is difficult for me to say if I chose my life as an activist or if my life as an activist chose me. Yet, for some of us, there is no choice, if we are to find our dignity and persevere. Perhaps, it is best to say that my life has been a true dialectic—choosing each step as it was choosing me. For many years, I was too young or naïve to be cognizant of this powerful relationship. But today I embrace my life fully knowing, as did Karl Marx, that we make history as much as we are made by history—which requires us to remain ever vigilant and yet humble. No doubt, Antonio Machado's often recited mantra "el camino se hace al andar," [2] resonates well with my life, although the path upon which I've walked has seldom been entirely of my own making. I say this in recognition that our personal histories are always tied to the larger social, political and economic realities of the time. None of us lives in a vacuum. Mine is a history of struggle and resistance, in which the politics of colonialism, capitalism, migration, racism, and sexism have been instrumental to my understanding of the world and my emancipatory efforts as a working-class feminist, living the many contradictions of the Puerto Rican Diaspora. As such, mine is a life often betrayed by translation.

Where and when did your life journey begin?

They say that witches are born on days when the sun is shining in the sky, while the rain showers down on the earth. I was born, on such a day, in Vega Baja, a poor rural community in Puerto Rico, in the midst of the McCarthy era and the Korean War. My birth in 1952 was the result of a liaison between a poor nineteen-year-old woman from Vega Baja and a 52-year-old wealthy, married man from Arecibo. The story goes that my poor grandmother and wealthy father entered into a financial agreement in which my mother was "sold" to him as his mistress, in exchange for a monthly stipend to support my mother's family.

Just prior to this transaction, my mother had lost her fiancé in the Korean conflict. He was a young, nineteen-year-old, Puerto Rican man who had been deployed immediately after his enlistment into combat. Sad and despondent over her lover's death, my mother fought with my grandmother over the transaction. Eventually, she acquiesced, seeing few alternatives for her life. Hence, her relationship with my elderly father was initiated purely on economic terms for the exchange of sexual favours. The loss of her early romance and the resulting mismatched liaison with my father was to leave an enduring mark on my mother's life.

The 1950s were the era of "Operation Bootstrap" on the island, a U.S. public policy initiative. A primary objective of the initiative was to reduce poverty in Puerto Rico. Overpopulation was deemed the culprit of the island's problems, while the disastrous impact of U.S. economic policies was left virtually unaddressed. Two state-sponsored tactics were widely enacted. The first was the mass migration of Puerto Ricans to large U.S. urban centres. So successful was this effort that by the 1960s one-third of the colony's population had been relocated to the mainland. The legacy of this mass migration is obvious today, with as many Puerto Ricans living in the Diaspora, as on the island. The second tactic was the mass sterilization of Puerto Rican women. By the 1970s, over thirty-five percent of all Puerto Rican women of my mother's generation had been sterilized.

So it came to pass that my mother at twenty-one was sterilized immediately following my sister's birth—a procedure orchestrated by my well-connected father who already had no intention of continuing his relationship with my mother. Unwilling to leave his wife, my father once again used his government connections to obtain inexpensive airfare tickets for my mother, my sister and me to leave the island. With our departure, we left behind not only our extended family, but all the familiar sounds, sensations, and being-ness of a cultural milieu in which we belonged, along with a lived connection to a history that was to elude me throughout most of my life.

What were your first years of the diaspora like?

We arrived in Chicago during the winter of 1954, remaining in the area less than six months. The inhospitable cold of the Midwest winter and difficulty finding full-time employment caused my mother much unhappiness with our conditions in Chicago. Hoping that things would improve on the West Coast, my mother desperately pulled together the money to purchase one-way airline tickets to Southern California, where two years earlier my grandmother had migrated.

Life in East Los Angeles, however, also proved to be a hardship. We lived off and on with my grandmother or moved from room to room for years, as my mother tried to find a place to settle down. My mother alternated between living on welfare and working in the sweatshops of Santee Street in the Los Angeles garment district. When on welfare, we lived in fear that the county social worker would show up unexpectedly and discover my mother was living with a man or that she was making a little extra money sewing for the neighbours—both "justifiable" reasons for terminating all welfare benefits from the State. When working in the factory, my mother spent long hours hunched over a sewing machine in a dirty, dusty, and crowded warehouse. In this way, she earned the piecework tickets that would be added up at the end of the week to determine her pay—pay without benefits of any kind. Occasionally in the chaos of her life, she would lose or misplace the little tickets. Pandemonium would strike! My knees would shake, as I watched my mother anxiously ransack the house. Furiously, she would fling things about, cursing loudly, her rage oozing from her eyes—no tickets meant no pay.

It was common for my mother to arrive home tired and angry at the exploitation and degradation she felt at the factory. "I'm nothing but a slave chained to a machine," she would yell. She thought of herself as the mule of the boss who made the money and paid the workers pennies for their hard labour. Yet in spite of these conditions, I recall several occasions when the union tried to organize workers in the factories where my mother worked. The workers, who were mostly women and undocumented, were intimidated by the bosses who threatened them with loss of their livelihood or a call to immigration. Unfortunately, on every occasion, the workers acquiesced, leaving them with a greater sense of powerlessness.

Along with the exhaustion and frustration felt at work, my mother's romantic relationships were tumultuous, with a long string of men coming and going throughout my childhood. The unfortunate conditions of poverty and her many troubled romances contributed greatly to my mother's disabling anxieties. Her pains and maladies are consistent with those of so many disenfranchised people—namely, depression, alcoholism, diabetes and emotional and mental instability. Yet despite her difficulties and emotional suffering, my mother was unable to secure treatment for her alcoholism or for her violent outbursts against her children or anyone that happened to cross her path. Hers was a miserable existence—an ambitious, intelligent girl forced to drop out of school to help support her family. Like so many oppressed women, she found herself imprisoned by the futility of underclass hopelessness, discouragement, and despair.

The conditions of poverty and injustice were marked on my mother's body—her sallow swollen skin, the ceaseless tension in her face, the dark circles around her eyes, and the brusque and impatient manner of interacting with others. Her features became emblazoned in my mind. Her uncontrollable rage and violence terrified me. Yet, the abuse I endured at the hands of my mother was the same violence she had received from her mother. If all this was not bad enough, both my sister and I became victims of child sexual abuse, perpetrated by several of my mother's lovers. I was molested for three years, from ages six to nine, and my sister was molested once when she was eleven.

My sister's molestation was to mark a pivotal moment in my life. During the years that I was molested, I had been too terrified to speak. I lived those years silently imprisoned in a surreal existence, in which I felt dirty, violated, isolated and unprotected. So, when my sister told me she had been molested, I felt my fury surge and I jumped to her defense. At thirteen years old, I summoned all the courage that my fury could harness to tell my mother—who I deeply feared—that her boyfriend had sexually molested my sister. Unable to save myself when I was younger, I now felt a sense of vindication. For the first time, I took a stance against my mother's blazing emotional fortress. Unfortunately, it was a very short-lived victory.

Sadly, for my sister and me, my mother regrouped quickly. She let the man back into our house and intimidated us into "forgiving" her boyfriend, because this was the Christian thing to do. Simultaneously, she began to send us off to a Seven Day Adventist Church (although we were Catholic) with a co-worker on Saturdays for religious instruction—as if my sister and I were in need of salvation. In the absence of my mother's protection, my sister and I grappled for footing. The scars of violence and emotional neglect in our childhood, not surprisingly, followed us into adulthood. It took decades before I could talk with my mother frankly about the physical and sexual abuse of those early years. For my sister, this was never to happen.

What does early schooling mean to you?

In the midst of the instability and isolation of our experience as Puerto Rican migrants living far from the majority of our extended family, school represented a mixed bag. Upon entering school, I felt more lost than ever. I only spoke Spanish and was unable to understand the teachers. Only my fellow classmates spoke Spanish, but this was the 1950s and we were prohibited from speaking Spanish in school—a linguistically oppressive practice that in U.S. schools seems to be gaining popularity. Consequently, I began to develop a terrible ambivalence about my language and my identity as a Puerto Rican. Constantly moving from school to school, I remember the humiliation I felt when I tried to speak English and the teacher would harshly correct me or the other children would laugh. Even my last name, Darder, became an issue. It was always mispronounced and I hated the sound. Even when I tried to correct my teachers, they insisted on anglicizing the pronunciation, which made it seem that I didn't even know how to pronounce my own name. This made me feel stupid and unwelcome.

Yet, school also represented a sort of respite from the pain and confusion at home. School was a place where I didn't have to worry about being beaten or sexually molested. As I learned English, I worked hard to adapt to the expectations of my teachers and peers. On a couple of occasions, I had teachers who took interest in my learning and my abilities. However, despite my enthusiasm, I often felt out of sync with teacher expectations. So, in many ways, I lived two lives. One of the eager child anxious to learn at school, while contending with the racialized attitudes of my teachers who knew little about (im)migrant Spanish-speaking children. The other of the very frightened and insecure child at home, fending off the attacks of a mother completely unprepared to ward off the hostility and brutality of a deeply racialized and unequal society.

This duplicity, however, actually served as an effective survival mechanism to withstand the cognitive dissonance of a child barely able to critically decipher the world around me. This tactic worked until middle school. In primary school, I worked to excel and did well. During recess and lunchtime, I loved to play kickball and basketball. The movement of my body released my anxieties and, for a moment, let me feel free. However, conditions in my life began to deteriorate at home during my early adolescence. My mother was hospitalized several times for schizophrenia. The more demanding curriculum of middle school required more concentration. The opportunities for running loose in the schoolyard disappeared. I became depressed and my grades suffered. Yet, no one in the school seemed to notice. No one ever asked about my home life nor inquired into the changing quality of my academic work. In many ways, I felt invisible and without direction.

In eighth grade I was assigned to an art class. I was excited by the possibility that I would learn to paint and draw. In kindergarten, painting was my favorite time. In third grade, a teacher asked us to draw a picture of ourselves in the future. I drew myself as a painter in Paris. I don't even know where this image came from. Maybe an old movie I had seen somewhere. My mother, however, did not approve of my interest in art. When ready to sign my middle school eighth-grade course list, she became undone when she saw I was assigned an art class. In her mind, we were poor and I had to learn something that would help me get a job. This was the first and last time that I remember my mother actually calling the school. In her deeply accented English, she cursed out the counsellor and demanded that I be changed to a typing class. Needless to say, I hated typing class and to this day can only peck away at the keyboard.

How did you "awake to politics"?

It is important to note that some of the tensions and frustrations of this period of my life were also linked to what was happening on the streets. At age ten, we moved from East Los Angeles to an area now known as South Central Los Angeles. The face of poverty was present everywhere—children and adults in worn tattered clothing, tired drawn faces, drunks visible on the street, youths fighting in the alley, and even a junkie on the stairwell shooting up.

On television, civil rights and Vietnam War images were juxtaposed. In 1964, the Watts riots erupted around us. African-American organizers came knocking at our door warning us that the riots were going to happen and that we should remain indoors. We were afraid but survived the burning and the closure of businesses in our neighborhoods. Again, we watched on television the images of burning buildings and the convulsion of people on the streets. Through it all, I found silence at home and silence at school. Few conversations provided us with a real understanding of what was happening in our community. We just knew that we were suddenly afraid, and then the fear dissipated as life re-normalized. And in spite of all the official promises made following the Watts Riots, very little seemed to change in our tiny corner of the world.

Overall, my family was politically invisible and powerless. In fact, the only presidential election in which my mother voted was that of John F. Kennedy. Of all the national political campaigns, Kennedy's was the only one in my childhood that inspired the wide participation and support of disenfranchised people. For a moment, that campaign touched and inspired poor, uneducated people of colour like my mother to believe that another world was possible— a world where their presence would count. The fact that Kennedy was a member of the ruling elite seemed overshadowed by a campaign of vitality and a glimmer of hope that life in the barrios and ghettos could be transformed. Along the same vein, when Kennedy was assassinated everyone around me mourned, but for many their grief turned into political cynicism and despair— a despair that my mother was to carry with her to her grave. Not only had she lost hope in electoral politics, she felt duped and betrayed by a political system that she saw working for the rich, while leaving those most in need to fend for themselves.

By the late 1960s, my mother's rejection of all political activism echoed the fatalism that Paulo Freire so poignantly described in many of his writings. With the deaths of Martin Luther King Jr., Malcolm X, and Robert Kennedy, along with the atrocities of the Vietnam War, my mother's contempt for all political activism solidified. Not surprisingly, my early involvement in community politics was discouraged and maligned at home. To my mother, politics and art were a complete waste of time—neither could pay the rent nor relieve our poverty. Perhaps, it was no coincidence that later in my rebelliousness I readily embraced both political work and art as a way to deal with the pain and anguish in my life.

Unhappy in a home filled with constant turmoil and chaos, I turned my attention to a boyfriend who was six years older and who my mother forced me to marry at sixteen, for fear that I would become pregnant. Although a coerced and misguided action, this proved to be an effective escape from the insanity of my mother and the futility of life on Magnolia Street. But shortly after my wedding, I became pregnant. Eager to continue my studies, I stayed in school and managed to earn my high school diploma before my son was born. I attended Whitney High School, a continuation programme for students with behavioral problems and pregnant teens.

The control of a poor woman's reproductive rights in the U.S. was not unlike the colonial legacy of my mother's generation in Puerto Rico. For example, when seeking contraceptive advice, I was simply prescribed birth control pills, without clear information. When the pills caused nausea, I stopped taking them and immediately became pregnant. After the birth of my second child, an IUD was inserted at the county clinic, to prevent conception. I experienced much bleeding and discomfort. Yet when I complained, the doctor told me that it was "normal" and to just take a couple of aspirin for the pain. Within a month, I had become pregnant again. Upon examination, the doctor was unable to find the device. Rather, than carry out further examination, he insisted that it must have been *expelled without my awareness*, despite my efforts to protest his conclusion. Three years later, when I was suffering from pain and distension in the abdomen, a simple X-ray revealed that the IUD had perforated my uterus and become lodged in the abdominal cavity. This now required major surgery. The attending physician at the time treated me like an idiot. How could I have not known that the IUD had become dislodged? Upon the birth of my third child, I was lectured in the hospital about either staying on birth control pills or being sterilized. Given my mother's history, I refused a tubal ligation and accepted the pills. It was in nursing school that I learned about natural means for contending with unwanted pregnancy. However, even in this female-dominated training context, there was an implicit message that poor women were not to be trusted with control of our bodies, and hence this method was heavily criticized and discouraged.

Although by age 20 I had given birth to three children, my hope to attend college remained an ever-burning desire. I still believed that education was the only path out of the poverty that I had known all my life. In fact, in the only letter I was ever to receive from my father, he urged me to get an education because it was "lo unico que nadie te puede quitar."[3] My mother repeatedly urged me to get an education so that I would "not be a slave" like her. I decided education would provide me with the tools to help myself and to struggle for change. There is no question that the liberating messages and actions attributed to the student walk-outs in Los Angeles, the growing anti-war movement, and the civil rights initiatives across the nation had an enormous impact on my aspirations and dreams as a young woman. Unfortunately, my aspirations were not shared by my husband, a working class Mexican-American man, who although kind, manifested recalcitrant patriarchal expectations—a wife should take care of the home, cook the meals, and tend to the children. This conflict caused me much frustration and anger. I acted it out by becoming involved with a college student and separating from my husband of six years. Hence my academic dreams and immaturity to contend with our difference led to a divorce, and thus began my life as a single parent and full-time student.

Your profile as an academic is complemented by a life dedicated to community activism. What were the highs and lows of your experience within different communities?

At 21, I enrolled into a community college with the hope of becoming a medical doctor in the community. I was quickly discouraged, however, by a counsellor who authoritatively pronounced to me that "You people do much better in vocational programmes," urging me instead to earn a certification as a licensed vocational nurse. Yet, another counsellor advised me to consider the registered nursing programme because I was a single parent and ten years of medical school would be too difficult for my children to endure. Taking his suggestion, I completed the registered nursing programme at a community college. While a student there, I became involved in student and community activism and worked as a peer counsellor for students with similar personal histories as my own. Community college was, indeed, a blessing. For given my economic conditions and lack of knowledge regarding higher education, it served as an important entry point to begin my academic journey.

After graduation from nursing school, I worked as a pediatric nurse with children and their families in a hospital setting. Unhappy with the racism and cultural insensitivity I both experienced and witnessed among the medical staff, I opted for a pay cut, left the hospital, and went to work for the Head Start Programme. At Head Start, a federally funded educational preschool programme for low-income children, I provided basic health assessments and educational information for Latino children and their parents. I believe it was during this time that my community activism deepened, an activism rooted in my struggle to create options for families with scant resources—families very similar to my own. I also became acutely aware of the manner in which the early childhood curriculum and assessment tools used were actually complicit with the programme's inculcation of middle-class, market values upon young impressionable minds. Through my practice at Head Start, I came to recognize how the middle-class values of parent education programmes were unrealistic and inappropriate for poor working-class Latino families, as they unwittingly reinforced a message of cultural deficit. This stirred me to begin advocating in new ways, recognizing my interventions demanded greater attention to cultural and class issues if my efforts were to create the conditions for families to empower themselves.

Within a few years, I began working towards a degree as a marriage and family therapist, while employed at a community mental health centre. As part of my duties, I counselled Spanish-speaking clients who came to the clinic and worked in the community with immigrant children and their families. My emphasis was to reconstruct parent education programmes to meet the needs of working class Latino families. During that time, I conducted rap groups in public schools with Spanish-speaking children, as they struggled to integrate themselves into the mainstream of classroom life. I also became active in anti-racism work, conducting workshops for counsellors, teachers, and community workers. Outside of my practice as a therapist, I served on the staff of an alternative community newspaper and was involved with an anti-nuclear organization, organizing and demonstrating against the proliferation of nuclear arms and power plants, with my three children in tow.

There is no doubt that my children played a significant role in my development as a woman and an activist. As a young mother, they anchored me and kept me focused. With them, I hoped to redeem my life, by working to change the course of our destinies. When my children were born, I made a deliberate decision that the child abuse that I had known would not be repeated. However, to keep such a promise would take more than my resolve—I would have to face the madness from which I was running. So not surprisingly, in an early relationship, I saw the physical and emotional abuse being reproduced in front of my eyes by a partner. Again, the fear of an earlier time consumed me. It took me several years to completely extricate myself from this destructive liaison—something that I was able to accomplish only with therapeutic intervention. In the process, I set out very consciously to create an atmosphere of open communication, one in which my children might experience the love and security that I had never known. As I struggled to be a good mother, I came to learn so much from my children about human resiliency and the meaning of unconditional love—a love where intimacy, honesty, and commitment are central. Moreover, it was my children who gave me the strength to struggle internally with my personal demons and gave me the impetus to struggle politically out in the world. Fighting against the suffering and injustices I witnessed all around me became a very personal affair. I wanted a different world for all children, but most tangibly for my own.

Meanwhile, my work with community organizations and schools revealed more clearly how racialized, gendered, and homophobic class relations were inextricably linked to the reproduction of inequality and social exclusion, particularly in poor communities. More importantly, I began to understand the manner in which "professionals" not only manage and control working class populations but also buffer and mask the manner in which ruling class interests reproduce economic and political impoverishment. As I attempted to challenge and change the mental health practices of the organization, I experienced much resistance from the Anglo director and clinical supervisors. Agency officials insisted that I follow traditional protocols dictated by institutional mental health practices—approaches that were not only inappropriate but proved to be further oppressive to the lives of poor Latino men and women.

Latino bilinguals and Spanish-speaking clients who came to the center were generally court-referred for alcoholism, child abuse, or domestic violence. Unfortunately, the treatment protocols utilized by mainstream therapists at the clinic often did little to build on the existing cultural knowledge and strengths of Latino clients. Rather, their interventions further alienated Latino clients from the very therapists who supposedly were there to "help" them. During my tenure at the mental health center, I consistently urged officials to hire more Spanish-speaking mental health workers with an intimate understanding of Latino cultural values and knowledge of the immediate community.

After several years of struggling vociferously over these issues, I found myself marginalized by the administrative and clinical staff. Although initially praised for my therapeutic prowess, when I began to question the legitimacy of mainstream intervention strategies used with Latino families, I was not only characterized as a political radical, my mental stability was called into question. Upon completing my Master's degree and receiving my license as a therapist, I decided to leave the mental health center to seek employment where my knowledge, skills and sensibilities would be more welcomed. In an effort to channel my energies into community work, I took a job at a family support center in East Los Angeles that focused on mental health intervention for child physical and sexual abuse. Although Latinos directed the organization and attempted to conduct culturally appropriate intervention practices, major difficulties existed in the center's advocacy efforts within schools and the courts. This led me to critically question if mental health practice was the most effective political venue for working toward minority community empowerment. Hence, my concern for Latino community empowerment led me to accept a new position with a Latino non-profit organization working for the rights of Latino and immigrant Spanish-speaking populations.

How do you reconcile politics with art and spirituality?

This was an enormously creative and vibrant moment in my life. In fact, it was during these years that I began painting, writing poetry, and learning music through a completely organic process. My artistic expression proved to be my salvation through many difficult personal and political moments. I became immersed in the poetry of Jose Marti, Julia Burgos, Pablo Neruda, Nikki Giovanni, Maya Angelou, Rumi and others. I began to develop as a poet through my participation in a weekly barrio writers' workshop for Chicano/Latino activist writers in Los Angeles organized by Luis Rodriguez and the late Manazar Gamboa. Music was always a mainstay in my life, since my early years dancing, singing, or lip-syncing to the music of Celia Cruz, the Grand Combo, Tito Puente, The Temptations, Martha and the Vandelas, the Beatles,

Janis Joplin, the Rolling Stones, and later Bob Marley and Peter Tosh. With friends, I learned a little percussion and began writing simple songs of struggle and love. My painting literally began after my first visit to the La Casa Azul, the Frida Khalo museum in Coyoacan. As I walked through the house, I became completely swept away by her paintings and the stories of her life. Similar to Khalo, my deep anguish found in painting a medium in which to project my fears, angers, hopes, and political vision. From that time on, my artistic expression became central to my survival and to how I came to experience my aesthetic relationship to the world, as an educator and political activist.

My conscious spiritual quest also began during the early 1980s. As a child I had reached beyond our immediate tangible existence, to find solace in my loneliness. But catechism classes at Resurrection Parish had rung hollow in the midst of the turmoil at home. Perhaps the memories of that time prevented me from discovering real meaning in the Catholic Church. Now as a young adult, I sought more earnestly to explore spirituality and its role in both my daily life and political work. I read books on Zen Buddhism, Taoism, shamanism, Santeria, and indigenous spirituality. Over the next twenty years, I would become involved with a variety of spiritual traditions, searching to reconcile the anger, pain, conflict, and anguish within. I attended prayer circles, sun dances, moon meditations, vision quests; I danced, I prayed, I sat alone in the dark. But just as earnestly, I sought to integrate my intellectual, emotional, physical and spiritual faculties in my revolutionary practice and political vision of society—a daunting project in the midst of radical political ideas that rejected the legitimacy of such a quest.

Politics, art and spirituality evolved as parallel dimension within me. Art and spirituality teachings gave me an inward focus, politics an outward focus; all providing me with the sustenance to interrogate the contradictions, to speak the unspeakable, to persist even when all seemed lost. In many ways, this intermingling gave the artist and poet a place to exist. From my outrage and anguish, I struggled to create beauty and possibility. The spiritual cast a light within. The political cast a light on the world. These interacting forces, now, exist dialectically. Politics, art and spirituality intermingle in my life, rooting out my inconsistencies and humbling me to see the poet in every life—keeping my life supple and fluid, even in the most disheartening times.

Your passage to academia followed a period of political conflict and strife. Can you describe the period in question?

As director of the community agency, I worked with others to develop popular education programmes for children and adults, while simultaneously learning to raise funds to expand the organization. I became more politically involved with efforts related to worker rights, bilingual education, women's rights, and immigrant rights. I participated in a multitude of political projects, from street demonstrations against U.S. intervention in El Salvador and Nicaragua to community forums on education and cultural festivals that celebrated Latino community life and political solidarity. We organized the Latino community against land developers, in support of bilingual education, and to demand health services for impoverished residents in the city. For several years my work with the organization seemed tremendously successful. I felt happy and extremely fulfilled. However, in the third year of my tenure all hell broke loose!

In 1985, the organization lost several important sources of funding which required the difficult task of cutting programmes and reducing the staff. Upset by how the crisis was handled, some of the staff became disgruntled and broke off, staging a series of protests. I was shocked by the actions taken against me and felt tremendously betrayed. Suddenly, all that I had worked so hard to accomplish for the organization and the community appeared to be in ruins. A campaign of harassment was launched against me, using the Spanish media and the local newspaper (which quickly obliged). Wherever I was asked to speak or perform my poetry, the event organizers received phone calls slandering my personal and political integrity and threatening a boycott of the event. This was probably one of the darkest moments in my life. In retrospect, I recognize that given the difficulty of what was occurring within the organization, I became immobilized with fear and failed to create the conditions for sufficient dialogue among the staff before decisions were made regarding the crisis—an error in judgment that I will always regret.

Nevertheless, there is little doubt that the viciousness with which I was persecuted and attacked, by people whom I considered to be my comrades, was equivalent to a witch-hunt. This caused me great turmoil and anguish and its negative impact on my self-esteem and confidence, given my personal history, took years to overcome. Over time, many comrades that were initially swept up by this vendetta returned to apologize. Some actually spoke of both the inherent sexism (a woman in leadership in a traditionally male-dominated arena) and the sectarianism (a Puerto Rican working in a predominantly Chicano community) utilized to fuel the campaign against my work. They noted that I had been attacked in a manner that seldom is experienced by men. In fact, the campaign never targeted any of the men who were also involved in the decision-making process of the organization. In an effort to assist the organization to regain some equilibrium and to personally recover from the blows, I decided to remain for another year trying to pick up the pieces of the fiasco, while beginning a doctoral programme in education.

From 1982-1986, I taught courses in Chicano literature, bicultural development, and anti-racism as an adjunct professor in a variety of colleges. In 1986, I decided to leave the organization and accepted a full-time faculty position. The first year at the college was exhilarating, but also frustrating. While attempting to incorporate my knowledge of community into my teaching, I encountered, among some faculty and students, significant resistance to engaging more critically with issues of social justice, particularly those related to racism and poverty. Suddenly without notice, I was again embroiled in controversy. I was given notice that my contract would not be renewed in the middle of my second semester.

The dean often seemed uncomfortable when interacting with me, perhaps disturbed by both an ideology that made power explicit and a communication style that was more direct and intense than her own. Nevertheless, following a protest by students against my firing and a threat of a lawsuit against the institution—pointing to the lack of due process, since no warning or evaluation was ever issued to substantiate the decision—I was offered a contract renewal. I accepted the contract with the understanding that my bicultural development programme would become an independent specialization within the larger curriculum. Accordingly, I went on to establish the first human development programme in the country that was specifically grounded in the contexts and realities of subordinate communities and thus, central to the core curriculum of the programme.

Who were your key intellectual mentors?

As a Master's student in the early 1980s, I was strongly influenced by the work of Carol Phillips and Louise Derman-Sparks. Their work critically examined human development and schooling in terms of sociopolitical context that included culture, race, class and gender. Carol Phillips, an African American professor, particularly influenced not only my conceptual understanding of these issues, but inspired me to believe in my own intellectual capacity. Louise Derman-Sparks, a longtime radical activist, feminist, and educator grounded my initial understanding of capitalism and mentored my teaching for several years. In addition, writers such as Paulo Freire, Franz Fanon, Albert Memmi, Kenneth Clarke, Angela Davis, Rodolfo Acuña, Mario Barrera, Gloria Anzaldua and Cheri Moraga influenced my thinking.

During my doctoral programme, I again returned to the writings of Paulo Freire. In 1987, I had the good fortune of attending a critical pedagogy conference where Freire and many of the major critical educational theorists of the time were presenting their work. This experience fundamentally changed my life, as I came to know personally many of these thinkers. Freire opened his heart to me as a teacher, mentor, and friend. He was to become *my father* in the struggle. For the first time, I had discovered critical principles that provided me with the theoretical tools for engaging in a more systematic examination of education—an approach that brought together history, culture, politics, and economics to formidably challenge class and racialized inequalities.

Paulo Freire's *Pedagogy of the Oppressed* was a particularly significant text to my intellectual formation as both an educator and political activist. His capacity to politically embrace the concept of love as our vocation and as a fundamental ingredient in the struggle for liberation has underscored my work and my own writings in the field ever since. Over the next few years, I also became immersed in the work of Karl Marx, Antonio Gramsci, the Frankfurt School, as well as the critical pedagogy literature of Henry Giroux, Michael Apple, Peter McLaren, Ira Shor, Donaldo Macedo, bell hooks and others. My dissertation, which focused on culture and power in the classroom, was greatly influenced by my reading of these powerful texts, which I combined with my knowledge as a therapist, educator, cultural worker, and community organizer.

My teaching practice in both the classroom and community has been not only a central aspect of my political work and a source of great joy, but an important site for my intellectual formation. Whether within the community or university classroom, students have been instrumental to my political understanding of the world and the pedagogical needs of students. Recognizing my authority within the classroom and my power to use this authority in the interest of my students, I worked with them to develop innovative democratic approaches to create ongoing intellectual spaces for dialogue and reflection. They taught me the power of listening and being present to students as a collective learning community, as well as individuals with particular needs for their development of consciousness. More importantly, in my relationship with students I discovered the power of intimacy and love in the act of teaching. Hence, to teach critically was not an act of political indoctrination but rather the liberating of public space for dialogues that brought the alliance of theory and practice to the centre of our learning together.

However, there is no denying that my consistent focus on issues of racism, sexism, class inequalities, and other forms of exclusion has also made teaching a challenge. Students often enter the classroom with many conditioned notions that move contrary to emancipatory ideals. Yet like all of us, they generally are unable to recognize readily their own internal contradictions. Efforts to enliven consciousness and to engage authentically are not easy tasks, particularly, since we can seldom leave our life experiences (good or bad) out of our interactions with students. Many times this caused me great emotional upset when working diligently in the classroom to examine conditions of oppression—many conditions that I had personally endured during my lifetime.

It is only honest, at this juncture, to note that at times I responded to my students' comments too personally, feeling the pain too acutely, and inadvertently pushing them too quickly with my own political urgency. This led me to not only approach my work from a commitment to a larger political vision, but also, unwittingly, from emotionally self-righteous anger, frustration and rage over the oppression I had witnessed and experienced in my own lifetime. So although, in such moments, I may have been politically correct, I was pedagogically ineffectual. My brashness and tendency towards an indulgence of my victimization, unwittingly, displaced the needs of students and pushed them away from engagement. This shortcoming in my teaching and political practice has proved to be one of my greatest challenges: to move beyond the arrogance and ego-driven survival mechanisms I learned as a child to a place of greater compassion and critical understanding as an activist scholar. This demands not only critically comprehending emancipatory theories and revolutionary practices but also contending forthrightly with my internal contradictions in clear and open ways. Sometimes I do this well and sometimes not.

Your academic life is also marked by political struggle...

Yes, very much so. After years of fighting with the ravages of oppression in my private and public life, I found myself within a privileged university context. The dissonance I experienced during my beginning years as a Latina, working-class, female professor in an all-Anglo department is a feature of junior faculty life that is seldom discussed in any substantive manner within the academy. There were many personal doubts and insecurities I faced in my efforts to find a place for myself in the university. Patriarchy, class, and racism within the university function nearly invisibly to those immersed within the contours of privilege. But this is not so for activist scholars, particularly women, from historically disenfranchised populations. Given the trajectory of our uneven development, we are often acutely aware of the racism and elitism that underscores university relationships, even with the most supportive of colleagues.

Hence, as a working-class, Latina professor I often felt acutely aware of the racism, sexism, and elitism of administrators, faculty and even students. In essence, I found the academy to be, on the surface, hospitable, while in practice a brutally political arena where the oppressive structures of the larger society were systematically reproduced. More disheartening has been the politics of silence, where faculty members deem major ideological differences within a department to be simply a matter of competition. The primary concern here is to steer themselves free of conflict, despite the most unjust conditions. In short, there is an absence of lived moral courage. Even esteemed progressive colleagues can become more concerned about not tainting their reputation, in order to preserve the power or influence they feel they've garnered along the way. Hence, on more than one occasion I found myself completely isolated and alone, surrounded only by the echoes of liberal social justice rhetoric and books filled with lovely radical ideas by colleagues-authors missing in action. This may help to explain one of the reasons why the structures and practices that reproduce inequality remain intact. All social change requires the insertion of the body into the struggle; our ideals are thwarted by inaction.

The struggles within the academy were to become central to my work as a professor. For example, the university I joined proved to be very supportive during my early years as a junior and associate professor at the institution—perhaps partly spurred on by a multimillion-dollar lawsuit for discrimination filed by an African American professor against the department. However when I became a senior professor, the faculty and administration did not appear to respond as positively to the influence that my teaching and writings were having within the university and the larger community. Tensions began to ensue with faculty members who held more conservative notions of education and who feared the loss of control over the curriculum, student formation, and the intellectual direction of the department. As I attempted to challenge and vie for changes in a department that was quickly moving from a more progressive to a more conservative educational agenda, I found myself under fire once more.

When a group of graduate students protested curricular changes that portended a more conservative teacher education curriculum, I extended my support in a brief email that later was circulated. This public support for a more critical curriculum became the tangible act necessary to orchestrate a faculty hazing, where I was falsely accused of trying to destroy the department and damage the reputation of the university. Colleagues contended that I had proven myself to be non-collegial and could never be trusted again. Following the meeting, I learned that covert actions were taken by some faculty members to work toward forcing my removal. I was alerted that those in power had gone to university attorneys to discuss the possibility of rescinding my tenure, an action that was discouraged since there were insufficient legal grounds to carry out such an action.

I learned quickly that the marginalization I had experienced from my colleagues in the past was only child's play compared to the fallout I now faced.

A group of students were organized to meet with the dean and the president of the college regarding the injustices at work in my case. I made repeated efforts to discuss the matter with the provost, dean and colleagues. All efforts were to no avail. Eventually, most of the students became confused by what they were told by other faculty members, who wished to keep matters under wraps. Legitimate concerns and important ideological differences were reduced to personality conflicts. After 10 years of superior university, department and student evaluations, suddenly my research was questioned and maligned. The tension was thick enough to cut with a knife. Finally, in an effort to step out of the eye of the storm, I asked for a leave of absence. Supportive colleagues at another university were able to create a visiting appointment for me, which provided the space I needed to recuperate from the assaults of this unexpected attack.

You give a lot of importance to personal community...

Personal community—family, friends, comrades and colleagues—has played an important role in my life and my scholarship. For example, despite the hardships I endured in my early years, I continued to make efforts to reconcile my relationship with my mother. Although it took many years to make peace with those early years, our relationship blossomed during the last 10 years of her life. I learned to see and appreciate my mother as the suffering soul she was and from there began to accept her history as also part of mine. In the process, I discovered who my mother was and grew to understand more fully the impact of racialized and gendered class oppression upon an individual life. I also found the room to let my mother be herself, to enjoy her raunchy humour, to appreciate her skill as a seamstress and cook, and to recognize that in spite of her personal demons, she loved my sister and me dearly and was haunted by enormous shame and remorse.

Given my difficulties with intimate relationships, the power of community has been a saving grace. Yet, I don't want to leave the impression that my intimate relationships and love affairs with men were bad. For, in fact, I was quite fortunate to be in the company of many intelligent and creative men. However, it is not surprising that oppressed souls find one another. And in the midst of intimate relationships, we often act out the most irrational and violent aspects of our violated bodies. For some of us, it takes a very long time to grapple with the disowned rage and grief that sits just beneath the mask of social niceties. For me, it has been only very recently, that I have found the strength and wherewithal to begin actually enjoying my life with a man. It has required facing my shame for all the mistakes that I have made and embracing each relationship as a moment in which I learned something new about myself.

None were a failure. Yet, it is not surprising that a history of four marriages easily lends itself to humiliation and brutal judgement, particularly in those who would commingle their moralism with their envy. This speaks to a colonizing shame rigidly constructed by social conventions that disregard the alienating impact of capitalist society and the hardships of just staying alive. To struggle for liberation then requires that we disrupt the tyranny of shame in our own lives, so that we will not repeat it in our relationships with others. My personal community is comprised of individuals who also aspire to such a politics of human emancipation.

My friends and comrades over the years have also been key to my development and sustenance as an educator, political activist, and scholar. They encouraged and challenged my work, inspired me to persevere, and embraced me during hard moments with their love and solidarity. Although too many to mention here, my friend and comrade Rudy Torres is an example. His intellectual prowess and extensive knowledge of Marxism filled an important theoretical gap in my scholarly formation. Through our dialogues, I came to interrogate more deeply my constructions of "race" and more firmly anchor my understanding of political economy. We worked on a variety of scholarly collaborations that contributed to the field of Latino studies and helped to carve an argument for a critical theory of racism. The latter writings sought to shatter reified notions of "race," which function to stifle the formation of political solidarity across class and cultural differences. It was in my relationship with Rudy that I learned much about constructing healthy working boundaries, while struggling in concrete ways with the sexual politics so prominent in relationships between women and men. At times we fought over ideas or personal differences. Yet, our friendship and scholarship, grounded in our shared political commitment to the struggle for economic democracy and social justice, have withstood the test of time. Moreover, our intimate familiarity with poverty and its devastation and the painful histories of our childhood could not help but become inextricably inscribed in our work together.

My personal community has been my lifeline during moments of extreme personal and political turmoil. They have seen me through political struggles, broken relationships, major illnesses, my house burning, and my mother dying. They are my extended kin of the heart and through them I have found the way to stay open and alive. These are the people that have known me at my best and my worst, yet continue to love and appreciate me for the woman I am. They support and challenge me to live my life in concert with my values and beliefs. Yet, when I falter, they never expect or require more from me than I am able to give. These relationships are lifelong, nourished by politics, food, conversation, notes, books, music, art, dance, love, and, most importantly, the knowledge that we are growing old together in a history we share. But more importantly, this comprises a personal network of relationships that is not anchored in repressive interpretations of reality or the unrelenting drive for material gain. Instead, our anchor is our love for the world, which drives our revolutionary dreams.

How do you see your future?

Well, in 2002, unable to return to the politically strained environment of my former university, I began a job search and was offered a faculty position at a university in the Midwest. I now entered a department in a large public institution with a very diverse faculty working on many of the issues that were close to my heart. Yet, even within this more hospitable context, many of the same concerns I found in a small private institution continue to be at work, but with an enlarged bureaucracy. Despite very gracious interactions among the faculty, there clearly exist contesting notions of identity politics, "race" and racism, the political economy, gender differences, and the role of activism in graduate education. Yet, seldom are tough intellectual issues engaged in any substantive manner among the faculty. As is so common within university environments, there exists little time for sustained dialogues. This is generally coupled with an unspoken competition over ideas, which unfortunately is indirectly waged through the mentorship of students—making scholarship an issue of personal loyalties, rather than of the larger intellectual and practical concerns of emancipation.

Furthermore, despite the large number of faculty of colour in the department, questions of elitism and sexism continue to go unaddressed, and we have been unable to establish a consistent democratic governing practice, although the majority espouse democratic empowerment and hold expressed commitments to social justice. However, in this instance, these concerns seem less about unwillingness or resistance. Here the issues are more tied to institutional expectations of productivity, university service, and external professional contributions. These expectations ultimately result in placing major time constraints on faculty—time constraints that subsume collective interrogation of academic ideas, structures, and practices, as well as the building of a solid intellectual community. The key to making a change in the university requires surrendering our proclivity to chase after new intellectual experiences for the mere sake of obtaining individual professional recognition or reward. Instead, the faculty would need to link collectively our labour within universities to actual community conditions and events, with the very clear purpose and intent of transforming these conditions in concrete and meaningful ways.

After 20 years in the academy, I've come to firmly believe that the fundamental structures of inequality that shape university life make it next to impossible to construct an emancipatory political practice, even in the presence of radical scholarship. For what is necessary is a critical mass of scholars at a university who embrace emancipatory ideals in practice and, this, unfortunately, is very difficult to find. The structures of individualism, competition, and rewards within the academy work effectively to counter such a phenomenon. Hence, the obdurate structural reality of the university challenges us, as radical intellectuals, to wrestle with what at times seems the futility of our context. What exactly is the contribution of university professors to an emancipatory political vision? How do we contend with the complicity of our faculty role? What are the limits and possibilities of radical scholarship in these times? How do we link our scholarship to the everyday realities of oppressed people's lives? And how can we even measure the extent of our contribution to the ongoing struggle for social justice, human rights and economic democracy? Important questions in the midst of the internationalization of capital, the fascism of the media, the current evangelizing campaign of the Right, and the deceptive political repression of dissenting voices.

It is also important here to speak for a moment about the link between the scientism and racism of the academy. There is no question in my mind that the penchant for employing scientific paradigms of precision and objectivity for interpreting human conditions works to harden consciousness. We are taught (and teach our students) to accept a static science and the static vision it affords. As an abstraction of life, our research freezes everything, including the motion of our imagination and all social relationships. Struggling to disrupt this hardened consciousness has been one of the most difficult tasks of my labour as a professor. Colleagues and students educated in the "classical traditions" are often more resistant to a pedagogy that shifts the centre of power from elite traditional readings of society to a critical understanding of the world.

My efforts to crack disciplinary borders and counter static scientific methodologies within the academy have closed many doors. For example, as a visiting instructor at a very prestigious northeastern university, I asked to meet with the chair of the department to discuss the possibility of my remaining once my contract ended. Within moments of beginning the meeting, the chair told me, in no uncertain terms, that "not even in my dreams" should I think that I could remain for another year. His contempt and disdain were spurred by my efforts to "politicize the curriculum with multicultural rhetoric." In his eyes, this "weakness signalled a deep flaw in my scholarship." It took me some time to recover from the condescending manner in which he spoke to me. As a loyal gatekeeper of the institution, he deployed his power and influence to protect the tradition of positivism, a tactic I have seen repeated in a thousand ways, throughout my tenure in the academy.

Hence, despite my accomplishments, I must confess that I am terribly disheartened with my work as a professor. I seek a life where books are not the primary source for making meaning, but rather where relationships nourish and sustain our capacity to live fully the dialectics of our existence. Yet, I know that in my effort to renew my work, I'm forced to confront my contradictions and acknowledge how the economic advantage and privileges of university life are the carrot that keeps me on course with the university's hegemonic function in the larger world. It is the price I pay for my stressed-out, always-so-busy life, lived isolated and alienated from the vitality of the streets and just outside of the suffering and anguish of so many. It is the reward that keeps my eyes seeking the elusive prize—being deemed an *important* radical intellectual of our time. All this, while I am supposedly tearing down the master's house? Isn't this the fallacy that Audre Lorde warned us about? Didn't she say that we couldn't dismantle the master's house using the master's tools? In my misguided zeal and arrogance, I guess I thought I could.

So, after so many years of dedicating myself to what now seems a futile endeavour, I must extricate myself from academia and reenter the world that, unbeknownst to me, I tried to escape by dancing with ideas in my head. Instead, I need to be more outward in the midst of nitty-gritty commonplace problems. Where will this lead me? I can't really say. But it must be toward a life where happiness, even in the midst of struggle, becomes revolutionary purpose. And where the freedom to express my humanity, as I am, is welcomed—whether in the company of people or on a blank sheet of paper—where my voice can flow freely and the colours of my being explode into a million shades of love.

How do you envisage the struggle for greater social justice from now onward?

Over the years, my struggle for consciousness has always brought back home to me the body. This is particularly true for those of us who exist, as Henri Levebre contends, in a world where every aspect of our daily life—birth, death, marriage, family, school, work, leisure, parenthood, spirituality, and even entertainment—has been colonized. Under such a regime of power, our bodies become alienated, disconnected and compartmentalized, leaving us unmercifully vulnerable to the whims of capital. Meanwhile, the marketplace fools us into believing that democracy equals capitalism and consumption equals happiness. As our consciousness becomes more and more abstracted, we become more and more detached from our bodies. The consequence is a deep sense of personal and collective dissatisfaction generated by a marketplace that cannot satisfy authentic human needs—human needs that can only be met through relationships that break the alienation and isolation we live.

Throughout my life, I have seen how injustice, both personal and institutional, blocks, disrupts and corrupts the free and fluid participation of subordinated bodies within society. In a myriad of forms, oppression reifies exclusion in the interest of economic imperatives, without regard for the violated bodies left behind. When human needs such as food, shelter, meaningful livelihood, healthcare, education and the intimacy of a community are not met, bodies are violated. Violated bodies easily gravitate to whatever can provide a quick fix to ease the pain and isolation of an alienated existence. I witnessed this in my own life. For years, I repeatedly tried to erase the pain and grief with temporary quick fix solutions. But illicit drugs, excess food, and a multitude of troubled relationships only dug me deeper into the hole of my despair, making it more difficult for me to participate fully in coherent struggles out in the world. We need, instead, fully integral bodies expressing our humanity from a place of wholeness and love, rather than fear and uncertainty, if we are to transform our personal and political madness.

When I recall my mother's life or the lives of many students and comrades, I can't help but conclude that to summon the power of consciousness requires the development of a moral and ethical understanding that can safeguard the dignity and integrity of all human differences. Moral here should not be confused with moralism. Being moral means exploring and being self-vigilant of all our sensations, ideas, and practices. This is a process that is impossible to accomplish by abstracting our current conditions from our ideologies and histories of survival. It requires that we bring together the moral and political, as well as the particular and the universal, acknowledging that all life exists interconnected.

This entails an understanding of politics that begins with the needs of the body. For without our bodies to enact the principles we embrace, any notion of an emancipatory democracy is meaningless. Moreover the origin of emancipatory possibility and human solidarity resides in our bodies. For as Terry Eagleton reminds us, it is the moral, fragile, suffering, ecstatic, needy, dependent, desirous, and compassionate body which furnishes the basis for all moral thought. And it is, in fact, moral thought that places our bodies back into the political discourse. Yet, discourse here extends beyond the notion of *voices*; for genuine democracy is about the body's interaction with the world. Thus, it must exist as a practice, in which human beings interact as equals in order to contribute to the world the best of what we have to offer. And this practice must take place in the field of unfettered human interaction—the social and political medium for struggle and the development of consciousness.

Throughout my life as an activist scholar, I have worked to embrace the tradition of *revolutionary love* as did Che Guevara, Paulo Freire, and others in the past. This is a love that compels us to become part of an emancipatory politics and pedagogy that cultivates human connection, intimacy, trust and honesty, from the body out, into the world. Here again, Eagleton provides the direction. Revolutionary love means to comprehend that the moral and the material are inextricably linked. And as such, our politics must recognize love as an essential ingredient of a just society. Love as a political principle motivates the struggle to create mutually life-enhancing opportunities for all people. It is a love that is grounded in the mutuality and interdependence of our human existence—that which we share, as much as that which we do not. This is a love nurtured by the act of relationship itself. It cultivates relationships with the freedom to be at one's best without undue fear. Such an emancipatory love allows us to realize our nature, in a way that allows others to do so as well. Inherent in such a love is the understanding that we are never at liberty to be violent, authoritarian, or exploitive.

My life has shown me that love is revolutionary when it is empowered by consciousness. And the power of our consciousness exists within our bodies. It is in our freedom to speak and act collectively that our power commingles with one another. It is this commingling of emancipatory consciousness that oppression seeks to contain, or halt altogether. However, once our freedom to exist is unleashed, the beauty and power of the decolonized cannot be pimped by the whims of political tyranny or the greed of capital. Instead consciousness sustained becomes human energy to produce change in the existing conditions which shape our lives, as both individuals and social beings.

Most importantly, it is through such collective struggle that consciousness is born. The poet Muriel Rukeyser reminds us that "a true consciousness is the confession to ourselves of our feelings; a false consciousness disowns them."[4] This disowning leads to the corruption of the mind and the body. Often, it is the outcome of seductive resounding images—via a celluloid screen, a third grade teacher, a social worker, a college counsellor, a doctor's diagnosis, a "beauty" magazine, the evening news—colonizing images in disguise that tell us our lives, as they exist, are worthless, or at best deficit. Consciousness distracted by the false yearning and desires of the marketplace corrupts our political will. With promises of an easier life, we are rendered passive citizens of the empire.

Hence, the struggle for me has always been to fight against the inertia of passivity inspired by capitalism, so that I might find the moral courage required to voice dissent, even when standing alone. In the mining of my own grief, I have heard the grief of our humanity. With great effort I have fought to contend with the blinders of complacency, the indulgence of my victimhood, and the political righteousness of my oppression. In so doing, I have found that the path to a revolutionary struggle must be grounded in shared kinship, political self-determination, and economic justice. It is a struggle that holds no guarantees or promises yet finds in our collective consciousness the seeds of our liberation and in our buried histories, the quickening of our power. Oppression would love them to remain forever hidden; perhaps this is why it takes madness, something of the insane, to redeem the power from all that we have lived.

Notes

1. Rukeyser, Muriel, 1996. *The Life of Poetry*. Ashfield, MA: Paris Press (1).
2. "we make the path by walking"
3. "what no one can take from you"
4. Rukeyser, op. cit. (49).

Fascism, Colonialism and the Promise of Critical Education

Interview with Luiza Cortesão

*L*uiza Cortesão *is a much respected educator in the Portuguese-speaking world. She lived through the years when Portugal was under the grip of fascism and her family suffered directly because of their anti-fascist politics. In this interview, Luiza Cortesão relives this period in Portuguese politics and assesses its impact on the Lusitanian country's educational scene. She also examines its legacy as well as the impact of the so-called 'revolution of the carnations' in 1974. The impact of Paulo Freire's writings are also discussed in this context (Professor Cortesão is very much involved in directing the Paulo Freire Institute of Portugal). In addition, she discusses the current challenges for Portuguese education in an age of globalisation and at a time when, as with many other Southern European countries, Portugal is shifting from a country of emigration to a country of immigration.*

Given that, historically speaking, the Portuguese experience of fascism came to an end not so long ago (1974), are there still any legacies of that experience that need to confronted by the critical educator today?

One has to start by briefly describing the complex historical, political and geographic contexts that provide the framework for an analysis of the Portuguese educational scene, in order to be able to reflect on the challenges facing education in Portugal today. At the start of the 20th century, after a short period that followed the establishment of the Republic, the need to seriously invest in education was underlined. Such an investment was particularly focused on teacher training, on the improvement of the teachers' status and work conditions, as well as on the development of a 6-year compulsory education period. Education was then considered to be a priority area for investment and also a possible key to the solution of some social problems. Following a coup d'état, the short-lived First Republic was replaced by a fascist dictatorial regime that managed to stay in power for almost fifty years. From the beginning of this period one could notice a great lack of investment in education. Everything seemed to move in the opposite direction as far as education was concerned. The teacher-training period was reduced; the curricula began to be very limited, the compulsory schooling period was reduced first to four years and later to three. Curiously, some time later, it was increased to four years for boys and maintained at three years for girls. It was only later that a period of four years was established for both sexes. The program contents led to indoctrination, and delivery was of the type that Paulo Freire calls 'banking education'. The teachers' authority and discipline were strongly reinforced, while teacher-training schools were closed for several years.

So-called "teaching posts" were established to co-exist with those already available in schools. One did not require any teaching qualifications to occupy these posts. The weight of the Catholic Church was strongly felt throughout the curricula and adopted disciplinary codes. Needless to say, fifty years of this orientation left an indelible mark on the Portuguese educational system. As a result, the changes that started to take place at the end of the dictatorship and especially after the 25th April revolution met with a lot of difficulties given the existence of conservative structures and mentalities. These were a feature of the habitus of teachers and the population in general, a habitus that had been structured in an oppressive context. Besides, Portugal is, nowadays, a semi-peripheral EU member state. Like other countries it was faced with an economic globalisation context before it had developed into a modern country. This being the case, it is common to find people in positions of responsibility who search for 'scapegoats' to account for the economic problems that beset the country in this late modernity context. Education was made to blame for the economic and social ills experienced by Portuguese society. So a 'school crisis' was said to exist in a country where public schooling had as yet not been consolidated. It took a long time for mass schooling to be consolidated. While in post-war Europe, especially in Northern countries, the welfare state was developed and strengthened, Portugal was under a dictatorship that outlasted other European fascist regimes. It regarded popular education as a 'menace' that needed to be restrained. This gave rise to what my late colleague, Steve Stoer, and Helena Araújo call the "simultaneous crisis and consolidation of mass schooling." This fragile situation is more likely to lend itself to the uncritical acceptance of modern day educational proposals governed by the ideology of the marketplace with the emphasis being placed on profitability, effectiveness and low costs incurred. It is difficult for the views of critical educators to be accepted in this context, and their proposals are often dismissed as being utopian, unpractical and not in tune with "present world needs."

To what extent did your formation as a critical educator entail your confronting Salazarism?

As you are aware, the first steps in one's teacher formation are taken during one's schooldays. My schooling occurred during the worst period of the dictatorship. My family and peer-group, however, that provided an important support framework during my infancy and adolescence, somehow served as a bulwark against the incorporation of certain ideas and values that were being conveyed by the educational system at the time. I must mention that I am the daughter of a political emigrant who actively engaged in revolutionary activities against the dictatorship. Falsely judged and condemned, he was forced to migrate, as an exile, to Brazil, when I was still a very young child. I only really met my father when I was seventeen, having spent one year with him in Brazil. So I can't forget the oppressive social and political context in which we were brought up. This made my family regroup into a kind of clan that allowed us to resist and live a life, as children and adolescents, of great quality. All our friends were in opposition to the regime, and this relational and interactive context must have served as an antidote to the teaching context provided by the schools that sought to inculcate the dominant conservative values in students.

I must confess however that my exposure to a one-way transmission, dogmatic and magisterial mode of teaching conditioned my approach to pedagogy during my initial years in the profession, without my being aware of this. It was due to an effort to bridge the gap between my ideological convictions and professional practice that I recognised the importance of engaging in research with regard to teaching. Afterwards, I understood how crucial it was to question my own practice, to develop an attitude of critical vigilance and to try to help students and teachers, with whom I worked, develop the same attitude. It is obvious that such a change in my approach to education was also made possible through my contact with other Portuguese and foreign colleagues that came about as a result of collaboration in the areas of educational research and intervention. This made me realise the importance of being aware of international debates and research in the field that, in turn, enhanced my reflections with students and colleagues. I must also mention the enlightening influence of certain authors whose works I read, notably those who forcefully exposed the reproductive function of schools. I understood that only a critical disposition would enable one to oppose this process.

Above all, however, it is important to highlight the tremendous effect that the period that followed the 25th April, 1974, the 'revolution of the carnations,' had on all of us, educators and other citizens. We enthusiastically questioned everything, debated and analyzed everything. We shared ideas in a spirit of hope with a view to contributing to the diminishing of the social injustice that had engulfed our country until then.

You have for years been engaged in the formation of educators in Portugal. What is your vision for teacher education provision throughout Portugal in the forthcoming years?

Within a globalized world strongly influenced by structures and institutions such as the World Bank, education and consequently schools and teachers are increasingly becoming subject to the pressure of rendering teaching processes more 'efficient' and 'technical-rational'. This is affecting, with greater or smaller intensity, not only educational structures, such as the curriculum and teacher-training but also funding that, in turn, affects the possibility for developing research in education. One can therefore envisage these orientations becoming even stronger in the years to come. Because of these orientations, greater importance is arbitrarily given to greater effectiveness and profitability and the lowering of costs involved. These trends tend to give larger impetus to the ideology of competitive individualism. There would be less room in which to manoeuvre in such a context. The autonomy of teacher-training institutions, schools and teachers would be curtailed. Teacher-training would thus be seriously threatened. In these circumstances, there is the danger that teachers will become less significant since, in keeping with the logic of neoliberalism, 'appealing' technical-rational processes, involving the Internet, television, distance learning and teacher-proof packages, will take over.

Fortunately, as I said earlier, there are movements that assert the importance of education and the teachers' role in the process. They argue that teachers should not submit passively to the onslaught of technical-rational processes but, on the contrary, should use the technical means involved for critical educational purposes. To summarize the attempt is here to shift from the idea of simply an informed subject to one who is formed more holistically. The concern is with stimulating creativity and developing a critical disposition as well as generating an awareness of citizenship rights and fostering a sense of social solidarity. There are pockets, here and there, where people make these the goals of their efforts in education.

You are very much involved in the direction of the Instituto Paulo Freire in Porto. How significant is Paulo Freire in education and social thinking in Portugal today?

Paulo Freire exerted a great influence in the literacy and popular education efforts in Portugal following the 'revolution of the carnations' of the 25th April, 1974. His influence and importance became less evident in the 80s and 90s. This having been said, one can detect Paulo Freire's influence in diverse contexts, works, projects and activities that were and are developed at different levels. These have, though, been re-appropriated and are sometimes not even recognized as Freirean. However, as Paulo Freire himself argued, the best way to appraise a thinker is not to follow but to re-create him or her—experiments cannot be transplanted but must be reinvented!

One can nowadays detect an increasing interest. This is partly evident in such activities as those developed by the Instituto Paulo Freire de Portugal through its links with other Paulo Freire institutes and Paulo Freire research centres, particularly the Instituto Paulo Freire in São Paulo, Brazil.

Can you introduce the non-Portuguese readers of this volume to some of those whom you consider to be the leading critical educators in Portugal?

This is quite a difficult question to answer. If we think about those educators who strongly influenced the Portuguese educational firmament but who have already died, there are some names that deserve to be mentioned. To provide a few examples, I would mention António Sérgio, Adolfo Coelho, Rui Grácio, Maria Borges Medeiros, or even Lindley Cintra, the last mentioned having played an important role in adult education. It is not easy to identify the ones who engaged in a critical approach to education since such an approach does not favour those who seek to take on a leadership role.

There are, though, some institutions, research groups, schools and even isolated teachers whose work is characterized by critical action and reflects a critical disposition. I would rather not mention any names here since there would be the risk of my leaving out some important movements or persons, either through lapses of memory or because of my ignorance of their work. It is important to say that significant research, intervention and action-research work is being developed in some research centres and universities. One should also refer to the existence of movements, schools and teachers who have survived in their efforts to provide a problematizing education where the concern is with students' citizenship rights, the development of critical awareness and democratic educational action and social relations.

One must however recognize the existence in Portugal of a complex hegemonic conservative presence that, simultaneously, values technocratic competencies and skills' acquisition, as well as the use of so-called innovative methodologies and relational patterns that lend support to a hidden curriculum that is predominantly normalizing and domesticating.

The Portuguese colonial situation suggests that ideas from the colonized countries (e.g., the ideas and writings of Paulo Freire and Amilcar Cabral) can have a transformative effect on the colonial centers. The liberation of Portugal's African colonies has often been viewed in this light. Would it be fair to state that the Portuguese overthrow of the Caetano regime and the independence of Portugal's former African colonies together represent a case of the oppressed liberating the oppressors while liberating themselves?

This is the most difficult of all your questions! I might not be the best person to answer it.

It is known that the "Captains' Movement," that was responsible for the 25th April revolution, was very much the result of the enormous uneasiness felt within the armed forces owing to the Colonial War that took place in Africa. There were strong and violent liberation movements in the so-called 'Portuguese colonies,' and many of the soldiers who were sent to fight against them had or acquired the awareness that not only was this a 'lost war' but one which brought about a lot of unfair hardships and violence. They acquired the consciousness of having been the oppressors. Such an awareness conditioned and favoured the emergence of the so-called "Captains' Movement," which, on the 25th April, deposed the regime led at the time by Marcelo Caetano, as Salazar was already dead by then. In that sense, it can be admitted that the "colonies," liberation movements also helped to liberate Portugal from its oppressive dictatorial regime. I am not convinced, however, that the political events that led to the ex-colonies' independence managed to have a strong and profound effect on the Portuguese people in general, one which would have given rise to a critical consciousness, a consciousness that would have dismantled the insidious *habitus* structure that had been built throughout 50 years of dictatorship. Although we now live in a formal democratic regime, humble and submissive attitudes, myopic views, and low civic participation in confronting social problems are still quite a general feature of our society.

On the other hand, as many are aware, in many former colonies (the colonised world cannot be read as an homogeneous whole due to each colony's specificity) the period of time subsequent to independence was particularly difficult and violent as is always the case when civil war breaks out. So, there is need for reflection on the extent to which such a civil war context allows for a genuine liberation of the people involved, bearing in mind the influence of foreign powers in these situations and the ever-so-strong presence of neo-colonialism.

How is the Portuguese education system responding to the needs of a society that is increasingly becoming multi-ethnic as a result of the experiences of immigration that Portugal is currently sharing with other Southern European states.

Portugal has been, for a long period of time, a country where subsequent waves of strong emigration currents could be felt. Mainly Brazil, USA, Canada, Africa and Europe were, at different times, the targeted destinies of many of our emigrants. There is recurring emigration mainly to other European countries. This notwithstanding, Portugal has gradually become an immigration country. Straight after the decolonisation process, Portugal became the destiny of several immigrants from Africa. Nowadays, we have immigrants mainly from Brazil and the Eastern countries and also from Africa and Asia.

Portugal was not used to catering for immigrants in its educational system. The only group that was significant in numbers and distinguished itself from the mainstream Portuguese, in the first years of primary school, were the gypsies. These were 'naturally' excluded from the educational system that, in its rigidity, did not and still does not accommodate the gypsies' needs and interests. Nowadays, the ethnic and national variety is much greater. Furthermore, with effectively nine years of compulsory schooling, members of several Portuguese minority groups that once didn't go to school, such as children and teenagers from distant rural surroundings, fishing communities and rundown suburban environments, are now at school. Because of their presence, schools are experiencing difficulties in the way they function. Though there have been some changes, Portuguese schools still maintain strong monocultural features. The curricula and methodologies used, as well as the established pedagogical relations, have a strong ethnocentric character. A lack of appreciation of the 'multicultural rainbow' in which it operates has led to the 'massification' of schooling. This favours, in terms of school achievement and success, those persons who have traditionally been benefiting from this type of school, namely white, middle class, urban males.

Explicit racism and xenophobia are still being felt throughout Portuguese schools and society in general. Nevertheless, there are studies intended to sensitise people to the problems arising out of the emergence of a multicultural society. Multicultural education is beginning to make its presence felt in Portuguese education with reasonable success.

Studies in the Postmodern Theory of Education

General Editors
Joe L. Kincheloe & Shirley R. Steinberg

Counterpoints publishes the most compelling and imaginative books being written in education today. Grounded on the theoretical advances in criticalism, feminism, and postmodernism in the last two decades of the twentieth century, Counterpoints engages the meaning of these innovations in various forms of educational expression. Committed to the proposition that theoretical literature should be accessible to a variety of audiences, the series insists that its authors avoid esoteric and jargonistic languages that transform educational scholarship into an elite discourse for the initiated. Scholarly work matters only to the degree it affects consciousness and practice at multiple sites. Counterpoints' editorial policy is based on these principles and the ability of scholars to break new ground, to open new conversations, to go where educators have never gone before.

For additional information about this series or for the submission of manuscripts, please contact:

> Joe L. Kincheloe & Shirley R. Steinberg
> c/o Peter Lang Publishing, Inc.
> 29 Broadway, 18th floor
> New York, New York 10006

To order other books in this series, please contact our Customer Service Department:

> (800) 770-LANG (within the U.S.)
> (212) 647-7706 (outside the U.S.)
> (212) 647-7707 FAX

Or browse online by series:
> www.peterlang.com

ADVANCE PRAISE FOR
Public Intellectuals, Radical Democracy and Social Movements

"An inspirational collection of interviews with some of the world's most courageous, committed and strategic popular educators and activists....thanks to Borg and Mayo's incisive questions we have honest, moving and analytically profound accounts of lives, contexts and strategies—a testimony of hope in popular education...from the toil and anguish of these brave women and men across the globe...redemptive in its scope..."

Mary Darmanin, University of Malta

"Borg and Mayo have created an utterly fascinating and unique window into the depths of learning, self, collectivity and political change. This book is one of the most important ever written on the role of agency, social movement learning and political transformation. This is the best product yet by two internationally respected scholars of critical pedagogy and popular education. Borg and Mayo bring readers inside some of the most powerful movements of the late twentieth and early twenty-first century. Their dialogues with women and men who have given their lives to learning and struggle for a better world reveal new dimensions of pedagogy, common sense and love."

Budd Hall, former Dean of Education, University of Victoria, Canada; former Secretary-General of the International Council for Adult Education

"This beautiful book of interviews organized in Gramsci's spirit is a powerful reminder of two facts: first, that public intellectuals of democratic persuasion exist in all global regions, no matter their particular political conditions. Second, that it is the clarity of vision and analysis of critical intellectuals at the periphery of the centers of cultural power which accelerates the drive for global transformations in a genuinely democratic key: a drive in solidarity for human dignity."

Renate Holub, University of California, Berkeley

"I am immensely excited by this book. It is a timely response to the pressing need for a more critical engagement with ideas that expose neoliberalism's common sense as making no sense at all. Between the covers lies a feast of critical ideas from a diversity of people and places. All have a unity of purpose, ideas for realistic, practical utopias. The book compellingly takes us on a journey through the lived experiences of these authors, setting their life stories in their cultural and political time as the basis of their praxis. The particular niche for this book in mirroring critical dialogue through the written word is to stimulate ideas and action in the world. This is the latest work to emerge from Malta out of the Borg and Mayo partnership, and it excels. It is essential reading for all those who work toward a just and sustainable world."

Margaret Ledwith, University of Cumbria, United Kingdom

Advance Praise continued

"During the twentieth century, many predicted the demise of the public intellectual. These insightful interviews with seventeen committed women and men show that, in the twenty-first century, public intellectuals continue to be engaged in critique and construction all over the world…In ***Public Intellectuals, Radical Democracy and Social Movements,*** Borg and Mayo have assembled a great collection of thoughtful and inspirational dialogues…delicious reading for all those interested in building more democratic and just societies."

Daniel Schugurensky,
Ontario Institute for Studies in Education, University of Toronto, Canada

"***Public Intellectuals, Radical Democracy and Social Movements*** is both intellectually challenging and politically inspiring. In documenting the intellectual thoughts and practices of a wide range of publicly engaged egalitarian intellectuals, including leading feminist activists, Borg and Mayo's work brings hope and encouragement to all those who struggle for social justice. The book also demonstrates the power of ideology and resistance, and the crucial role that scholarship plays in promoting a more egalitarian world when it is wedded to activism."

Kathleen Lynch, Professor of Equality Studies,
University College School of Social Justice, Dublin